"All sensible Americans are rightfully horrified by the treatment of the Jews of Europe by the Nazi Regime. We also dare not forget that the Armenian nation and people faced Genocide early in this century under the swords and gunfire of the Ottoman Empire. We cannot again permit any people to suffer such atrocities as those documented in this book."

                George Deukmejian
                      Governor
                State of California

The CROSS and the CRESCENT

Publisher: UCS PRESS
         3531 W. Glendale Ave., Suite 202
         Phoenix, AZ 85051

All rights reserved, including the right to reproduce this book or any portions thereof in any form.

Copyright © 1989 by Lindy V. Avakian

Jacket design by Wayne Horne

Jacket photo by Dan Hemesath

Printed in the United States of America

First Printing: 1989

Library of Congress Cataloging-in-Publication Data

Avakian, Lindy V., 1927-
   The cross and the crescent / by Lindy V. Avakian
     p.   cm.
   Originally published: Los Angeles, Calif: DeVorss, 1965.
   Includes index.
   ISBN 0-943247-06-3
   1. Tehlirian, Soghomon, 1896-1960. 2. Armenian massacres, --1915-1923. 3. Talaat Pasha, 1874-1921--Assassination. 4. Assassins--Armenia--Biography. 5. Armenia--Biography. I. Title.
DS195.3. T44A95   1989
956.6'2--dc 19   89-4759
                                                                          CIP

The CROSS and the CRESCENT

by

Lindy V. Avakian

Published by UCS PRESS
Phoenix, Arizona

"And God shall wipe away all tears from their eyes; and there shall be no more death, neither sorrow, nor crying, neither shall there be any more pain; for the former things are passed away. Behold, I make all things new."

Rev. 21:4

DEDICATION

First and foremost, to my Father, God; His Son, Jesus; and the Holy Spirit.

To Glynna Mae, my wife, for her inspiration and unflagging encouragement, and whose loving interest was so much needed during this writing; Melessa Lynn, my daughter; and Jason David, my son—with love and appreciation for sharing their lives and love with me.

To the memory of Avak Zakar Avakian, my father, and the spiritual and moral richness he symbolizes in the sons and fathers of Armenia—a spirit that will endure forever.

To Surpoohi, my mother, who symbolizes the daughters and mothers of Armenia, whose devotion to noble causes was always based on infinite tenderness.

To the millions of Armenian souls, wounded during centuries of oppression, in the name of Humanity.

And, especially, to the one-and-a-half million Armenian Christians who, in 1915, were slain by the Turks at the foot of His Cross. Planted in the likeness of His death, may they also be in the likeness of His resurrection.

SPECIAL ACKNOWLEDGMENTS

Soghomon Tehlirian, for his contribution and dedication. **Yeranouhi Danielian,** for her contribution and her unselfish dedication. **Larry Acker,** for his tireless efforts, faith, and sound advice; and to his lovely wife, **Suzanne.** **Jim Dobkin**s, for his faith in me and encouragement; and his lovely wife, **Marty.** **Jim Porter,** for his faith and effort; and to his wife, **Barbara.** **Irwin Zucker,** for his encouragement, assistance, and belief in me. **Steve Adler,** for his assistance. **Henry D. Spalding,** noted editor, author and reviewer. His advice and guidance were invaluable in the completion of this book. My heartfelt appreciation is extended to him. **Sam Avakian,** my brother, for his encouragement and untiring efforts in obtaining research data and translating difficult Armenian writings. His assistance, guidance and advice helped make this book possible. **Roger H. Tatarian,** Editor-in-Chief, United Press International, for his advice and encouragement. **Shahan Natalie,** member of the Ninth Assembly Meeting, one of the masterminds of the Plan to mete out justice to war criminals, for his valued information. **Misak Torlakian,** an executioner, for his valuable information towards this writing. **Arshavir Shiragian,** an executioner, for his assistance. **Ronald Allen,** and his charming wife, **Carol,** for their assistance, valued information, and encouragement. **Berg Avakian,** my brother, and his lovely wife, **Queenie,** historical research and translations. **Girard Avakian,** my brother, noted artist; and assistance from his lovely wife, **Sylvan.** **Hoosig** and **Queenie Antoyan,** for their assistance. **Harry Avakian,** my brother, and his wife, Sue, for their assistance and encouragement. **Rosalind** and **Nori Avakian** for assistance, faith and encouragement. **John S. Alexander** and his adorable wife, **Linda,** for their faith, inspiration and encouragement. My deepest appreciation to them both. **Reuben Darbinian,** Editor-in-Chief; **James H. Tashjian,** Editor; and **Sarkis Atamian,** author, of the *Armenian Review*, Hairenik Association, official organ of the Armenian Revolutionary Federation. **Donald Kitterman** and his lovely wife, **Irma,** for their faith and encouragement. **James H. Cox,** Library Administrator, University of California at Los Angeles—the "Armenian Chair of U.C.L.A." **George Mason,** Editor-Publisher, *The California Courier*, Fresno, California. **National Geographic Society,** Washington, D.C. *New York Times*, New York, N.Y. *Christian Science Monitor*, Boston, Massachusetts. *The Fresno Bee*, Fresno, California. *Los Angeles Times* and *Los Angeles Herald-Examiner*, Los Angeles, California. **Dr. K. L. Martin,** German Bar Association—*Bundesrechtsanwaltskammer*, Bonn, Germany. **Andre Amourian,** Editor-in-Chief, *Asbarez*, Fresno, California; his assistance and encouragement were invaluable to this writing. Counsul-General **Hans Rols Kidderlen**; Cultural Minister **Dr. Volkmar von Zuehlsdorff,** Consulate of the Federal Republic of Germany at Los Angeles. **Associated Press,** New York, N.Y. **Reuters International,** London, England. **Mustafa Aksin,** First Secretary, Ambassador **Urguplu** (later Premier), Turkish Embassy, Washington, D.C. **Krikor Amirian,** former Adjutant to the Commanding General of the Armenian Volunteer Regiment. *Chicago Tribune*, Chicago, Illinois. **Hovannes Babessian,** Historian and friend, research and translations; an associate of the Armenian College, Beirut, Lebanon. **Frank Arthur,** for his assistance and encouragement; an excellent writer, and an outstanding radio and television personality. My appreciation to him and to his charming wife,

Genevieve. Rev. Father **Yeghishe Mekhitarian** of the Armenian Apostolic Church; data on personal experience and that of the clergy during massacres. **Alex Eskendarian**, translations and research. **Witold S. Sworakowski**, Assistant Director, Herbert Hoover Institution on War, Revolution and Peace, Stanford University, California. **Armenag Melik**, Editor and Armenian War Correspondent. **Lillian Avakian**, my sister, for her assistance, faith and encouragement. **Los Angeles** and **Hollywood**, California Public Libraries. **Dick Avakian**, my uncle, for his efforts and faith in this writing. **Frank Cooke**, photography, in part. **Mrs. Parantz** (Khamroin) **Ohanessian**, survivor of the death march from the city of Bitlis, Armenia, to the Syrian desert of Der el Zor. **Mrs. Anahid Tehlirian**, lovely widow of Soghomon Tehlirian, for her faith and encouragement. **Lucy Ohanian**, data concerning Soghomon Tehlirian. **Anthony Prince**, French translations. **Mrs. Araxie** (Danielian) **Sebilian**, sister of Yeranouhi Danielian, featured in this book, for her assistance. **Hazel Flynn**, Editorial, *Hollywood Citizen*; data, Armenian victims of massacre. Her experience while with the Herbert Hoover Commission and Near East Relief offered me a wide scope of information. **Al Weymouth**, photography, in part. **Steven Gaal**, noted artist-sculptor; appreciation for his advice. **Guy Chookoorian**, translations. **Orville Andress**, for his advice, guidance and encouragement. **Les Kaufman**, writer-publicist, for his encouragement and assistance; and his lovely wife, **Mary**. **Gabriel Injejikian**, principal and educator, Holy Martyrs Armenian Elementary and Ferrahian High School, Encino, California, for his assistance and guidance; and his lovely wife, **Rose**. **Alice Mudurian**, survivor of massacre at Smyrna, for assistance and information. **Vartan Thomasian**, and his charming wife, **Florence**, for their assistance. **Mr.** and **Mrs. Hrand Simonian**, for assistance, information and encouragement. **Douglas Phanco, Virgil Mitchell, Jack Evans** and my brother, **Koch Avakian**, for their encouragement. **Haugen's Magnum Visual Communications**, photography, in part. **Mr.** and **Mrs. Archie Dickranian**, for assistance, information and encouragement. **Ardythe Hitchcock**, editor, for her direction and inspiration. **Armenian Holy Trinity Apostolic Church**, Fresno, California: to the Very Rev. Father **Vahram Yeghiayan** and Rev. Father **Papken Kasparian** for their contributions to this book. To my family, **Nori** and **Lilly Avakian, Mary** and **Harry Avakian, Larry** and **Cathy Avakian**; my sister, **Alice**, and husband, **John**, and my nieces, **Nancy** and **Norene**, and **Smiley Avakian** for their faith and encouragement. To the more than 200 survivors of the Genocide of 1915, whose personal testimony played a major role in establishing data for this writing. To the countless others who I am unable to mention by name, your efforts made this book possible.

Grateful Recognition to his Excellency, The Honorable **Simon Vratzian**, former Premier of the Repubic of Armenia (1918-1920), for the series of interviews in which he contributed factual and official information exclusively for The CROSS and the CRESCENT.

CONTENTS

	Introduction	10
I.	The Execution	14
II.	Massacre	16
III.	Armenians Strike Back	33
IV.	Ashes In My Fist	41
V.	The Quest	47
VI.	Death Of A Renegade	54
VII.	Executions Authorized	63
VIII.	A Tear For Yeranouhi	68
IX.	The Path Of The Hunter	75
X.	Requiem for Armenia	89
XI.	The Lair	93
XII.	A Bullet For Talaat	110
XIII.	Portrait Of A Prisoner	116
XIV.	The Trial Opens	124
XV.	Parade Of Witnesses Begins	131
XVI.	Atrocities Introduced	146

XVII.	Turkish Horrors Proven	160
XVIII.	Key Witnesses Disclose Atrocities	169
XIX.	Intermezzo	184
XX.	Talaat Exposed As Author of Genocide	192
XXI.	I Demand To Testify	205
XXII.	Prosecution And Defense Rest	211
XXIII.	The Verdict	242
XXIV.	Conclusion	246
	Epilogue	251
	Index	252

INTRODUCTION

The CROSS and the CRESCENT extends far beyond the factual account of a twenty-four-year-old Armenian executioner who emptied his Mauser into the body of the man who authored the Genocide of the Armenians. Although my account begins with a fatal shooting of a fugitive Turkish leader, my intentions were to express history as scholarly historians of old portrayed the facts: with emotional purity and intensity.

The CROSS and the CRESCENT, in essence, is intended to transcend the unremarkable, as Jesus transcended Barabbas. It reaches far beyond the single but important incident of an execution of a Turkish war criminal. It is the story of Armageddon prematurely bestowed upon the people of the first nation to adopt Christianity, in 301 A.D. It is a panoramic view of an Armenia in its former splendor, in its finest hour, suddenly thrust into its death throes by 20th century barbarians; militarists who exploited the deep religious feeling of their own citizens—Turks—through a diabolic plan of fear and hatred, distorting religious differences.

The history of Armenia is an important one. These ancient people, blessed with the wealth of territory beneath Mt. Ararat, unselfishly contributed to the development of a civilized world. Emerging from the birth canal of the Indo-Europeans, they were the pioneers of Alchemy, presented the "Queen Translation" of the Holy Bible, and numerous other important developments which historians have failed to document. They have been in the forefront in defending the Christian faith since the months following the Ascension of Jesus to the heavens, to take His Place beside His Father, God. A scripture borrowed by the late U.S. Senator Robert Kennedy expresses the reason why the Armenians, and the Jewish people, have suffered—not as victims—but as the chosen and selected peoples. Kennedy said, in effect, "To those God has given much, much is expected of them."

The overall view of the Armenians, from ancient times to the present, is history written in blood. Unlike a sacrifice without reason, the Armenians defended the Cross; rather than surrender their faith, they chose to stand boldly against insurmountable odds to defend the faith; devoted stewards of the Dominion. A Dominion which was bestowed upon them at the Upper Room where Jesus directed Saint Bartholomew and Saint Thaddeus to travel to Armenia to introduce Christianity to the peoples whose sacred mountain lovingly held Noah's Ark years before. Their first century ministry led to the inception of the Christian faith into that ancient nation. To this date, it remains the essence of the Armenian worldwide, the mainspring of close ties which permeate the family; an inner radiation which I refer to as the <u>Armenian Spirit</u>. It is a spirit that reaches beyond the nationality referred to as Armenian; rather, it is a blood-tie, a deep Christian love the ancient Greeks called "Agape."

The story of the young Armenian patriot and executioner, Soghomon Tehlirian, fascinating as it is, has deeper implications than the guilt or innocence of one lone man on trial for a fatal shooting. Here are the Crusades brought to the 20th century; the never-ending war of the spiritually right and the morally wrong. This was a life and death struggle, not between personalities, but between irreconcilable concepts of morality. Soghomon Tehlirian was symbolic of the Cross. Talaat Pasha, the murderer of a million-and-a-half innocent Christian men, women and children, represented the Turkish Islamic Crescent. It is difficult to realize that, in this the 20th century, the Turkish *Ittihad Terraki* Regime—the Young Turks—exploited the Turkish Moslems, and with unparalleled bestiality, attempted to annihilate the Christian Armenians in the Turkish Empire—within their own, ancient homeland of 4,000 years—and nearly succeeded before the eyes of the civilized world.

When the holocaust was over, 80 per cent of the Armenians within the Empire were dead (1,500,000); the 350,000 survivors driven from their homeland and that nation erased from the face of the earth, as though some catastrophic earthquake had suddenly devoured the men, women and children in their homes, villages and towns. Some 45 billion dollars of property was destroyed; 2,050 Armenian Apostolic churches, 203 monasteries, 127 Armenian Catholic priests, several hundred Armenian Gregorian (Apostolic) priests, and 57 nuns were lost; as well as countless Protestant churches and ministers were victimized. Only one prelate escaped the frenzied Turks; the others were killed in cold blood. Yet not only has Turkey, to this date, failed to right that wrong, she continues to deny her monumental crime.

Turkey's former premier, Suat Urguplu (Inonu's successor), while ambassador to the United States in 1963, called the 1915 Genocide "alleged massacres." Ismet Inonu, who left the post of premier in February, 1965, and who was responsible for the mass-murder of 250,000 Armenians, Greeks and many Jews, in 1919 and 1922, was a candidate for the 1965 Nobel Peace Prize. It is a shame that Turkey is the only country in history not to accept guilt for such a mass-criminal act; yet she was one of the first in the United Nations to sign the act outlawing Genocide. To date, despite mounds of documentation internationally, Turkey continues to deny the Genocide.

Twenty miles south of Madera, California, my birthplace, lies the city of Fresno and its environs, with its sunny vineyards, orchards and farms, which support a population of many ethnic groups. The Americans of Armenian vintage among them number some 40,000, making it one of the largest communities of this warm-hearted, industrious people in the United States.

Avak Zakar Avakian, my father, was a fearless man of vision, with an acute sense of the heritage and destiny of his people. He held a deep love and respect for an America that had given him and his fellow Armenians refuge. He was a proud American. He was a dedicated father, husband and community leader. But he had a burning love within that fueled his dedication for a lifetime for the re-establishment of a free, democratic nation of Armenia. It was natural, therefore, that his circle of friends and associates would be worldwide, including most organizations and prominent individuals who shared his beliefs and aspirations.

Inevitably his path crossed that of Soghomon Tehlirian, and in the course of their years of corresponding and the time they spent together, their friendship grew and ripened to warm intimacy. My recollections are deeply etched with the inspiring memory of countless discussions with or about Tehlirian, held in the old-fashioned parlor of our home at 422 South Fulton Street in Fresno by representatives of the Armenian Revolutionary Federation and my father, who was a founding officer of the Pacific Coast Council of the A.R.F., and instrumental in forming regional offices throughout the United States, and a key official in the International Congress.

As the years unfolded I learned the facts behind the importance of Armenia in history, shared with me by my father, mother, grandparents, brothers, sisters, political leaders, military leaders, and officials, including members of the clergy that frequented our home. Eventually I came to know and revere the man who was referred to as "The Avenger"—the man who executed Talaat Pasha, the Turkish author of Genocide who, in 1915, boasted: "I shall strike the Armenians such a blow that it will take them fifty years to recover—if they ever do."

April 24, 1989 marks the 74th Memorial of the 1915 Turkish

Genocide, the loss of one-and-a-half million men, women and children, and subsequent loss of their homeland; victims of Talaat's reign of terror. Although the term "Genocide" was not coined until 1944, its grim meaning was known to the Armenians at the turn of the century.

From the wealth of innumerable anecdotes, captured Turkish, German and Soviet documents and communications, interviews with eyewitnesses, and first hand knowledge, this book has been painstakingly written.

Here is the story of Armenia, the cradle of civilization, where existed the Garden of Eden and Noah's Ark upon Armenia's sacred Mt. Ararat; bludgeoned to death at the hands of the modern barbarians, the Turks, as told through the eyes of Soghomon Tehlirian. Although the vivid contents of this true story may prove embarrassing to the Turks, its true purpose is to show how, in this the 20th century, the first Christian nation was made extinct by the century's first act of Genocide. Carried out by a plan so diabolical that it not only destroyed the most productive citizens of the Empire but victimized the average Turk by robbing them of the wealth of their Armenian neighbors. If the world had tried and punished the Turkish war criminals for their crimes against Humanity, would there have been a second Genocide in Hitler's Germany and throughout Europe?

It is this author's wish that this "carefully forgotten" story take its proper place in history and contribute to a world that is free from such heinous criminal acts. And perhaps, in some way, reach the modern Turkish people, especially the young, many who fought alongside me in Korea, and influence positively the need to accept their nation's past error, as have the modern Germans with the Jewish Holocaust, and break the yoke of guilt visited upon the sons and daughters, and grandsons and granddaughters of the perpetrators of the 1915 Genocide. Inasmuch, putting to an end the vicious cycle of misinformation and guilt that must breed itself in modern Turkey under those circumstances. It is then—and only then—that we, as human beings, can rise above the nature of the beast and evolve into a world that God has blessed; a world that places emphasis on caring, and sharing, for the benefit of all—a truly civilized planet, despite differences in ideology and religious beliefs.

Lindy Vahag Avakian
February 14, 1989
Fresno, California

I. THE EXECUTION

The Berlin sky was overcast and leaden on that dreary morning of March 15, 1921. I have good reason to remember the date, for I, Soghomon Tehlirian, was stalking the killer of a million-and-a-half of my fellow Armenians. I watched as he minced through the gathering powder of new-fallen snow. My quarry was the former Prime Minister of Turkey, Talaat Pasha, the first modern architect of the crime of genocide.

Now I was but twenty feet behind the mass-murderer whose trackdown had taken me three long years. I slowed my pace, turned my coat collar up as a shield against the snow that was now turning into a drizzling rain. Just ahead of me an overfed, porcine-faced man waddled through the slush, unaware that he was being followed. The street was almost deserted except for a few stragglers whose heads were hidden beneath their black umbrellas. A beggar wheedled me for the price of a cup of coffee, and I gave him the equivalent of a quarter. Not that I felt philanthropic, but I was anxious to get rid of him.

Why?

I was about to execute a man.

I was now within firing range. My finger tightened on the trigger but I was unable to fire. I simply could not shoot a man in the back, even such a fiend as I knew Talaat to be. An Armenian security agent in Boston once told me that a human being will instinctively turn around at the moment of impending death. I remember experiencing a fleeting hope that he would do so, but no—my obese prey continued to slog through the snow, undoubtedly warmed by the inner glow of satisfaction that he was responsible for the deaths of a million-and-a-half of my people, the forcible deportation of the survivors, and the destruction of my beloved Armenia. Here was the engineer of death, guilty of the massacre of my family. An ungovernable need for retribution engulfed me.

Hurriedly, I crossed into the street and doubled back. Now Talaat approached, only a few yards between us, a grey phantom rising out of the mist. I raised my Mauser automatic and pointed the muzzle at his head, waiting until he was full upon me. I had no intention of missing.

Although he had thought he was well hidden in the teeming city of Berlin, where he lived under the assumed name of one Salieh Bey, and had even altered his features through surgery, it was evident that the dread of ultimate judgment was always with him. I had not uttered a word, but there was no question that he instantly knew me to be an avenging Armenian. His eyes widened in fear. His mouth opened as if to protest. Suddenly he turned to run, the unholy fear of death in his pudgy face.

I fired—Once!

There was no need for a second bullet. He collapsed as though a rod had been pulled from his back. I wondered about my own feelings. It had often occurred to me that, given the opportunity, I would fire shot after shot into Talaat's warped brain. But now I could only stand there quietly, the smoking gun in my hand forgotten. It had done its work.

Talaat's body was sprawled at the curb, his face half submerged in a puddle of water that overran the sewer. Somewhere I could hear the terrified screams of a woman. I was scarcely conscious of the crowd of indignant citizens who surrounded and then mauled me. *"Der Moredehr!"* someone shouted in German. The epithet brought me up sharply.

"Murderer? No! . . . " I thought fiercely. "A million-and-a-half Armenian Christians in their unmarked graves were mute testimony that this had not been a murder—but an *execution.*"

The human who walked the earth on all fours was dead.

II. MASSACRE

My little country of Armenia was no stranger to persecution, having endured six hundred years of merciless oppression under the heel of the Ottoman Empire, whose Turkish warlords enslaved our people, as well as the citizens of other lands.

Like most other Armenian children I learned of the countless Turkish barbarities just a few years after my birth on April 15, 1896, in Erzinga, Armenia. Khachador Tehlirian, my father, and Hnazant, my mother, were Christians, as were all other Armenians. (COMMENT: Armenia is the world's first Christian nation, having adopted Christianity as its national religion in the year 301 A.D.) The Turks, who profess the Islamic faith, seized on this contrast as a pretext and conducted a series of *Jehads*—so-called "holy wars" against us, although it was plain that they really wanted to exploit our land, its resources and our population. Although a young child, I can still recall my three elder brothers—Misak, Avedis, and Setrag—talking about our arrogant conquerors.

My father and uncles were in Serbia (Yugoslavia) attending to their coffee distributing business. They were later joined by two of my brothers. I visited them briefly in 1913, planning to study mechanical engineering when my work there ended. My third brother, Avedis, was studying medicine at the American College in Beirut, Lebanon. The scattering of our family, it was understood among us, was temporary. We planned to unite as soon as our financial condition improved. We Armenians are a clannish people, so it was natural that my mother would be quite happy among our relatives. Joyously we awaited the time when our family would be together again—a dream that was never to be fulfilled. Kaiser Wilhelm had embarked on his scheme of conquest, ushering in World War I. He was soon joined by Armenia's long-time oppressor—Turkey.

Destiny now took a cruel turn. The Turks swept across our beloved Armenia—beneath the very same Mt. Ararat where Noah built his Ark—burning, raping, pillaging, and murdering; soaking our virgin soil with the blood of our vastly outnumbered countrymen. The barbaric deportations and mass killings of peace-loving citizens mounted in intensity and fury; the agony of a nation of civilized people, in pain, unheeded by a world involved in its own problems. The unholy Turk set his plan to annihilate the entire 1,850,000 Armenians of the now Ottoman Empire into motion. Before the nightmare was over, one-and-a-half million of us were murdered, and 350,000 exiled to alien lands, and our country gutted and ravaged.

Here is the bitter report written in September, 1915, by Henry Morgenthau, former United States Ambassador to Turkey: (COMMENT: Mr. Morgenthau was Ambassador to Turkey from 1913 to 1916. He died on November 26, 1946. His son was Secretary of the Treasury under President Franklin Delano Roosevelt.)

> "After 450 years, the evil Turk has come to the end of her misrule of her Christian subjects. Her dominion over the Christians and Jews has been one of savagery. They stand convicted of wholesale murder in the first degree, of committing the most atrocious crimes and beastly tortures of the age and maintaining an unjust, incompetent government.
>
> "They have demonstrated their absolute inability to govern themselves or the nations they have conquered by using sheer brute strength. They have given nothing to these people, no culture, no literature, no architecture, no art, no progress of any kind. They have sapped the lifeblood and energy of their subjects and deprived them of their security and more often their lives. They have ruled by might and fear, depriving themselves of the best part of their population. They have robbed, pillaged and murdered; a conscienceless breed of barbarians unique since man's appearance on earth."

A month after the Morgenthau Report, on October 6, 1915, England's Lord James Bryce, a member of Parliament, rose to his feet in the House of Lords and delivered a blistering attack against Turkey. He said in part:

> "The whole nation of Armenia is nearly extinct as the

result of the Turkish massacres. Nevertheless, I ask that every effort be made to send help to the unfortunate survivors, hundreds of whom are daily perishing by want and disease. It is all that we in England can do; let us do it, and do it quickly.

"Let the German Government tell its friends, the Turkish leaders, that they are preparing themselves a well-earned retribution, and that there are some things which the outraged opinion of the civilized world will not tolerate."

Granted that the atrocities were, in fact, committed, by what right, you may ask, does an individual take it upon himself to slay another as I have done, not once but twice? Surely, it may be argued, executions are the sole prerogative of the State. Still another question may be raised: what possible crimes had they committed which were so heinous as to earn me, an ordinarily peaceful man, the title "The Avenger"?

The men I executed were instrumental in bringing upon my people the greatest tragedy to befall us in all our ancient history. By sword, axe, gun, starvation, abuse and deportation they were responsible for the near-annihilation of the Armenian race and the dispersal of the few survivors across the face of the earth.

The holocaust that despoiled our peaceful little country occurred just prior to and during World War I. It must be remembered that there were no international courts of justice to whom we could appeal. To all intent and purpose we were forgotten or ignored by the countries who could have helped us as we lay bleeding. In 1946 the Allied Powers established a pattern of international law which culminated in the Nuremberg trials where the war criminals of Nazi Germany were tried and sentenced. But—that was 1946, a quarter of a century too late to indict and try the Turks who actually supplied the blueprint for genocide to the Nazi Germans. Hitler, on August 23, 1939, at Obersalzburg, stated: "In 1915 the Turks exterminated the Armenians—who remembers the Armenians now?"

The world knows and looks upon with horror the genocidal attack against the Jewish people during the reign of Adolf Hitler. Six million souls were murdered in the gas chambers and disposed of in the crematoria. The parallel between the Jewish and Armenian holocausts is striking, but comparatively few have ever heard of the inhuman acts committed by the Turks against a helpless Christian population—acts so unbelievably satanic as to revolt the sensibilities of decent people everywhere.

* * * * * * * * * *

It is difficult to pinpoint the precise time that Armenia was bludgeoned to death. One might say it was not a single blow that proved fatal, but a continual rain of skull-shattering concussions. Simple arithmetic tells its horrendous story. When Armenia first was invaded by the Turks in the 14th Century, its population was a flourishing 18,000,000 souls. Through the centuries of relentless attrition the Armenians, who had been in Asia Minor 3,000 years before the advent of the Turks, were finally decimated in the period 1915 to 1918 when 80 percent of the 1,850,000 Armenians who remained were slaughtered and the rest deported.

The summer of 1908 brought with it a short-lived ray of hope that the cruelties might cease. In that year an organization calling itself the *"Ittihad-Terraki Party,"* commonly known as the "Young Turks," seized control of Ottoman Turkey and compelled Sultan Abdul Hamid II to establish what they cynically termed a "constitutional" form of government. (COMMENT: The first appointed Prime Minister, Prince Said Halim Pasha, was later replaced by Talaat Pasha, Minister of Interior.) The Young Turks managed to obtain a favorable press reaction throughout the world. They were lauded by writers as well as nations and described in glowing prose. Their slogan, "Liberty, Equality and Fraternity," struck a responsive chord throughout Europe and America and they were offered material, moral, and financial help.

But while a few of the more optimistic Armenians, especially those living in or near Adana, hoped that the new regime would permit them to live unmolested, the vast majority, alone among world opinion, knew that the snake still retained its fangs.

Six months later the cobra struck!

The city of Adana in April, 1909, was an intellectual center whose Armenian population soon began to feel the oppressor's mailed fist, this time gloved in the superficial "democracy" of the new regime. The unfortunate residents naively believed some of the Turkish declarations and dared to expect the widely-trumpeted declarations of equality and freedom advertised to a gullible West.

The first massacre under the Young Turks ended with the death of 30,000 civilians in the Adana area, thousands of whom were disemboweled and decapitated by the sword-wielding soldiers of Islam. A wave of terror gripped the hearts of every man, woman and child of Armenia. They knew from bitter experience what to expect in the future. The brutal assaults so infuriated Britain's Lloyd George, who was later to become Prime Minister, that he said: "The Turks are a human cancer, a creeping agony in the flesh in the lands which they misgovern. With satisfaction I look forward to a final account."

What lay at the root of the psychopathic hatred held by the Turks against the Armenians? Researchers agree on two primary causes: Turkish moral degeneration and religious fanaticism.

For more than three hundred years the Turks of the Ottoman Empire have done nothing but destroy. Intellectually they were unfit to govern the peoples whom they conquered, practically all of whom were intellectually superior to their conquerors. Like a pestilence, they destroyed large areas, slaughtering the peoples of Greece, Nestoria, Syria, Bulgaria and Armenia. Illiteracy among the Turks has always been high. Venereal and other diseases were often of epidemic proportions. Morality, honesty and common decency were almost unknown virtues in that graft-ridden and corrupt nation. Turkey was justly labelled "The Sick Man of Europe" by the Western nations.

The contrast between the immoral, internally rotten structure that was Turkey could hardly escape critical comparison with its enslaved dominion of Armenia. Here Armenian schools, some of which were sponsored by American and European educators, were filled to the overflowing with eager, bright youngsters intent on an education. (COMMENT: There were 785 Armenian educational institutions and over 85,000 students as compared to only 150 Turkish schools with an enrollment of 17,000.) Because of the influence of the traditional Christian home environment for which the Armenians are noted, morality, literacy and respect for the law were a way of life. In addition, Armenian students in ever increasing numbers were studying at the great universities of Europe and the United States. Thus, while the Turks remained semi-barbarian, existing only by right of conquest, without labor or intelligence, the Armenians were growing culturally and intellectually, greatly respected wherever Christians maintained high standards of ethical, moral and spiritual awareness.

It was inevitable that the Turks would seek to destroy this neighboring people who were their superiors in every branch of the arts and sciences, for they knew that they could not long subjugate an educated, freedom-loving population.

It has been said that more people have been tortured and killed in the name of religion than for any other single reason. If that be true, the Turks have contributed more than their share, for to them, murder of the "non-believers in the true faith" is a divine command with Paradise as the reward. The fundamental reason for this religious insanity will be found in the holy book of Islam, the Koran. (COMMENT: Islam in Arabic means submission to (God) Allah. The religion is based on a book, the "Koran." Mohammed was a prophet of Allah and the adherents are called Moslems, Muslims or Mohammedans. Mecca is their holy city.)

Those of the non-Islamic faith will find it difficult to understand a religion which, in effect, encourages the killing of Christians and Jews. Indeed, their murder is considered to be Allah's holy edict. It was this monstrous religious belief that led to the massacre of 325,000 and the deportation of another half million Armenians in the period of 1894 to 1896, for no other reason than that the victims followed the cross instead of the crescent.

Unbelievable? Let us examine the Koran so that we will understand the religious climate that condoned and even approved, in the name of Allah, torture, treachery, theft, and genocide. We shall then better understand the collective mentality of a nation that still believes it will find eternal joy, promiscuous love, and other uninhibited heavenly rewards as divine gifts for having destroyed the lives of the "infidels," as the Koran describes Christians and Jews.

Here are excerpts and chapters of eight injunctions as they appear in the Koran, which Talaat and his henchmen used to inflame the fanatically "religious" Turkish masses against the non-Moslem world. As translated from the Arabic:

1. Fight therefore against the infidels until there be no more temptation to idolatry, and the religion be Allah's. (Ch. 2)

2. War is enjoined you against the infidels. But this is hateful unto you; yet perchance ye hate a thing which is better for you, and perchance ye love a thing which is worse for you; but Allah knoweth, and ye knoweth not. Restrain their hands, then seize them and kill them wherever you find them. And against these, we have given you a clear authority. (Ch. 2)

3. Ye are also forbidden to take to wife free women who are married, except those whom your right hand shall possess as prisoners or slaves if they become Moslems. (Cp. 4)

4. Those who believe, fight in the way of Allah; those who disbelieve, fight in the way of the Devil. Fight against the friends of Satan, for the stratagem of Satan is weak. (Ch. 4)

5. They are surely infidels who say, verily God is Christ, the Messiah, the son of Mary. (Ch. 5)

6. O true believers, take not the Jews and Christians for your friends; they are friends the one to the other. And whosoever amongst you takes them for friends, he is indeed one of them. Surely Allah guides not the unjust. (Ch. 5)

7. And when the months wherein ye are not allowed to attack them shall be past, kill the idolators wheresoever ye shall find them, and take them and besiege them, and lay in wait for them in every ambush. (Ch. 9)

8. When you encounter the unbelievers, strike off their heads, until ye have made a great slaughter among them. (Ch. 47)

"Churches were burned or turned into stables," wrote Rev. Frederick Greene, a missionary. "Other churches, their crosses ripped away, were converted into warehouses in which personal and household effects, stolen from the massacred Armenian people were held."

The *Hamidehs,* Kurdish tribesmen, in conjunction with their fellow Moslems, the Turks, also committed unspeakable crimes in the name of Allah. According to many published press dispatches, they not only raped mere children but were seen sexually violating the dead bodies of women. These ghouls apparently had an affinity for corpses. They would murder priests, shred the bodies with bullets and swords, and publicly mangle the private parts of the dead clergymen. All the while they would laugh hideously as they ripped the bodies to pieces like wild animals, loudly challenging Christ's intervention.

The British Blue Book, an official documentary on the Turkish atrocities against the Armenians, reports that the Turks, singing the praise of Allah, placed children in a row, like dominoes, and then fired their rifles through their little bodies to see how many would fall dead from each bullet. After that, in order to win their places in Paradise, they bound the wrists and ankles of the still-living children, soaked them with kerosene and burned them alive—their exultant laughter mingling with the agonized screams of the dying boys and girls.

The list of crimes committed against the Christians by the Islamic savages in the name of Allah is lengthy enough to fill this and several other volumes. I do not itemize those which I myself witnessed nor the eyewitness accounts given by scores of my countrymen. For the purposes of this chapter I confine my reports to those facts which have been documented. For example, I refer to the United States Congressional Record:

> "Columns of soldiers, their Turkish and German officers watching smilingly, held children aloft by their hair as others, bayonets affixed, galloped past the youngsters in a devilish game to see if they could sever their heads from their bodies with one cut. Those youngsters who somehow managed to remain alive, were used in another game to test the strength of the soldiers. The strongest Turks vied against each other in a contest which called for bare-handedly ripping the children's jaws apart in the shortest possible time. The quivering bodies were casually thrown to the ground and left to writhe in torture until merciful death brought an end to their suffering."

Multiply these diabolical instances a thousandfold and the total will represent but a tiny part of the atrocities done in the name of the Islamic faith.

Another substantiated instance published in the world press tells of a Gregorian church in which nearly a hundred Armenian girls, ranging in age from nine to fifteen, were held captive by fifty Turks. Outside, fathers and mothers of the girls were horrified to see blood seeping through the crevices of the front door and trickling down the church steps to the street below. The children had been raped and slaughtered.

There is the documented account of the priest who was flayed alive, his skin stuffed with hay, and left to hang on a crude cross as a mockery to the "infidel" God.

Many Armenians remember the seventy-eight-year-old priest who was disemboweled when he refused to embrace the Islamic faith. *"Yehs Heesoos chem guhnar ooranall* —I cannot deny my Jesus," were his last words.

"Then let Jesus stop this, the wish of Allah!" they screamed, thrusting their bayonets into his abdomen.

This, then, was the much-vaunted Moslem Holy War—*Jehad* —whose righteousness was, and still is, fervently defended by the average Turk. But the "spiritual" and political leaders, such as Talaat, Enver, Djemal, Khalil, Halim, Shekir and others, believed no such nonsense. They used religion as a pretext to incite the Turkish masses against the Christians so that they, the instigators, would be free to plunder and loot, robbing the Armenians of their possessions and their very lives. Hypocrisy, "religion" and greed were the handmaidens to the Turkish ambitions that erupted in the near-extermination of my people.

* * * * * * * * *

The atrocities perpetrated by Turk religious fanatics were not merely confined to the 1915-18 period. Indeed, the acts of barbarism against non-Moslems (Jews and Christians) stemmed from the very beginning of the Ottoman Empire. Nor were the deeds always committed in the name of Allah, but often through the sheer blood-lust which has characterized the Turks for so many, many centuries.

April, 1915, represents one of the blackest months in modern history. It was then that the Ottoman Empire's Talaat Pasha launched the Plan to exterminate the Armenian people—now a minority—within its borders. In six months nearly a million human beings were killed; victims of an unparalleled program of systematic destruction.

(COMMENT: Veteran news analyst Raymond Gram Swing, the American War Correspondent at Dardanelles in 1915, stated: "The biggest blunder of the 20th Century occurred in March, 1915, when the Allied warships were withdrawn after one was struck by a single torpedo. They withdrew from the Turkish straits in the belief that Turkish and German land torpedo stations were in existence. The fact was: they had none. World War I could have ended there and then." This statement was corroborated by

Armenia's former premier, Simon Vratzian, in an exclusive interview with this author on February 12, 1963, in Los Angeles. The former premier added: "One-and-a-half million of our fellow countrymen might still be alive; our country still our own. Millions throughout the world might yet be alive.")

Here is a press dispatch released by the "American Committee for Armenian Relief" in May, 1915, and republished throughout America:

> "The city of Kharpert, Armenia, the home of many of Armenia's professional and cultural leaders, has become a burial ground for thousands of victims of the Turkish mass slaughters. From all directions they have been brought to Kharpert to be buried. There they lie, and the dogs and vultures devour their bodies. Now and then a glassy-eyed man throws some earth over the corpses.
>
> "In Kharpert and Mezre the people have had to endure terrible tortures. The women have had their eye-lashes pulled from their lids, their breasts cut off and their nails torn out. The Turks hack off their feet or else hammer nails into them just as they do in shoeing horses. This is all done at night, and in order that the people may not hear the screams and know the agony, Turkish soldiers are stationed around the prisons, beating drums and blowing whistles. It is needless to relate that many died in these tortures. When they die, the soldiers cry: 'Now let your Christ help you!'"

I have never been able to erase the soul-shattering memories of that summer when, as a seventeen-year-old youth, I encountered dozens, then scores, then hundreds of fleeing refugees from the Turkish terror. The reports which I heard from countless lips still return to me in nightmares.

"The entire Armenian population of Erzeroum has been banished," a priest told me. "In town after town the Turks smashed into private homes, driving the inhabitants into the streets, throwing them into prison and putting them to death after terrible tortures. The younger men were marched to the outskirts of the town and slaughtered."

"Were none left alive?" I gasped.

"A few," he said sadly. "Mostly old men, women and children."

It was from many others that I learned the horrifying fate of the survivors. All over Armenia they were being sent on death marches, driven like cattle to the distant areas of Asia Minor or more frequently to the Der-el-Zor desert, east of Aleppo. Unmercifully whipped as they marched, many perished from the beatings. Countless others died of starvation. Thousands were robbed of their very clothes and then axed to death. Women were sold to the slave traders or raped and then beaten into insensibility, their unconscious forms loaded on wagons and hauled away, never to be seen again.

It sounds incredible, but the verified truth is that at least on one occasion, in the city of Trebizond, 15,000 Armenian captives were herded aboard ships, some packaged alive in wooden boxes, and then thrown overboard to drown in the Black Sea. Those who clung to the sides of the boats were shot. The few women who were spared death by drowning were, as usual, raped and marched hundreds of miles into the desert to die.

Here is how the *London Times* described the frightening event:

"London-June 5, 1915:
"Turkish authorities are driving hundreds of Armenians southwards towards Syria in a merciless wholesale deportation program that already has taken an estimated half a million lives.

"Thousands are dying daily from hunger and mistreatment during death marches across the country. Others are being taken outside their home towns, slaughtered and thrown into mass graves.

"Secret accounts coming from Turkey indicate that in many cases the men of Armenian towns have been rounded up at night and taken away. Women and children then have been forced to leave all their belongings behind and begin marching toward remote parts of the Ottoman Empire.

"Joining guerrilla bands, Armenian men of other cities have managed to escape and fight back. Turkish forces have been unable to subdue them, despite the fact that the Armenians apparently have few arms and little ammunition. They were disarmed by order of the government long ago.

"In some districts, such as Bitlis and Van, there is said

to have been hardly any organized deportation. Instead there has been outright massacre. In others, such as Erzeroum and Trebizond, deportations have begun and then the convoys have been butchered systematically at an early stage on the road.

"Thousands of refugees are streaming out of Turkey, pushing on to other parts of the Ottoman Empire such as Syria or escaping into the Caucasus or Georgia.

"Estimates of the number who have been killed or have died of hardship have passed the half-million mark and are still rising."

United Press (later *U.P.I.*) reporter Henry Wood, on the scene at the time of the massacres, sent this cable to *U.P.'s* New York office:

"It is now apparent that the order for extermination of the Armenians was issued early in April, 1915, and was put into effect with the cruel genius of the Turkish police and army troops. Telegraphic orders, in addition to sealed orders, were dispatched to administrators throughout the Empire. Lists of Armenian civic leaders were sent from Constantinople and they were quickly arrested and killed. The entire Armenian population is in danger of annihilation."

And on October 8, 1915, the *New York Tribune* editorialized:

"With callous equanimity Germany has allowed its Turkish partner to continue the extermination of the Armenian people. Germany's attitude of indifference is not mere injury to written law; that is a minor detail. She has allowed, in the twentieth century, a condition of the Dark Ages. But whatever Germany does now, she must do it quickly, because the judgment of humanity refuses to allow the oppressors as well as their counterparts to go free without retribution. That is the indictment. Let Germany cease to deserve it."

A secret, unusually emotional report for a diplomat, marked "urgent," was dispatched to Rome on August 25, 1915, by the Italian Consul-General, Signor Garrini. So outraged was the King of Italy that permission was given to publish the account in the *Journale IL Messagooro* :

"The slaughter of the innocents, a black page stained with the flagrant violation of the sacred rights of humanity, has been ordered by the Central Turkish Government. I saw 15,000 Turkish troops, armed with the finest equipment, and thousands of Turkish civilian volunteers move on this peaceful community and rain devastation on the Armenians. After the Turkish slaughter of July 23, 1915, I can no longer eat or sleep. I have been given to seizures of nausea and nerves. I even sobbed because there was nothing I could do to help those defenseless, innocent creatures. They fell before my very office window, their prayers and cries for help silenced by the Turkish soldiers, mobs and gangs of fiends who were killing them wholesale.

"All the Armenians are dying.

"Their possessions, their homes, are being given to Turkish civilians. The Armenians who survived the axe, the sword, the rifle, have been bound and taken to the Black Sea and the River Deyirmen and drowned.

"I am almost driven frantic to describe the happenings here. For one month I endured this dreadful sight. I can no longer compose myself. If the great Powers knew what I know, they could not for a moment hesitate to come to the rescue of these Armenians; at least in the name of Christendom. World, rise up and cry anathema against these inhuman Turks! Those who assist Turkey, or her loyal Germany ally, I say that they should be marked forever as a shame, a horror and a disgrace to mankind."

Blood curdling and factual as I knew these reports to be, they were as nothing as compared to eyewitness accounts that tore at my heartstrings. As a soldier with the Armenian Volunteer Regiment I remember meeting one old man in a desolate area bordering Persia, a venerable grandfather who told me of his own personal tragedy. He held a little girl on his knee. She was about seven years old. The child had been shocked into speechlessness and could not regain her voice. The grandfather explained:

"Her mother—my daughter—was killed two weeks ago because she tried to protect her little girl from the Turks and Kurds. When they attempted to molest the child, her mother interfered.

For that they took her to the mountain and buried her up to her neck in the earth. When this child was released the next day, after she had been violated, she crept to the place where her mother had been almost buried. Wolves had chewed and then torn her head from her living body. Friends found my granddaughter and brought her to me. She hasn't uttered a word since." The old man covered his face with his hands and wept bitterly. The child just stared vacantly and smiled a little, mercifully lost in a private, kinder world of her own.

The massacres had attained such a degree of ferocity that President Wilson, in the autumn of 1915, was advised of its seriousness in a special dispatch from a newspaper correspondent, Armin T. Wagner:

> "Hon. Woodrow Wilson
> The President of the United States,
> The White House,
> Washington, D.C.
> Your Excellency:
> "Armenians from the highlands, numbering in the thousands, have been force-marched to Aleppo by the Turks. On arrival, only a few hundred were in any semblance of health. Blackened, swollen corpses are strewn in the fields, the decomposing bodies befouling the air. The corpses are bound back-to-back and naked, having been robbed of their clothes. Hundreds upon hundreds of Armenian dead are floating in the Euphrates.
> "Turkish militia are withholding food from their victims who are being starved to death. I saw several of the guards tantalize the unfortunates by tossing scraps of food to them and howl with laughter as they fought among themselves like wild animals for the morsels. Even as they chewed they were beaten with clubs and whips, some of the victims dying with bits of food clutched in their fingers.
> "At the gates of Aleppo they were held at bayonet point, compelled to remain on their feet without rest even though some had been on the road for forty-five days or more. They were driven on, barefoot, almost without clothing, in shrunken parties, for hundreds of miles, through stormy defiles, over pathless steppes, and increasingly enfeebled in their wilderness of desolation. During their

march nearly all died. Most of the survivors were slain.

"The few men who were left were robbed of what little clothes they still possessed and then hanged, shot, axed, poisoned, stabbed and strangled. The others met death through drowning, thirst, starvation and disease, their bodies left to putrefy or be devoured by jackals. The women were forced to disrobe and then were violated before their terrorized sisters, mothers and children.

"The Turks have taken children of all ages and dashed their brains out against the rocks. Men have been herded to the mountains where they were butchered like swine. Women with hymns on their lips were driven into the Euphrates River where, together with their infants, they were drowned.

"The Armenian people, at the hands of the Turks, have died all the deaths on earth. Those who still live implore you in the name of God and your great nation to hear their cries.

Respectively,
Armin T. Wagner"

The Turkish butcheries resulted in another torrent of indignation in newspapers throughout the world. The *London Daily Express* published one of the most scathing editorials ever written about an entire nation. Under the heading, "The Huns of The East," the newspaper said of the Turks:

"They are still the blind destroyers. They have contributed nothing to the life spirit. They can burn and massacre, but they cannot build or create. The Turks have no place in modern Europe, nor indeed, in the modern world. The Young Turks are a thousand times more detestable than the old Turks."

The Turkish atrocities touched off a gusher of anguish which could not adequately be conveyed by the cold ink and newsprint of the world press. People everywhere were revolted at the reports coming out of stricken Armenia. Even I found it difficult to absorb the shocking fact that my people were being murdered by the thousands and tens of thousands. But the horror of it all was brought home to me by Parantzie Khamroian (Later to become

Parantzie Ohanessian, she is a member of the author's family and lives in Fresno, California.), a simple girl of nineteen, a young mother of two small children. Although history establishes the massacres of the Armenians by the Young Turks as having started in the Spring of 1915, she related her experience of the first deportations which had taken place in the Spring of 1914—a year before the official extermination decree was even ordered by Talaat. I can still recall her story.

"It was a few days after Easter," said Mrs. Khamroian. "I was nineteen. I was in my kitchen baking *lavash* bread. My two-year-old daughter was staying with my mother in a village several miles from our native Bitlis and my one-year-old son, Joseph, was asleep. I was terribly worried about my husband, Ahbet, a cabinet maker, who had not returned from his job. We knew that nearly five hundred men had been jailed without reason. All of a sudden a squad of Turkish police, their swords and rifles swinging from their belts, burst into my home and arrested me. The squad captain snatched my little Joseph from his crib and hurled him into my arms.

"Driven into the street at bayonet point I looked on with despair as an officer affixed the black seal of the Turkish government on the door; silent proof that our property had been confiscated and would be given to a Turk. I could not know, of course, that I was the first deportee in Bitlis and that one year later, in April, 1915, the entire Armenian population was to be exterminated or deported by the Turks.

"'Where is my husband, Ahbet?' I pleaded, terror-stricken.

"'*Sesehn Kass!*—don't complain!' an officer shouted, smashing me to the ground with a rifle butt. Half insensible I retrieved my now bleeding baby and, prodded by the sharp bayonets, I was forced to march through the streets. Friends and neighbors who attempted to intervene were slashed and stabbed.

"I never saw my husband again.

"Hours later," Mrs. Khamroian went on, "I was whipped to the outskirts of Bitlis where I joined hundreds of others, captive young mothers and girls who had been rounded up in surrounding towns and cities, their husbands, fathers, brothers and sweethearts murdered, as was my husband. Wearing nothing but my housedress I was forced to march in the blistering sun with the other unfortunate women, the bayonets of twenty-five or more Turkish policemen stabbing us onward to the hills outside of Bitlis. All day and throughout that horrible night we plodded along the rocky roads until the sun rose again over the mountain crests. Those who faltered from sheer exhaustion were shot and callously dropped over the cliffs. Some of the young girls, many who had not yet reached their teens, were raped and then killed. I breast-fed Joseph as we walked. I was not even allowed to stop long enough to nurse my baby.

"In the morning we passed several mountain streams but I dared not risk a drink. The Turkish guards had already shot down three desperate girls who sought to quench their agonizing thirst. All that day we marched beneath the blazing sun, without food or water. Most of us became ill. I pleaded for water, not for myself but for my infant. My answers were bayonet stabs.

"Little Joseph, with only eleven months of life on God's earth, died in my arms. My parched breasts, their milk turned to dust, were unable to to give him the nourishment his tiny soul needed to retain the spark of life. When my baby died . . . I wanted to die, too."

Her story unnerved me. Like most men I can absorb the sufferings of adults but wanton cruelty to sucklings is more than I can bear. I tried to comfort young Mrs. Khamroian. Together we said a prayer for baby Joseph.

Moving with Armenian guerrilla forces I journeyed onward, hearing tales of almost incredible tortures, consoling the living victims when I could, and all the while an awareness of the savagery of the Turk grew within me—a feeling that was to change the course of my life.

III. ARMENIANS STRIKE BACK

The people of Armenia, what pitiful remnant was left of us, rose in anger against the oppressors, determined to forfeit our lives in an effort to drive the Turks from our land. But within the borders of the Ottoman Empire, the Armenians had long since been stripped of all weapons and prohibited from possessing anything which might be used as arms. Most of the males between twenty-one and forty-five years of age had been conscripted into the Turkish Army. They were never given weapons but were, instead, dispatched to remote areas where they were put to work building roads, digging tunnels and draining swamps. The Armenian population, possessing no arms, their fighting youth conscripted, were left without any means of self-defense, and virtually at the mercy of the Turks.

Systematically the widespread butchery began, slowly at first and then increasing in ferocity. The 200,000 young Armenian males who were forcibly taken into the army were axed, stabbed or shot to death by their Turkish officers. It was plain enough by now that the Turks had never intended to use the Armenian men as soldiers in their war against the Western Powers. The entire recruitment was a hellish device to lure the young men away from their homes and communities where they could be murdered in the tens of thousands. The purpose behind this appalling program was twofold: first, to decimate the Armenian population of its potential fighting men and, secondly, to destroy the biological basis of a possible future Armenia.

None of these atrocities came as a surprise to General Antranik (Ozanian), Supreme Commander of the Armenian Volunteer Regiment, comprising a total force of about 10,000 men. It is interesting to note that the volunteer regiment, which fought under the banner of the Armenian Revolutionary Federation, was organized and staffed by the handful of survivors who comprised the *Fedeii*—the Armenian Fighting Elite. These were a small but valiant band of guerrillas who had been fighting the Turks ever since the massacres of 1894. Now they imbued the volunteer regiment with an esprit de corps that pervaded all four of our comparatively small divisions. *Zoravahr* (General) Antranik had already set up headquarters in Tiflis, in the province of Georgia, where he organized the nucleus of the Armenian Volunteer Regiment. Shortly thereafter, in October, 1914, the first of his field headquarters was established at Diliman, on the southeastern border of Armenia where it meets Persia (Iran).

Eventually, Commanding General Antranik established four divisional headquarters staffed by officers selected from the Fighting Elite. The field headquarters at Diliman, in the province of Salamaust on the Persian-Armenian border, was under the commands of Generals Sumpat, Mourad, Gaidzag, Sebouh and the latter's adjutant, Lt. Amirian. The region surrounding Igdir was commanded by General Dro. General Hamazsasb commanded at Kagizman, while the Field Headquarters at Sarikamis was under General Keri.

Said General Antranik, in a classic statement that merits a niche in history: "If our officers had been able to recruit the 200,000 youths whom the Turks had lured into the army and massacred, our volunteer regiment troops would have driven the Turks back to the gutters of Constantinople from whence they sprang." (COMMENT: Constantinople was renamed Istanbul in 1929.)

When my bleeding nation called, I immediately left Serbia where I had been working for my father's coffee distributing company, and journeyed through Rumania and on to Tiflis and then to Diliman. The volunteer forces did not include many men directly from Armenia, but comprised a force of patriotic young Armenians from the United States, Latin America, England and non-Turkish Europe, the Caucasus and the Middle East. Volunteers flocked to the symbol of liberty that was General Antranik, ready to fight for Armenia's destiny. Later, another 5,000 volunteers were to be formed to fight on other fronts bordering Armenia, making for a total of 15,000.

I immediately attempted to join the irregulars. I was almost seventeen years old then, but I had grown a mustache in order to appear older so that I would be allowed to fight beside my countrymen. When I finally managed to enlist in the infantry my pride knew no bounds. It was enough for me to know that I was one of General Antranik's fellow fighters. It was here also that I began a lifelong friendship with a daring, rugged, yet cultured gentleman, my immediate commanding officer, Lt. Krikor

Amirian. (COMMENT: Lt. Amirian resided with his family in Los Angeles, California and was an active official of the Federation until his untimely passing in August, 1964.)

There were 250 men in our outfit and we all loved and respected Lt. Amirian. Truthfully, I was almost rejected from military service. Lt. Amirian, a veritable Samson of a man, took one look at me and snorted, "Go home and put some meat on your bones, Junior. You're too skinny to be lugging a rifle. If you ever did meet a well-fed Turk you'd need a lightweight pistol, not heavy army gear."

His words were prophetic, although I could not, of course, have known it then. *"Mee mudahokneer eem voskornehroos* — never mind my bones," I retorted audaciously. "Skinny or not, just put me in the front lines where I can get some Turks."

Lt. Amirian scowled blankly for a moment at my impudence and then his square face slowly softened in a wide grin. He rose to his feet, snatched a rifle from a rack, and threw a cartridge-laden bandoleer across my shoulder. "Go get the Turks, Junior! ... Say, what did you say your name was....?"

After a hurried preliminary training we moved to the front lines where, to my surprise, I met my brother Misak. But we were soon separated. I never saw him again.

From that moment on it was one ferocious battle after another as we fought our way into the hills, the mountains, finally advancing deep into Armenia. Eventually we reached the city of Van where we met our converging volunteer forces from the north and east. From Van we advanced westward to the cities of Bitlis and Moush, smashing the numerically superior enemy who often outnumbered us ten to one, and at times even more.

I will never forget the Battle of Diliman in April, 1915. The massacres were now taking their bloody toll throughout Armenia. Our 10,000 irregulars were confronted by more than 75,000 well-trained Turkish regulars. During the first few hours of fierce fighting we were driven back from the Diliman Hills by their sheer numbers. But we quickly rallied. Indeed, we had no alternative— the Turks took few live prisoners. Regrouping our forces, we attacked. It was soon evident that the Turks had no heart for shooting at people who could shoot back. They retreated. Within twelve hours we killed three thousand of them, pursuing them as they withdrew in panic. For three days and nights, without rest, we fought the massively superior enemy forces as they fled in disorganized retreat. We clashed with them in the valleys and on the slopes and rugged mountain terrain of Diliman, pursuing them until we had reached Van, about a hundred miles distant.

For us it was a joyous victory. For the well-equipped Turks, their crack cavalrymen notwithstanding, it was a disastrous rout. Against their superior German military equipment, ours were only grenades and rifles. In contrast to their smart uniforms we wore khakis made by Armenian women, and crude, lamb-skin hats, exactly as worn by General Antranik himself. Although our officers' uniforms were of better material than those of us enlisted men, no rank marks were displayed. Here was an ideal example of a numerically small, democratic force, imbued with the fervor of liberty and moral right, vanquishing a great host of brutish, would-be assassins. We also were pleased with the knowledge that we had rescued more than 25,000 Armenian men, women and children from certain annihilation at the hands of the Turkish murderers.

There were many valiant battles throughout Armenia in which I did not participate. Many of them were fought, not by our volunteer regiments, but by the civilian population itself in a last ditch effort to save themselves from extinction. These heroic resistances occurred mainly in those towns and villages where word had been received that the inhabitants were about to be massacred. Among them were Shabin Karahissar, the area of Shadakh, Pesan Valley, the five villages of Musa Dagh and the cities of Zeitoun, Ourfa, Bitlis, Van, Moush and Sassoun.

History will undoubtedly record the Armenian defense of Shabin Karahissar as one of the most heroic and savage struggles in modern times. (COMMENT: Shabin Karahissar, the birthplace of General Antranik, Armenia's great military hero, was renamed Sebenkarahisar by the Turks after their — and the Soviet — conquest of the Republic of Armenia. Once a populated center of Armenian culture, not a single Armenian is alive there today. The population in the mid-1960's numbered 7,542 Turks. Shabin Karahissar, the site of the famous battle which bears that name, is situated 80 miles northeast of the city of Sivas and 40 miles south of the Black Sea.)

The resistance was hopeless from the beginning, but the courageous citizens bequeathed a heritage to the few who were left that, to this day, makes their hearts sing with pride. The city of Shabin Karahissar, nestled at the base of a mountain slope, has a history extending back to before the time of Christ. Above the peaceful town was an ancient fort constructed by the Romans in

60 B.C. Over the front of the main gate to the citadel, a Roman eagle, carved in the masonry, could be seen. It was here in the lofty nest of the eagle that the Armenian defenders were witness to the destruction of the Roman aerie by the Turks.

Word had just been brought to the inhabitants by the few escapees from nearby Poork that 13,000 Turks were assaulting every Armenian city in that area and that Shabin Karahissar was next. The city of 5,000 souls, robbed of their 300 young men who had already been massacred by their Turkish officers, prepared to fight. Surrounded by more than 13,000 Turks who were constantly reinforced, and who were armed with every modern weapon of war, the 5,000 men, women and children prepared to defend themselves. Of the defenders, less than 600 were armed with outmoded rifles and crude grenades. But they all fought; with bullets, rocks, sticks and stones, and then with their bare hands—for 26 agonizing days and nights. Only 47 souls, those who were on patrol, survived the massacre. They were to join the guerrilla bands of Mourad of Sebastia to seek retribution against the hated oppressor.

The Turks, accompanied by their Moslem priests, screamed "In the name of Allah!" as they converged on the helpless city like a great swarm of locusts. The defenders barricaded their homes to protect their women and children. The few who had weapons fought from the rooftops and the streets. But to no avail. The heavily armed, overwhelmingly superior Turkish forces could not be halted. Soon the cry, "Withdraw to the Fort!" was passed from family to family. Desperately they began the rocky one thousand foot ascent. But first, burning the city, a delaying action against the Turks. What their thoughts were as they saw their homes and possessions being consumed by leaping flames can only be imagined.

The Turks, however, quickly broke through the cordon of fire and closed in on the escaping civilians, shouting and hacking, their insane laughter drowning the terrified screams of the women and children. Countless bodies dotted the slopes of the *dagh* (mountain) before the survivors reached the lofty "eagle's nest."

The next twenty-six days and nights were filled with drama, a drama that will never end. Time and time again the Turks ascended the slopes of the mountain and time and time again they were driven back. Now the women and children joined the fight, shoulder to shoulder with their embattled husbands and fathers. Braving the constant change in the weather—from the burning heat of summer to stormy nights and summer rains—they fought from the mountain summit. Day after day, night after night, with grenades, rifles, sticks and stones, the Armenians repelled the ferocious onslaught of the Turkish attackers. The women worked shifts, alternately baking *lavash* —bread—in the caves and firing at the invaders who climbed the walls which surrounded the Fort. From the west, east, north and south, shouting and screaming, they were repulsed by the dwindling civilian defenders. In the darkness of night, patrols would descend the mountain to capture food and ammunition from the Turks. On one occasion a group of women, leading a few sheep up the side of the mountain, were caught and literally torn to pieces by the savage enemy.

As the days passed, Armenian observers, using binoculars, viewed with dismay the long line of Turkish reinforcements heading for the city. There seemed to be no end of them. Ammunition was almost exhausted. Women and children hurriedly refilled the few remaining magazines as the others held the attackers at bay. Now even the supply of food had shrunk to almost nothing. The day's lone meal included one egg, a handful of walnuts and a piece of bread. Sometimes there was a sliver of cheese and a few ounces of soup. The water supply, what was left from the winter snow, was being hoarded in crocks.

On the twenty-third day, a battery of enemy artillery had arrived, including a dozen or more cannons manned by Turkish soldiers but directed by German officers. For the next several days and nights the Fort was incessantly bombarded. Although the Armenian resistance had cost the Turks many casualties, the reinforcements quickly filled the ranks left open by the Turkish dead and further swelled the attacker's force with several thousand newly arrived troops.

On the night of June 26th, a patrol of forty-seven Armenians left the Fort to reconnoiter. They were never to return. Columns of Turks now blocked re-entry to their mountain bastion. They were later to join the guerrilla bands commanded by General Mourad and continue their fight against the Turks.

After twenty-six days and nights of unceasing struggle, on June 28, 1915, the siege came to its inevitable end. It was on that day that the soldiers of Islam made their last and most powerful onslaught. Under an umbrella of heavy shells, advancing behind a curtain of bullets, they progressed to within yards of the Armenian stronghold. The furious bombardment now increased in intensity, its deadly accuracy predetermined by the German military command. Almost completely demolished by the cannon fire, the walls of the Fort crumbled. The Turks, faces contorted, voices rising in a crescendo of lunacy, flowed like an avalanche into the compound that had been impregnable for two thousand years.

The defending men, women and children were clustered in the center of the Fort. They clung to each other, offering their final prayers to a God who, it seemed, had abandoned them. Wave after wave of sword-wielding Turks descended on the kneeling, little group, their "amens" smothered by the screaming, fanatical horde. The defense of Shabin Karahissar had come to a tragic, bloody end.

An Armenian fighter, one of the forty-seven survivors who had been on reconnaissance patrol, described the scene he and his fellow guerrillas witnessed when they returned to Shabin Karahissar weeks later:

"The Fort had been leveled to the ground. Wherever we looked were the scarcely recognizable corpses of our neighbors and loved ones. Hanging by their ankles at the main gate were the disemboweled, naked bodies of our two priests. Inside the caves where our wives, daughters and sweethearts had baked bread during the siege, were their charred remains."

There were many such heroic struggles in which my people refused to go like lambs to the slaughter. Often, in the face of certain devastating defeat, we resisted fiercely rather than be murdered.

Despite these losses there is little question that the Armenians who were defending their homeland would have completely demolished the enemy within the next few months had not the Russians, who had also been fighting on the Eastern Front against the Central Powers, defected into the new Soviet camp.

The Bolsheviks had just come into power, and under their leader, Nikolai Lenin, proclaimed themselves "Champions of the Minorities!" Within days, the self-styled "Champions" conveniently forgot the Armenians. They promptly abandoned their pledges, deserting us in our hour of peril—along with the other Allied nations.

Soon the void left by the withdrawing ex-Czarist Russians, now turned Communists, manifested itself on the battlefield. Along a 225-mile front line stretching from Van to Erzinga, the Turks under the command of Talaat's cohort, Prussian-trained Enver Pasha, struck with hammer blows in an all-out attempt to penetrate the Baku oil fields. It was this strategic area which their friends, the Germans, relied upon for fuel for their war machines. But somehow, we Armenians fought tenaciously, holding the Eastern Front for six months and preventing the Turks from seizing that rich source of oil. It was this courageous action that helped stall the Kaiser's war machine, thus contributing to the Allied victory in the Second Battle of the Marne.

But it was not long before our supplies and equipment had become so scarce and our ranks so decimated by the continuous warfare that our volunteer regiment had no recourse but to disband. Like most of my comrades-in-arms I joined the guerrilla bands of Mourad of Sebastia and successively with Generals Gaidzag, Arakel, Sebouh and others of the Fighting Elite—*the Fedeii*.

The battles grew increasingly brutal. This was soldiering such as few men anywhere, at any time, were to know it. We were hampered by minute supplies, fighting over unimaginably difficult terrain, sometimes in constant thirty-below-zero weather, at other times in the blistering heat. My comrades and I went through incredible hell, fighting our way into Garin, Papert and finally into my home city of Erzinga, gathering the few Armenians who still remained alive. These homeless stragglers we escorted to safety, and then to the Caucasus. I do not know the precise number but in this manner we saved well over twenty-five thousand of our people who would have otherwise been slaughtered.

One would think that our triumphant re-entry into Erzinga, the only home I ever really knew, would have filled me with joy. But the opposite was true. Within a few hours, I was to know the most shattering grief that a man can feel—an experience that was to ultimately place me on trial for my life in another country, surrounded by a strange people whose language I did not even understand—a trial that was to be headlined in every metropolitan newspaper on earth.

IV. ASHES IN MY FIST

My youthful pride in having helped recapture the city of my childhood, Erzinga, was tempered by the utter devastation of the city. A language has yet to be invented that can adequately describe the shambles and the extent of Turkish brutality evident all around us. How does one convey the horror of finding only two Armenians alive in a city that once boasted a population of twenty thousand?

The fate of the family I had left behind was obvious to everyone, I suppose, but me. Hoping against forlorn hope, I made my way to the street where we lived, praying that I would soon hear the familiar voices of my mother and brother. I turned the corner and brought myself up sharply. A sickness grew in me as I looked upon what had been my home.

Ashes!

For several moments I stood there in a state of dull, uncomprehending shock. Yes, I had seen war. I had seen people die. But somehow the essence of the Turkish lust to kill and destroy had not fully penetrated my mind until that soul searing moment of personal tragedy. I sobbed aloud as the terrible thought occurred to me that somewhere in that pile of ashes were the charred remains of my mother and brother, Avedis—cremated.

Finally, as though from a great distance, I heard the voice of a friend and fellow soldier, Corporal Girar Antoyan:

"Soghomon," he called.

I tried to focus my attention on his words, but the numbness within me had robbed me of my ability to understand, let alone speak. I nodded dumbly and pointed to what had been my home. I brushed the tears from my eyes.

Antoyan put a comforting hand on my shoulder. "Come, Soghomon, it is better that we go on," he said sympathetically. "*Koo guskeeds zanoenk yaid chein gurnahr yaid berell* —Your grief will not bring them back."

His words tortured me. I desperately wanted to believe they had somehow eluded the Turkish murderers. I grasped the lapel of his jacket. "My family may be alive and well, at this very minute; perhaps in another house, on another street."

"Soghomon," he said in what was almost a frightened whisper, "Erzinga is a city of ghosts and memories. I heard today that only two remain alive."

"Two?—only *two* alive in all Erzinga?" With an effort I brought my eyes back to the still warm ashes before me. Had this terrible thing really happened to my loved ones? I prayed that it was only a nightmare from which I would soon awaken.

But, no! The grisly evidence was everywhere. I stood there frozen. For a moment I could see my mother baking *lavash* — bread on the hearth. I could see my brother Avedis studying, and I could almost hear my father reading passages from the Bible.

I suddenly realized I was still clutching Antoyan's lapel. I released my grip. "I'm sorry," I muttered.

"It's all right, Soghomon."

"Girar, tell me, where are the two Armenians who remain alive?"

"They are talking to Zakarian, my squad leader."

"Take me to them."

Antoyan and I hurried over to where one of the survivors was seated, eating the first food he had had in days. I asked him what had happened.

"They murdered our people in cold blood," he said bitterly. "The Turks promised that they would move all of us to safety, away from the battle. Five or six hundred left as ordered, on a day-long journey outside the city." He hesitated. "We believed them when they said they were concerned for our safety."

"What happened?" I demanded.

"We were ambushed. Instead of the sanctuary they had promised, the Turkish militia and the police surrounded us. A few minutes after we arrived they struck down our men, women and children as though we were swine." He buried his face in the cup of his hands.

"My mother! My family!" I asked in panic. "You knew them. Did they escape?"

He answered without raising his head, his voice muffled. "There were no survivors," he said starkly. "Only my companion and I. If we hadn't sworn loyalty to the Islamic religion, we, too, would have been murdered." He lifted his head and his eyes held mine firmly. "I am an *Armenian*—and a *Christian*. I shall remain so."

Sadly I retraced my steps to where our home had once stood. There among the smouldering ruins the anguish within me was so intense that my mind began to whirl and my vision blurred. For the first time in my life:

I fainted.

When I awakened to the cold reality of the genocidal madness that had taken, in addition to my mother and brother, the lives of eighty-two close relatives, a fierce, red haze enveloped me; a fiery sensation surged throughout my body. I knew then that I must seek retribution. Bleakly, I vowed that as long as God allowed me a single breath, I would track down the fiend responsible for the murder of every Armenian who had fallen to the sharp blade of the Turkish crescent.

I sank to my knees and clutched a fistful of ashes. "Oh, God in Heaven, give me the strength and wisdom to act as your instrument. Let me punish the slayer—the man responsible for the murder of my people. This will be my mission. Help me, oh Lord, to find that one man. Guide me in this mission."

Shortly thereafter, our guerrillas moved on, leading the caravan of liberated Armenians to safety—those who had survived in other towns and cities. I was near to complete exhaustion, but like so many of my countrymen, I forced myself on. As long as there was one Armenian in danger of the Turkish slaughter I simply could not lay down my rifle.

There were times when the defense of our beleaguered nation looked hopeless. Our spirits were often low. To us, this was not a battle of international finance, a fight for oil—or any of the usual platitudes given by some large nations as an excuse to make war on others. We were struggling for our very homes and hearths, our personal possessions and the lives of our neighbors and kinsmen whose blood ran rich and warm in our own veins. It was a desperate fight for our very existence.

* * * * * * * * * *

On May 15, 1918, the Turks began their largest offensive against the Armenians, attacking Alexandropol and Chinkil, having as their objective the city of Yerevan (Capital of the Armenian Republic-to-be.). The Armenian forces, inferior in numbers and lacking proper equipment and food supplies, were driven back. To make the situation even worse for the Armenians, a new offensive began with a combined Turkish and Kurdish force attacking at various points. Several days later the entire Ararat Valley was swarming with enemy troops.

Miracle of miracles!

Commanding General Silikian, with a force of 10,000 irregulars, evolved a three-pronged counterattack against the 36,000 well-trained and fully-equipped Turkish troops who were under the command of Wehib Pasha. On another front, General Piroumian rallied his meager forces at Sardarapat while, completing the pincer movement, General Dro (Ganayan) regrouped his troops at Bash Abaran.

On May 23, 1918, General Silikian issued the long awaited order to Generals Piroumian and Dro to counterattack. A bloody battle followed. In a struggle for their very existence the Armenians struck simultaneously at Sardarapat, Bash Abaran and Karakilisseh. Over 6,000 Turks died in one of the worst defeats they had ever suffered. On May 28, 1918, the Armenian military staff sent this terse but revealing communication to Yerevan:

"The Turks have been defeated. They are in pell-mell retreat on every front and our troops are pursuing them."

On that same day the Turkish forces were routed on every front. General Silikian's strategy and Armenian courage had triumphed. The red, blue and orange tricolor was raised high and proudly above the city of Yerevan, establishing the new, Independent Republic of Armenia. The victorious battles of Sardarapat, Bash Abaran and Karakilisseh can rightfully be compared to any epic military triumphs of recorded history. Thus, May 28, 1918, marked the prideful milestone for us—Independence Day, the "Fourth of July"—for Armenia. For the first time since the fall of our country in 1375, we had freed ourselves of bondage.

In Armenian homes all over the world, toasts were exchanged. And if there were tears in their eyes and a catch in their throats as they sang *Mair Hairenik,* "Our Fatherland", who can blame them?

The Allied armies won their victory over the Germans and Turks and the Armistice of 1918 brought World War I to a close. Figurative hands clasped with the great democracies of the West—and particularly the United States of America which we all admired as the ultimate in political and spiritual freedom—the

Republic of Armenia settled down to a future of liberty and social justice. But I could not know, of course, that thirty-one months later, on December 2, 1920, our adored new, Independent Republic of Armenia would be crushed by combined Turko-Soviet forces under the leadership of the infamous team of Kemal Pasha of Turkey and Lenin of Communist Russia.

* * * * * * * * * *

The fight against the Turkish oppressors was over and I returned to civilian life. But for me, the battle had just begun. I had sworn a solemn pledge, and there was to be no rest for me until that vow was fulfilled. Time had healed the wound—only on the surface—but the scar served only to cover a deeper hurt that festered inside. Someone had ordered the wanton killing of a million-and-a-half Armenians and the deportation of 350,000 others of my people. The need to find the monster who was responsible for the atrocities was a fever in my brain. My mission now was a compulsion. I could not and would not rest until it was accomplished. The eventual conquest of our little Republic will always remain as an indictment against those other nations who preferred the kind of blind "neutrality" that would rather see a peaceful democracy conquered by professional militarists and dictators, than to display the courage necessary to rise to their defense. We were soon to learn that the Turks and the Reds had no intention of allowing our little nation to exist. While our newborn country was discarding its swaddling clothes and preparing for a healthy adolescence, with an eye to wise maturity (and meanwhile earning the respect of the community of free nations throughout the world), the Turkish and Soviet Governments were running true to form. Together, in secret conferences, they were already plotting their next act of aggression—this time the utter destruction of Armenia.

But I was a fighting man and still too young to be concerned with my new government's "political problems." I saw with pleasure that our new country was taking its rightful place in world society, but at that time, as are most youths recently returned from combat, I was preoccupied with my own readjustments to civilian life.

During my soldiering in the Guerrilla Regiment I had met a gracious and lovely girl, Anahid Tatigian, during a visit to Tiflis, Georgia. She, too, had suffered the tragic loss of some of her loved ones. This mutual grief initially brought us together. It was not long before we had fallen deeply in love. Visions of sweet Anahid filled my soul, bringing with it the promise of a joyous wedding and a happy life for both of us. Yet, while we whispered those precious endearments which lovers throughout eternity have always used, and even as her tender kisses were as honey on my lips, we both knew that before either of us could find happiness together I must yield to the compulsion to find and punish the arch-criminal who had so brutally ravished and murdered our families.

Who can forget the pathos of surrendering a beautiful love, even temporarily, to the necessity of fulfilling a secret vow? I shall always remember that pre-dawn meeting.

"Anahid, you know about this nightmare inside me. You know I can't rest until I find the killer." I took her in my arms. "Darling, I promise, when I've done what must be done, we'll have the rest of our lives together."

"Soghomon . . . I'll pray . . ." A tear gave her away.

I comforted her, my soothing words helping to cover my own sadness. I can only say that my heart wept at the thought of leaving her. But the very notion that she would remain anywhere near the reach of the Turks, who might seek vengeance upon her should I be captured, was frightening. We agreed that Anahid was to sail by ship to the Black Sea port of Novorossiysk and then journey by land to a remote area in the Caucasus where she would be safe with friends. I would have it no other way.

We clung together like two frightened children, weeping and knowing that the time for parting could no longer be postponed. The moon went into hiding as the heavy fog crept over the waterfront; dawn was near. Without a word, I left her embrace for another world.

Later that day I embarked on my mission, a well-oiled gun in my pocket.

V. THE QUEST

Constantinople!

The city was a bustling metropolis of many strange and familiar languages and dialects, colorful bazaars, shouting hucksters in the teeming marketplaces, winding camel caravans, busy waterfronts and the ever-present minarets and dome-shaped mosques. "Quite a contrast to the once-lovely, Armenian cities these barbarians destroyed," I reflected bitterly.

A mental image of Anahid's pretty face floated through my mind and I ached for the sound of her voice and the touch of her fingertips. Resolutely I put her from my thoughts and set about my primary objective—to stalk my prey and strangle it in its lair, as I would a rabid beast.

Contrasting emotions? Probably. I was alive with love even though I also bore the seed of revenge. I wondered how the garden that was my love could nurture that seed. Could it do ought else but spread weeds among my flower-thoughts? Yet I knew that the only way I could destroy that feeling was to remove the cause—to kill the seed. I could not purge myself otherwise. And through it all, my love for Anahid was constant, warm and tender.

First I had to have a base of operations. Luckily I found a modest apartment located conveniently near the office of the Armenian newspaper, *Jagadamard,* which had become a clearing house of information for Armenian displaced persons.

I have said we Armenians are a clannish people. It was that very feeling of kinship that impelled me to visit the office of the paper to seek any of my relatives who might have survived the massacres and who might possibly have fled to this Turkish metropolis. Many of my countrymen, I had heard, journeyed to this capital city in search of the remnants of their families. But my paramount goal remained: to find and punish the chief perpetrator of the Armenian bloodbath.

Although it was quite early, a dozen or more Armenians, looking for all the world like lost souls, milled about the lobby of the newspaper, waiting for word from their loved ones. I skirted the crowd and approached the youth at a desk behind the counter.

"I would like to place an ad," I told him in Armenian.

The young man reached for a pad and pencil. I explained my needs and after a few words of instruction an announcement was quickly completed:

> **SOGHOMON TEHLIRIAN:** Alive and well in Constantinople, thank God. Any relatives or friends in this area please contact me. Box 101, care of *"Jagadamard."*

The young man accepted my payment, gave me a receipt on which he had already stamped "December 18, 1919." He was returning the change when a comely, beautiful, though serious-looking young lady—she didn't seem to be much more than twenty—approached me.

"*Barri louiss, Barone Tehlair-ee-yuhn*—Good morning, Mr. Tehlirian," she began conversationally, speaking in Armenian. "*Announus Yair-on-ouhi Dahnel-ee-yunh eh*—My name is Yeranouhi Danielian. I work here." She smiled, revealing snowy teeth. "I didn't mean to eavesdrop, but I couldn't help overhearing your conversation. You're from Erzinga?"

"Yes, are you from there, too?" I was glad of the opportunity to speak in my native tongue.

"No, but I have friends in that town. Did you know a soldier named Levon Madatian? He served with the Volunteer Regiment in Erzinga."

I nodded. "I knew him well. We were in the same unit."

The girl was pleased. "His parents live right here in Constantinople. I'm sure they'd love to meet you."

"I'd enjoy meeting them"

"If you like I can introduce you today. I only work until noon. I know they'd be glad to see you; it's been several months since they've heard from Levon."

"Very well," I said soberly, "but Levon Madatian should have returned long ago." I certainly did not want to alarm Levon's family but I doubted if he had survived those last terrible days of warfare on the Eastern Front. In any case, I was anxious to make new friends and widen my contacts.

We found a delightful little restaurant, Hurire's *Ararat,* and over our *pahklava* and *sourge* (multi-layered honey pastry and Armenian powdered coffee), I told her I was a member of the

Dashnag Party (Armenian Revolutionary Federation), the leading political party in our country.

She laughed. "We're opponents," she said teasingly. "I belong to the *Hunchak* Party. But don't let it worry you; I even attend Federation meetings now." She tossed her jet-black curls aside. Her snowy teeth glistened whitely between her parted, rose-petal lips. A slight flush bronzed her tawny complexion. Diminutive, pert and alive as a little bird, she was as appealingly feminine as a length of perfumed chiffon.

We were of opposing political factions but it made little difference to us. The tragedy of the recent massacres had united all Armenians against their inquisitors. The disaster suffered by our people and the retribution which it demanded overrode all differences. We exchanged little pleasantries and Yeranouhi confided that she hoped some day to go to America where she could pursue her career as a journalist. We thanked Hurire, the attentive, undersized restauranteur, for his service and assured him that we had enjoyed his wife's baking.

The sun was high overhead when we made our way to the Madatian family home, talking animatedly. Suddenly she stopped.

"Is something wrong?" I asked concernedly. Her pretty face was pale, her full lips compressed into a thin angry line. She pointed to an ornate mansion on the other side of the street. "That is where Harootoun Mugurditchian lives."

The name meant nothing to me. "Who is he?" I asked curiously.

There was a note of impatience in her voice. "You haven't heard? Mugurditchian is the worst traitor in Armenian history—that's who he is!"

I could only stare. "Traitor?"

"During the worst of the massacres, that Judas, Mugurditchian, helped prepare a list of over three hundred names of our leaders here in Constantinople which was given to Talaat Pasha, the Turk. All but one who were on that list were murdered. The lone survivor was Bishop Krikorees Balakian of the Armenian Apostolic Church. Mugurditchian was rewarded for his part in the conspiracy by Talaat himself who assured him of protection against reprisals by his own people. He was also given this mansion and enough money to last the rest of his life. He still receives the same political protection by Kemal Pasha."

A cold rage gripped me. "How can he be allowed to live after conspiring with the Turks against his blood-brothers?" I demanded, "Are there none of our countrymen here to punish him?"

Yeranouhi Danielian patted my arm. "Perhaps, but—we will talk of that later. First, there are things you must learn and people you must meet," she said mysteriously. Although I pressed her, she would offer no explanation. In any case, we had now reached the Madatian home.

The meeting with the snowy-thatched Khosgrove Madatian and his sightless wife was one of sorrow. Only that morning the aged couple had received word of their son's death in an army hospital. I murmured a soft prayer. *"Der Asvadtz, Levonee hokeen hoke dar* —Oh, God, please care for Levon's soul." I wondered: Would I never see the end of the sorrow the Turks had brought upon us?

"Who is responsible?" I asked urgently. "Who is the *one man* responsible for the murders?"

The ancient one, his eyes hard, pounded a bony fist on the table. *"Talaat!"* he spat. *"Talaat Pasha!"*

Yeranouhi and I excused ourselves and left the elderly Madatians alone with their pathetic memories. Within twenty minutes we were back at the *Ararat* restaurant sipping so*urge.* I waved away the overly solicitous though amiable Hurire, and chose my words carefully as I voiced the dark thoughts that were troubling my mind.

"Yeranouhi," I began, "old man Madatian spoke Talaat's name as though it were a curse. I know Talaat used to be the Minister of Interior and then finally Prime Minister of Turkey and I suppose he is the most hated man in Armenia. But what has that to do with the death of my friend Levon Madatian? Why did the boy's father single him out?"

She answered slowly. "Talaat is the leader of the 'Committee of Union and Progress,' the *Ittihad-Terraki* Party."

"I know that," I interrupted. "They're known as the 'Young Turks.' We certainly cursed them enough in the Volunteer Regiment."

"Soghomon, Talaat was responsible for the mass-murder of our people," she explained quietly. "Rumors have it that he and other leaders of the 'Young Turks,' such as Enver and Djemal planned to wipe out every Armenian, adult and child, off the face of the earth. But Talaat was the chief assassin." She shuddered. "They almost succeeded." (COMMENT: Talaat, Enver and Djemal escaped to Moscow where they attempted to gain the support of the Communists for the establishment of a new Turkey, with themselves as the rulers. Their proposal partially unsuccessful, they went to Berlin. Enver was to return later only to be killed leading an army of *Ittihad*-Turks, supported by the Communists, in a border skirmish on the Russian border near Armenia.)

Her words inflamed me. Somewhere Talaat was still enjoying a life of luxury, breathing the fresh air of liberty, while a million-and-a-half of his victims mouldered in mass graves. Temples pounding, I half rose from my chair. "I *must* find him," I rasped. "If he is to pay for his crimes it will be at my hands—and mine alone." Fully cognizant of my melodramatic stand, I nevertheless continued. "Without that there is no life for me, Yeranouhi."

Yeranouhi talked to me for the better part of an hour, revealing a fund of information that held me spellbound. With fascinating (and macabre) detail she told how the Young Turks had plundered the treasury of their own country and how they had been forced to flee beyond its borders where they would be safe from arrest. I suppressed an urge to ply her with questions. Instead, I concentrated on her flow of words.

"What puzzles me," she was saying, "is that Prime Minister Kemal's present regime professes to be hunting for the three Young Turks, supposedly because they looted the treasury. The truth is that no one has made any effort to apprehend them. Turkey under Kemal isn't much better than when it was under Talaat. Remember the old Armenian adage, Soghomon? It tells the story of the Kemalists: The donkey is the same; only its pack has been changed." (COMMENT: This was the regime that succeeded Talaat's government. In 1918, Turkey and her wartime ally, Germany, were defeated by the Western Powers. Kemal Ataturk, himself a former Young Turk *(Ittihadist),* reportedly condemned his former cohorts to death in absentia. This condemnation on July 6, 1919, is said to have prevented Talaat, Enver and Djemal from returning to reclaim their reign of Turkey and unseating Kemal, who was now Chief of State.)

Six hundred years of Ottoman savagery had not culminated overnight in a modern breed of paragons. The only difference between this regime and the former was that the new government was temporarily tamed by Turkey's defeat at the hands of the Allies. Freedom for Christians living in Moslem Turkey was a word not to be found anywhere except in dictionaries. Whether or not the three rogues had embezzled their government's money was no affair of mine. But if, as Yeranouhi believed, they were responsible for the program of genocide against our people, then it was definitely my business. "You said," I reminded Yeranouhi, "that Talaat was responsible. How can I be sure?"

"There is one way . . ."

"And that is . . . ?"

"At the next meeting of the Federation I understand they are to discuss Talaat—and his punishment," she said meaningfully.

Every nerve and muscle of my body tingled with the awareness that I was drawing closer to my quarry. The once-hunted was now the hunter. I took her hand in mind. "Yeranouhi," I implored, "I must attend that meeting. (The Ninth Assembly of the Federation which was held secretly in Constantinople in December, 1919.) I do not ask you to understand now but there can be no talk of punishment unless I am there."

Yeranouhi looked at me, looked at me strangely, her dark eyes holding mine. "I think I do understand, Soghomon," she said levelly.

We parted after her promise that she would escort me to the Federation meeting sometime during the following week.

* * * * * * * * * *

The first rays of dawn cast a pale glow in my bedroom before I finally fell asleep. Yeranouhi Danielian was a remarkable young woman and I belatedly realized that she was uncommonly familiar with the activities of the traitors and murderers who had butchered us. How had she learned of the Federation's proposed meeting?—a clandestine assembly that was a tight-lipped secret—a meeting that is shrouded in mystery until this very day, several decades later. There were many questions I intended to ask this strange girl with the haunting eyes.

The look of pure venom in Yeranouhi's face as she described the turncoat Mugurditchian nibbled on the edge of my mind. What was it she had said? He made a list of three hundred of our most respected citizens, representing the cream of our society. Doctors, lawyers, teachers, artists, writers, scientists, clergymen and others were marked for death by the stroke of this betrayer's pen. "In return for his thirty pieces of silver," she said, "he had bartered his soul to Talaat the Turk who, in turn, had exterminated these leaders." Nor were Yeranouhi's accusations against Mugurditchian unfounded. In support of her statements she showed me documents that fastened the guilt on Mugurditchian just as plainly as though I had been an actual witness to his betrayal. In the years to come I was to learn how we Armenians managed to lay hands on secret Turkish papers.

Any attempt to analyze the thinking process of a man like Mugurditchian would only result in frustration. It is difficult, if not impossible, to attempt a normal explanation for an abnormal act. Talaat, for example, like his later imitators, Hitler, Stalin, Eichmann and the rest of their ilk, may or may not have been criminally insane. The normal mind cannot accept nor even understand their underlying motives. Talaat was evil incarnate and he would have to be eradicated for much the same reason that an infected rat is exterminated in order to prevent a recurrence of bubonic plague.

But Mugurditchian—ah, he was a criminal, but he was *not insane!* In cold blood, with calculated forethought, this renegade Armenian had deliberately planned the murder of hundreds of his own blood-brothers.

It was morning when I loaded my Mauser and placed it under my pillow.

The betrayer must pay for his crime.

VI. DEATH OF A RENEGADE

It was a beautiful Sunday morning. I breakfasted lightly and attended services at the Armenian Apostolic Church of Constantinople. The text that the priest had chosen was the Biblical phrase: "The meek shall inherit the earth."

In my pew, just a few rows from the altar, I meditated bitterly. Why had the innocent Armenian people, certainly among the most meek on earth, met such a devastating fate, even to the point of being denied marked graves? Down through the ages, men with far greater wisdom than I have asked the same question. My faith, I am ashamed to admit, was badly shaken, but the roots of Christianity are deep and sturdy and I sought comfort in the familiar quotation: "Faith is the evidence of things unseen."

The aura of reverence inside the church brought to me a tranquility of soul that was a soothing ointment to my spiritual wounds. Do not ask me why, but for some inexplicable reason I knew then that the million-and-a-half martyred dead understood the apparent incongruity of how a devout Christian, whose every fiber quivered like a violin to the bow in response to the teachings of the church, could at the same time nurture the feeling that must only end in the taking of a human life. I did not seek, nor did I expect, the understanding or tolerance of mortal man. I only prayed—oh, how I prayed!—that God Almighty would understand and forgive, if in His judgment I had wrongfully transgressed the commandment: "Thou shalt not kill."

I knelt and prayed that my Master would allow me the strength to do that which I had vowed in His name. I regained my feet, sat back in my chair and sighed as though a heavy burden had been lifted from my mind. Now I was just a humble Armenian among other Armenians who had come to worship God and to pray for the souls of our ravished people.

The mass had ended and the priest, when he had completed the prescribed ritual of our church, began his sermon—an account of the betrayal by our fellow Armenian, Mugurditchian, and ending with an impassioned plea to the congregation for the forgiveness of the traitor. Each of his words bit into me as though they were teeth on a saw.

"Mugurditchian, as you know, helped compile a roster of hundreds of Armenian leaders which was given to Talaat, who in turn ordered Bedri, Constantinople's chief of police, to arrest all of them," the priest said. "Bedri deviated not an iota from the mass-killer's orders, but followed Talaat's instructions explicitly. These Armenians, who represented the cream of our philosophical, cultural and scientific society, were herded in groups of fifty, brutally manhandled, and thrown into jail without any provocation, recourse to the courts, or any guilt on their part. Their only 'crime' was that they were born Armenians; destined to become Christians.

"The cells were indescribably filthy and cruelly overcrowded," the priest continued. "The tiny windows to the outside world were tightly boarded. Inside the small prison the victims pleaded for water, food and medical attention. But their pleas went unheeded by the drunken, carousing jailers who had been thoroughly indoctrinated to the proposition that all Christian Armenians merited this inhuman treatment. Talaat, the darling of the Turkish Moslem world, had publicized a passage from the Koran which proclaimed that 'those of the Islamic faith could serve Allah best by annihilating the infidels who followed the accursed Christ.' As Christians, the Armenian victims were considered on a level below that of swine awaiting the butcher's knife. It was because of this fanaticism that, when a few survivors of the original three hundred captives pleaded for the right to die with some semblance of human dignity, the Turks, grinning and shouting obscenities, battered their helpless prisoners' skulls into gray-pink, quivering nightmares. Some of the bodies were later thrown into rivers. It was a miracle that even one, Bishop Krikorees Balakian, survived the slaughter."

The priest bowed his head. "Let us pray that the departed souls have found eternal peace in Heaven."

I sat there frozen, as, one by one, the priest called out the names of each victim who had been murdered. Once again I experienced the same sense of frustrated anger and dizziness that I had experienced when I viewed the wreckage of my burned-out home. My temples throbbed almost unbearably and it was only by the sheerest of determination that I was able to keep from fainting; seizures which were becoming alarmingly frequent. I clapped my palms to my ears in an attempt to shut out the sound of the priest's voice as he droned the names of my countrymen whom Mugurditchian had turned in for slaughter. But I could not wholly deafen myself. Each name was a knife-stab in my heart.

". . . and also bless the spirits of Siamanto, Jongiulian, Zakarian, Larentz, Chavoushian, Tomajanian, Aknouni, Daghavarian, Ashubashian, Kajag, Sharigian, Pashayan, Varoujan . . ."

The last name snapped me to attention. "Varoujan? Oh, no! Not our country's beloved poet!" I cried silently, my mind in torment. The priest's incantations fell across my back like whiplashes. Now he went on to recount the atrocities of the others of my countrymen.

The priest was concluding his benediction:

". . . Finally, let us beseech God's mercy for Mugurditchian and—yes—even for Talaat himself."

Normally I am a merciful and Christian man and I can understand someone of the cloth imploring God's forgiveness, even for the Armenian traitor Mugurditchian. Also the priest had virtually verified Yeranouhi's accusation: Talaat was the master killer of all.

Forgiveness ? ? ?

Suddenly I could not bear to hear another word. Blazing with fury I hurried from the church into the streets of Constantinople. The now familiar dizziness was again upon me. It seemed to follow a pattern—at the peak of unrestrained emotion. I had no sooner reached the bottom of the church steps when my mind whirled and I sank to my knees. For the second time within an hour my vision blurred and a cloud of swirling black spots, like a swarm of gnats, loomed before me. Again the same images appeared; our family home in ashes; my hometown, Erzinga, sacked; my mother, my father and an endless procession of faceless Armenians marching to their doom. A moment before I lost consciousness the name of one man exploded in my mind:

Mugurditchian!

It is said that one's mind ceases to function at a time such as that. Not so with me. I seemed to hear a distant organ, faintly at first; soon its volume increased, moment by moment until I feared the rising crescendo would shatter my ear drums. Then, out of the fearsome dissonance the voice of the priest emerged, chanting an endless dirge for our martyred dead. Once more I relived those horror-filled months when I saw children raped by the perverted Islamic hordes; men disemboweled, women attacked and murdered; young boys castrated. Again I witnessed Armenian women set upon by the frenzied Turks as they plunged their swords through pregnant bellies, slicing into the unborn babies, spewing their remains onto the ground. I can still hear the hideous laughter of the Turkish beasts who decimated nearly all of my people.

Forgive? Even in my semi-stupor I knew nothing but a vital compulsion to seek retribution.

Later, at my apartment, I threw myself on the bed where I spent a feverish night. When I awoke it was with the conviction that without retribution, justice could be no more than a meaningless word. The next three days were fused into an alternating series of eating, sleeping—and planning.

The depression into which I had sunk was dissipated on that fateful Thursday morning when Yeranouhi burst into my apartment. She was distraught. Her hair was disheveled, her face flushed with anger and fear. She panted heavily as though she had been running. "Soghomon! Oh, Soghomon!" she wailed. "He's got Madatian."

"Who's got Madatian?" I asked sharply. "Wait a moment, Yeranouhi, take this brandy. You look like you need it." The stimulant helped. "Now," I said, "tell me what happened."

"Khosgrove Madatian was arrested early this morning."

"What for?"

"He was so upset over his son's death he denounced Mugurditchian and Talaat in the public square. Mugurditchian heard about it and complained to Military Police Chief Tekir, who took Madatian into custody. You know what that means."

I clenched my fists. "Oh, the fool! The utter, brave, wonderful Armenian fool! How could he do this, here in the very heart of enemy country? He knew they'd have no more compunction in crushing the life out of him than they would in swatting a fly. He must have known they'd kill him for speaking publicly about the massacres and denouncing Mugurditchian, let alone Talaat."

"Yes, Soghomon, he knew," Yeranouhi said bitterly.

A thought struck me. "What will become of his blind wife? Surely the Armenians here in Constantinople will take care of her. She's far too old to look after herself."

Again Yeranouhi's eyes filled with tears. "There's nothing we can do for her, Soghomon. The Turks took her, too."

"But *why?*" I asked, startled. "Why in the world would they arrest a blind old woman?"

"I know it sounds incredible," Yeranouhi wept, "but she tried to fight for her husband. She could hear them, of course. She reached out and by chance caught Mugurditchian's lapel. He pushed her away and cursed her in Armenian. Then she knew who it was. 'You're a disgrace to our people,' she told him. 'In the name of my dead son I curse our betrayer.' With that, Mugurditchian hit her with his fist and knocked her to the floor. She was trying to get up, and was on one knee, when Mugurditchian kicked her in the head. Police Chief Tekir and his men lifted her unconscious body from the floor and Mugurditchian waved them away."

"You witnessed all this, yourself?"

"Everything. I was told that the editor of *Jagadamard* would be handed a press release which he was to publish without change. He already has the story, Soghomon. But it makes no mention of Mrs. Madatian."

"Why not?" I asked.

Yeranouhi shook her head sadly. "Turkey is displaying Constantinople as a model city where Armenians live happily and without persecution. They don't want the world to know they are still making war on women. But as far as Khosgrove is concerned, the Turks are using him as an example to intimidate any other Armenians who might protest. It's their warning to us, even though I think they despise Mugurditchian for what he is doing to his own people."

Inside me a cold, blue light of resolution burned fiercely. The traitor must pay! I pocketed my Mauser automatic. It was almost noon when I reached Mugurditchian's mansion. As I neared his house my finger tightened on the trigger.

A young boy playing in the yard caught my attention. He was a sturdy lad with curly black hair and sparkling eyes set in a smiling face. But so preoccupied was I; so intent on my mission, that I dismissed the lad from my mind without another thought. The yard, I observed, was encircled by an iron fence, its huge gates making a fortress of the residence. It would take some doing and no little scheming to penetrate this refuge. Thoughtfully I crossed the street and entered a wine shop which Yeranouhi had told me was owned by Armenians. Here I had a vantage point from which to watch the mansion. At a small table I sipped a glass of good Armenian vintage, lit a cigarette and tried to relax. Across the aisle from where I was sitting, two elderly men played *tavloo,* a form of backgammon native to my country.

I could not help but overhear their conversation which, ironically enough, concerned the traitor, Mugurditchian. The subject of their discussion was not altogether surprising: every Armenian in Constantinople, it seemed, was talking about the betrayer ever since the priest had exposed him from the pulpit the Sunday before.

"*Daveed,* Khosgrove Madatian will not be playing *tavloo* with us today," the elder of the two said dejectedly. "It is printed in today's *Jagadamard* that he was arrested for denouncing Mugurditchian publicly."

The other's face grew livid. "*Denounced* him? He should have killed the sonofabitch!" he exploded. "If I were twenty years younger . . . " The old man's voice trailed off in helpless anger.

The two oldsters continued with their game of *tavloo.* As they talked my anger mounted. I had to make a move. The criminal must be punished—*now!*

My attention was diverted as the door swung open and a youngster scampered to the counter. The two backgammon players halted their conversation abruptly, stared at the child for a moment and then grumbled something to each other under their breaths.

The boy addressed the shopowner in Armenian: "My father is giving a party for Tekir Pasha and would like five bottles of Martel wine." Completing his purchase the boy hurried out.

The two players resumed their conversation, their first words holding me in a steely grip. "The boy does not look much like a Mugurditchian, for which he will someday thank God."

The other nodded in agreement. "You'd think that Mugurditchian would have more sense than to entertain Tekir Pasha so openly," he commented, "especially since it was only a few hours ago that Tekir's militia dragged Madatian from his home."

The boy! Why of course! I had just seen him playing in the yard. I leaped to my feet, threw a coin on the table and raced from the shop, determined to follow him through the open gate.

I was a heartbreak's second too late. The lad quickly closed the gate behind him and scurried into the house.

"Fool!" I berated myself. Had I only been more alert, the traitor, at this very moment, might have already paid for his crimes.

Inside the lavish residence I could hear the sounds of revelry. I sidled up to a fence, trusting that the gathering dusk would afford me a degree of protection. Through the wrought-iron palings I caught a glimpse of a large room within. An elaborate crystal chandelier reflected the lights of a hundred candles, its prisms glistening. A manservant, his tray laden with fine glassware and silver goblets, served the assembled guests.

At once, a grossly obese figure emerged from behind the parted drapes, his richly-tailored robe incongruously accenting his slovenly appearance.

I froze. Yeranouhi had given me an old tintype of Mugurditchian. I whipped it from my pocket and compared it with the man inside the house. There was no mistaking that repulsive figure. It was he!

I swayed, the old dizziness threatening once again to engulf me. "Oh, Lord," I beseeched silently, "not now!" The traitor was only yards away, an easy target protected only by a window pane. He was in the center of the room, rapping a spoon on the table to gain attention. His thick lips moved and the merrymakers joined him in a toast. Was he saluting Tekir Pasha for his arrest of the aged Madatian? Was he toasting his own success in having helped rob three hundred of my compatriots of their lives?

With an effort of will which I had not realized I possessed, I quelled my incipient fainting spell, knowing now only a cold deliberation of purpose. This was no time to falter. The ghosts of my murdered countrymen and the elderly Madatians pointed to the man in the window and silently entreated: "Vengeance!"

I fired! The explosion reverberated in the quiet of the evening as Mugurditchian's body slumped out of sight.

The resultant confusion within the room could be seen and heard even from where I crouched on the sidewalk, outside the fence. I must confess that had they not been drinking so heavily, it might have been impossible to elude my pursuers with so little difficulty, but by this time I was racing not only from Tekir Pasha and his military police, but also fighting wave after wave of nausea. Within twenty minutes I reached my apartment. I threw myself upon the bed and surrendered to the enveloping blackness. But before I finally lost consciousness I experienced a surge of exhilaration in the knowledge that a serpent had been crushed under the heel of justice.

A knock on the door awakened me several hours later. I cautiously admitted my neighbor, an Armenian named Koch whom I had met at the *Ararat* restaurant. Word-of-mouth had spread the news of the shooting so that the entire Armenian community of Constantinople was already discussing the affair.

"The police are searching for the man who almost killed

Mugurditchian," my new friend informed me.

I chose my words as carefully as though I were selecting gemstones. "Then he is alive?" It was with difficulty that I kept the bitter disappointment out of my voice.

"Yes, he's alive. Tekir Pasha, the chief of the military police, took him to the Army hospital," Koch explained.

Carefully I avoided any remarks which might have implicated me as the attacker. We discussed the case as any two Armenians might have done, and I dismissed him as gracefully as I could, feigning a need for more sleep.

In the darkness I asked myself how Mugurditchian could still be alive. Why were they looking for a man? He had been a good target; massive, and directly behind that window. The night was long, an eternity of hour-long minutes, and I was hollow-eyed from sleeplessness when the sun finally rose. A footfall sounded in the hallway and then came a hesitant knock on the door, bringing with it a wild fear that the police had somehow traced my steps. I remained deathly still. Of course! Tekir Pasha's men had questioned Mugurditchian's young son. They had probably interrogated the proprietor of the wine shop and the two elderly backgammon players. Fascinated, as a bird must feel under the hypnotic stare of a barnsnake, I watched the doorknob slowly turn.

I retrieved the gun from beneath my pillow, rose from my bed and opened the door.

Yeranouhi Danielian stood in the doorway, a half-smile arching her lips, a copy of the morning *Jagadamard* in her hand. My relief was so great I had to lean against the door for support. But she did not seem to notice my behavior. Instead, she rushed inside. I had thought she would be disappointed with Mugurditchian's escape, for she surely must have known it was I who had made the attempt. But to my surprise she threw her arms around me, and kissed me warmly. "Congratulations, Soghomon, I am proud of you. Every Armenian holds his head just a little higher today."

I drew back. "No, no, Yeranouhi," I said despairingly, "don't praise me. I failed you," I wailed. "I failed our people. Mugurditchian still lives."

Silently, but with eloquent response, she unrolled her newspaper and pointed to the bold headlines:

MUGURDITCHIAN SHOT
Condition Reported Serious

Yeranouhi tapped a dainty forefinger on the story emblazoned on the front page. "That headline is *passe*," she exclaimed, "he really *is* dead. My editor sent me to the hospital this morning for a follow-up story. Mugurditchian died a few minutes after I arrived. We're getting out a special edition."

I permitted myself a deep, gratified sigh. Yes, I had taken a life, but in exchange for the Madatian family and for the three hundred other lives that he had extinguished. I experienced no remorse; rather a feeling akin to that one might have when stepping on a tarantula. My act could not bring back the innocent victims who had perished because of Mugurditchian's perfidy, but at least I had prevented him from causing further atrocities.

Was it the sheer relief of knowing I had succeeded in ridding the world of a poisonous spider? Was it a sudden surge of physical awareness? I only knew that Yeranouhi was in my arms.

Her face, framed and ovalled by glistening black hair that tumbled to her shoulders, mirrored her thoughts. The moment was electric. And then, unaccountably, my beloved Anahid filled my mind. I struggled to gain my perspective.

My arms dropped to my sides. "I'm sorry, Yeranouhi."

Her eyes were brimming. She started to say something, faltered and then spun on her heel. She rushed blindly out of the apartment.

VII. EXECUTIONS AUTHORIZED

There was a feeling of rain in the air when Yeranouhi Danielian, a week later, took me to Berge Serkoyan's house where a critical, clandestine meeting was to be held. This, Yeranouhi told me, was the ninth general assembly of the Federation meeting secretly in Constantinople to deliberate the punishment of the war criminals now in hiding. We were ushered into Serkoyan's living room where Yeranouhi introduced me to the assembled guests.

Serkoyan was a large man, dynamic, with an intimidating pose. At his side was Shahan Natalie, a scholarly-looking man about five-feet-six in height, his face carved from granite. He was one of the masterminds of the Federation's Plan to carry out international justice. In the absence of a world body, the Plan was to seek out and execute fugitive Turkish war criminals the world over.

Nervously I sat back in my chair, reassured only by my escort's lovely smile. But whatever misgivings I might have had were quickly dispelled when Berge Serkoyan rose to speak.

"We Armenians had hoped that the Committee for Union and Progress—the 'Young Turks' as they are called—would bring some measure of security to our people," he began. "There is no need to detail the tragedy which this new group of Turks have brought upon us. We know now, through our intelligence sources, that the massacres of the past three-and-a-half years were instigated and conducted by that unholy triumvirate: Talaat, Enver and Djemal, who supposedly represented liberty, equality and fraternity."

I trembled with excitement. So Talaat had had helpers! Here was the confirmation to all that Yeranouhi had said. She had been right. I clung to the speaker's every word, hungry for information.

"I will not burden you, my sisters and brothers, with the evidence which is already etched in blood—evidence engraved in your own hearts. Here are but five brief reports of the many we have on file from the world press which will remind you of the horrors that our people have somehow been able to live through.

"First let me quote a 1916 editorial from the American newspaper, the *Christian Science Monitor* :

> 'Turkey, in its present state, occupies a unique position. By reason of her barbarities in Armenia, there can be no such thing as a neutral attitude in regard to her. Her conduct has long since ceased to be a domestic concern, or even the concern of a special group of nations; it is the concern of humanity.'

"And here is how the *New York American* condemned Talaat as the 'most notorious wholesale murderer of this or any other century.' This front page indictment reads:

> 'It was Talaat who conceived and carried out the policy of exterminating the Armenians. No assassin of ancient or modern times could compare in wickedness with this coarse, gross Turkish monster. Neither Herod nor Caligula nor any of the infamous tyrants of history could measure up in deliberate cruelty with him.'

"I need not remind any of you of Talaat's vicious boast of 1915, made in the presence of the representatives of the world's press, and one which he has never denied—a satanic statement attested to by the *United Press, Associated Press* and *Reuters* :

> 'I will strike the Armenians such a blow that it will take them fifty years to recover—if they ever do.'

"Here is part of the speech made by England's Lord Bryce to the House of Lords on October 6, 1915:

> 'Talaat Pasha's Committee of Union and Progress began by promising equal rights to all races and faiths. This was the 'Union.' It proceeded forthwith not only to expel the Greek inhabitants of Asia Minor and to exterminate the Armenians, but to Turkify the Albanians.
> 'This is what union in fact meant. What 'Progress' has meant, in the hands of assassins like Talaat and his fellow Prussianized Moslems, is worse than the older Turkish pashas ever demonstrated. No Turkish Government should hereafter be permitted to tyrannize the subjects of another

faith.'

"I can name dozens—no, not dozens but hundreds of condemnations made by neutral observers. But let me discuss the report made by the 'American Committee on Armenian Atrocities' of New York. This committee sent a body of twenty-five outstanding American statesmen to Turkey for an objective, impartial report. This committee included: Chairman Rev. James Barton, Cardinal Gibbons, Charles Elliott (ex-president of Harvard University), Rabbi Stephen S. Wise, Cleveland H. Dodge, Samuel Dutton and many other respected U.S. leaders.

"When the committee made its report, devastating to the Turks, the Turkish Consul-General in New York, Djelel Manif, airily waved aside the whole matter with: 'Prefabrications; lies; forgeries. We love the Armenian people.' This was his light dismissal of the murder of a million-and-a-half people, even though lists of Armenian dead, official unbiased reports, were heaped upon his desk.

"Enver and Djemal were the beasts who implemented the orders for the mass-murder of the Armenian people, but even beasts must have a leader," Serkoyan continued. (COMMENT: Enver, Minister of War, was trained at the Prussian Military Academy in Germany. He appointed Bronsart Pasha, an expert in German military strategy, as his Chief of Staff. Bronsart Pasha was an alias for German Field Marshall Erich von Shellendorf, whom Enver had met while training in Germany. Djemal was the Turkish Naval Minister.) "In this case the arch-assassin was the pig—Talaat Pasha—former Minister of Interior. It was he who was obsessed with the idea to exterminate every Armenian man, woman and child. It was Talaat who was later promoted to Prime Minister of Turkey as a reward for having slashed the jugular vein of the Armenian people. It was Talaat who authorized the insane plan of racial extermination. And it was he who stands indicted as the planner of the systematic murders. He is the criminal who is chiefly responsible for this crime against humanity."

Serkoyan's voice was steely. "The question before us now, my countrymen, is this: Who shall punish the guilty?"

Yeranouhi restrained me from leaping to my feet and shouting my willingness to carry out the punishment. In retrospect I can see that her presence of mind was timely. She rose slowly from her chair and faced the delegates. Her eyes locked with mine as she spoke:

"Gentlemen, I am sure that every one here knows what happened to the traitor, Mugurditchian"—she paused, with a fine sense for the dramatic—"and I am equally positive that you all know who it was who punished the betrayer."

I could sense a dozen pair of eyes quietly studying me.

Serkoyan faced me. "Soghomon Tehlirian, rise," he commanded. The room was as quiet as a mausoleum as I left my chair. "Yes," Serkoyan went on, "we know of Mugurditchian and we thank Yeranouhi for her part and for bringing you here. If you wish, you may express your views to the delegates."

I wasted no time in making my position clear to the Federation members. I told them of my vow and of my determination to stalk the killers to the ends of the earth.

"Gentlemen," I concluded fervently, "I volunteer without reservation to punish the man who massacred our people."

"Soghomon Tehlirian," Serkoyan directed, "you may leave the room while we consider your offer."

Outside, in the vestibule, I waited for the next half-hour in an agony of uncertainty. The decisions to be made were important and twofold. First, the meeting held historic significance in that it marked the first time that men guilty of genocide were to be punished by an official group representing the victims. Secondly, the decisions were important to my own peace of soul if I was to know a moment of tranquility.

A door opened and Yeranouhi called to me. I returned to the room. Once again Serkoyan addressed me in behalf of the delegates:

"Soghomon Tehlirian," he announced evenly, "the Ninth General Assembly has given careful consideration to your proposal . . ."

I sucked in my breath.

". . . and this Assembly, in the name of the Armenian people, has unanimously agreed that you, Soghomon Tehlirian of Erzinga, have been entrusted with the responsibility of bringing final judgment against the chief perpetrator of the crimes against humanity and crimes against the Armenian people."

My voice was so low I doubted if Yeranouhi, who was sitting in the back row, could hear me. "Thank you," I murmured.

"You are specifically charged," Serkoyan declared, "with the punishment of Talaat Pasha, formerly Prime Minister of Turkey. This criminal is now in hiding—not only from the vengeance which he knows the Armenians will exact but also from Kemal

Pasha's present Turkish regime. (COMMENT: Talaat, in an attempt to destroy all evidence of his official government policy of genocide—the *Teshkilati Makhsoussieh* —removed all the official Ottoman archives in October, 1918. Documents which included cipher telegrams in code and numerous orders which outlined in detail Talaat's diabolical plan. Talaat and his henchmen then hurriedly fled Turkey, escaping the advancing Allied Forces.)

"In all fairness we must tell you that the Federation can provide you with little if any support at this time. However," Serkoyan concluded, "we believe that we will be able to give you a measure of cooperation at a later date."

I could understand the reason for what, at first hearing, sounded as though they were reluctant to offer me the assistance I would need to carry out my pledge. As the leading political party of Armenia they could not publicly acknowledge, let alone assist in my assignment, else they alert the Turks to our program of retribution.

"Gentlemen," I asserted, "I will, at my own expense, seek out Talaat, and entirely on my own responsibility, I will make every effort to carry out my assignment."

Applause.

Yeranouhi served cups of steaming, heavy-bodied *sourge* and for the next half-hour we sipped the Armenian coffee, conjecturing as to the possible whereabouts of the fugitive Turk. Our little tete-a-tete ended shortly thereafter.

I escorted Yeranouhi to her home and then returned to my apartment. When I finally fell asleep my dreams were a confused montage of faces—the jowled features of Mugurditchian and the stern but friendly faces of the delegates I had met that night. Now Yeranouhi's lovely face floated toward me. But just as I was about to enfold her in my arms, I beheld Anahid, robed in white and wearing a gold tiara. She descended from the heavens and her sweet Mona Lisa face radiated love. Yeranouhi retreated into the shadows and disappeared as Anahid and I embraced.

It was high noon when I awoke.

VIII. A TEAR FOR YERANOUHI

It was not long after the Federation authorized me to execute Talaat when I was again reminded of the telegraphic speed with which word-of-mouth news, no matter how secret, leaped from tongue to tongue among the Armenian people.

Yeranouhi and I had planned to meet that Saturday afternoon, so I was not surprised to hear the sound of her knock on the door. Indeed, I had grown so accustomed to the gentle one-two-three-four tapping of her fingertips that I knew her signal as well as I did her throaty voice.

"Soghomon," she said, after we had exchanged good mornings, "Archbishop Zaven wants to see you. He asked me to bring you to his home."

I was astonished. What could the *Bhadriargh* —Patriarch— the highest official of the Armenian Church in Constantinople; in fact, the entire nation—want with me?

We were in his home within the hour. I bowed my head deferentially as we were introduced. Yeranouhi, always the typically feminine Armenian girl, immediately set about making coffee.

"Soghomon, I do not ask whether you are guilty or not," Archbishop Zaven Der Yeghiayan began, "but I have heard rumors that Mugurditchian met his death at your hands."

I cast a quick glance at Yeranouhi and then felt a sudden sense of shame. No, of course it was not she who had talked! The Prelate noticed my momentary suspicion. He stroked his white beard and smiled.

"There are few members of our congregations who do not already know or think they know the story of how Mugurditchian died. You have been in Constantinople only a short time but, I can tell you, young man, that the name Tehlirian is already becoming a legend."

Yeranouhi served the coffee and joined us at the table, listening attentively but saying nothing. I dismissed Mugurditchian from my mind. He had paid for his crime and I said as much to the

Patriarch. My concern now was to find Talaat.

"Your Reverence," I began, "last week Yeranouhi and I attended a meeting of the Federation..."

He interrupted me with an impatient wave of his hand. "I am familiar with all the events of that meeting," he said shortly.

"Then you know of my mission?"

"*Eteh doun Toorka guh madnaneeshess Talaat, aiyoe* —If you refer to the Turk, Talaat, yes."

At twenty-two, without the leavening of life's experiences, my impudence equalled my youthful naivete. "You have many channels of information, Archbishop Zaven," I burst out impulsively. "I want you to use your influence to help me find that man, Talaat."

The Patriarch shook his head, the barest hint of impatience in his voice. "I am sorry my son, but as a Patriarch I cannot bring dishonor to the Church. Remember, your purpose is to take a human life, and an eye-for-an-eye is not a tenet of our faith. True, I have compassion for your cause but that does not necessarily mean that I condone it." He hesitated and then laid a gentle hand on my arm. "Has it occurred to you to ask why you are here—why I sent for you?"

Before I could answer, Yeranouhi turned to me, speaking for the first time. "Do you remember Tekir Pasha, the chief of police?"

"I'm not likely to forget him," I growled. "He was an honored guest at Mugurditchian's house the night I caught up with that traitor. If Tekir and his militia had not been so drunk they surely would have captured me. Forget him? Hardly!"

"He hasn't given up," Yeranouhi said. "Tekir and his men visited the Church several times to question Archbishop Zaven."

I suppressed an involuntary shiver. "They know about me? They know where I live?"

The Patriarch answered. "I doubt if they do—yet. Even I did not know how to find you. It occurred to me that *Oreyourt* (Miss) Danielian, because of her newspaper connections, might know your address so that you could be warned."

"*Bhadriargh* (Patriarch) Zaven was certainly surprised to learn that we knew each other so well," Yeranouhi grinned impishly.

The Archbishop studied us both with a paternal eye, logically misunderstanding our relationship. "I know you both will be happy together. Shall I have the honor of performing the ceremony?"

I was taken aback at the unexpected question. "We do not love each other," I said brusquely. "Miss Danielian is helping me with my mission."

Yeranouhi's face turned ashen. Belatedly, and regretfully, I realized I had wounded her and I silently cursed myself for my impetuous, thoughtless answer.

Archbishop Zaven immediately perceived his error and changed the subject. We discussed the possibility that, because of Mugurditchian's death, I might be captured by the police before I could find Talaat and that it might be wise for me to seek new living quarters. I thanked him for warning me and, after he blessed us, Yeranouhi and I departed.

The following days and weeks were occupied with gathering data which might lead to the whereabouts of the Turkish assassin, surreptitious meetings with Armenians introduced to me by Yeranouhi, and fruitless investigations of every clue I could obtain. My evenings would have been dreary indeed had I not had Anahid's letters (which were received at the newspaper *Jagadamard* under a pseudonym) to comfort me. I spent hours pouring my heart out to my sweetheart, filling page after page with the tender endearments which young lovers use everywhere. At other times I scrutinized Turkish textbooks, studying their newspapers and other literature in the forlorn hope that I might read news of Talaat.

True, Yeranouhi spent a few evenings with me every week. She would prepare supper for the both of us, wash dishes and then sift through the meager information upon which I would act on the following day.

I began to notice a subtle change in her. Although she worked tirelessly in our common cause, she evinced less of the political zeal and intensity that had characterized her when we first met. Her voice had gentled. She attended to my needs even before I asked. But it was Anahid, far away in the Caucasus, whom I loved. My only prayers were that I would not hurt the faithful, loyal Yeranouhi, whose life was becoming so closely entwined with mine.

* * * * * * * * *

January 25, 1920, Yeranouhi's birthday, is a date that is etched in my memory. It started pleasantly enough, but ended on a note of horror.

I made my way to the *Ararat* restaurant where Hurire, the proprietor, and I had struck up a warm friendship. He clucked proudly, like a busy hen over a newly laid batch of eggs.

"Ah, good evening, Soghomon. Your order is ready." From the kitchen he brought an elaborately decorated cake which he proudly displayed. I could not have been more pleased. The roly-poly proprietor had inscribed the white frosting with pink sugar:

HAPPY BIRTHDAY YERANOUHI

Carrying the cake gingerly in the palms of my hands I hailed a carriage and rode in style to Yeranouhi's apartment. The clip-clop of the horses' hooves on the cobble-stone streets lulled me into a rosy sense of security and I relaxed contentedly. Yeranouhi's sister, Araxie, a nurse, would be on duty tonight at the hospital so that we would be quite alone. I had been promised my favorite dish, *dolma*, a combination of meat and rice, wrapped in succulent grape leaves. My mouth watered. It occurred to me that I had been taking her too much for granted. One of these days, I reflected, I must do something nice for her.

I paid the sycophant coachman when we reached Yeranouhi's house and approached the entrance, whistling a gay tune of the day. At her door I tapped once or twice, lightly. Then I rapped sharply and when I received no response I called her name. She was, of course, expecting me and I knew that my devoted friend would not have left.

Again I called: "*Eranoohi*—Yeranouhi, *Soagamoan eh*—it is Soghomon." For a long moment there was no answer and then I heard it—a low, tortured moan. A grey forboding possessed me. The door was unlatched and I burst into the apartment. The room was in darkness. Hastily I struck a match and lit the gas fixture, its yellow glow illuminating the room. At my feet were two bulging suitcases, fully packed. But where was Yeranouhi? Lighting a candle I searched the empty parlor and again I heard the agonized moan. I hurried into the bedroom.

"Yeranouhi!" I gasped.

Fully dressed, she lay sprawled athwart the bed, sobbing and half insensible. Her face was bruised, her eyes swollen and purpled; a trickle of blood ran from the corner of her lacerated mouth onto her throat.

It was several minutes before I could arouse her to a point where she could tell me what had happened. Fortunately, her sister, Araxie, kept a supply of soothing ointments and other medications on hand. With these, and a moistened towel on her forehead, Yeranouhi finally was able to answer my questions. Her head was nestled against my chest, her sobs now muffled. Deliberately I kept my voice calm.

"Who did this to you?"

"Tekir," she said weakly. "Tekir Pasha and his police."

The shock of seeing her in that condition had numbed my brain. For a moment I did not associate him with the military police chief who had witnessed Mugurditchian's death. "But why?" I asked falteringly.

Yeranouhi attempted a wan smile and then grimaced from the pain in her torn lips. She placed a tiny hand in mine. "He traced you to me. We weren't very careful, Soghomon; we were seen all over town."

Silently I cursed myself for not taking the precautions that might have protected her—the same precautions I had taken when I sent Anahid to the Caucasus where she would be safe from the police.

Yeranouhi read the self-accusation in my eyes. "Don't blame yourself, my dear. Neither of us were concerned for our own safety. Whoever would have thought that the Turks would attach such importance to a traitor like Mugurditchian?"

"They came this evening?"

She nodded. "Yes. I was preparing our birthday dinner—the *dolma* that you love so much—when without warning, Tekir and his gang forced their way through the door. Tekir grabbed me by the hair. His upper lip was curled back so that I could see his yellowed teeth. 'Where's the murderer, Tehlirian?' he shouted.

"I was terrified. When I told him I didn't even know you he threw me to the floor and began to beat and kick me, all the while screaming, 'We know better!'

"I fainted several times," Yeranouhi continued, "but each time they would revive me and begin the beatings and questionings all over again. It was a nightmare. The last words I remember were their warning that they would return in the morning and that I had better cooperate." She looked up at me through swollen eyes. "But I didn't tell."

My fingertips gently traced a bruise on her cheek. "Yeranouhi," I said, my voice choking with emotion, "you are the bravest girl I have ever known. How can I ever thank you?"

Her voice was like the texture of a rose petal. "It isn't your thanks I want, Soghomon." Her arms started to enfold to my neck and then, self-consciously her hands dropped to her lap. "You have important work to do and I wanted to help. Let's just say I did it for Armenia—" Her voice trembled. "—and for you."

I asked her about the suitcases.

Yeranouhi rose to her feet and, with her back to me, she began to brush her hair in front of a small mirror, the light of the flickering candle softening the ugly bruises on her face. It was some moments before she spoke.

"I managed to pack my things after the police left," she said wearily. Her arms hung at her sides. "I'm leaving, Soghomon; leaving Constantinople."

In the stunned silence that followed I could hear my own labored breathing. Somewhere in the distance a nightbird called— a sad song; a lonesome song. I placed my hands on her shoulders and turned her about. It would have been pointless to plead with her to remain. The police had warned her that they would be back in the morning. At this moment they might well be at my own apartment.

"Where will you go, Yeranouhi? What will you do?" It occurred to me that she might move to a city in the Republic of Armenia and I regretted the distance this would place between us. But her answer astonished me.

"I'm not sure yet. Who knows? To Paris perhaps. Maybe even America. The important thing is that I must escape—tonight. To be here tomorrow means certain death—not only for me, Soghomon, but for you."

It could not have been more than a half-hour since I had entered the apartment. Now, for the first time, the sense of urgency, the need for decisive action to escape the Turkish authorities brought me to a sharp realization of our immediate peril. But once again I knew a moment of admiration and respect for this girl who had risked her life to save mine, and who had remained behind to warn me when she could have fled for her life.

I blew out the candle and lifted the suitcases. "I'll get you out of Turkey somehow," I said grimly.

"Wait, Soghomon, I can't leave without my sister. The Turks would surely persecute Araxie if she were left behind."

I agreed. Quickly we planned our next step. Yeranouhi was to go to the hospital where her sister was on duty and together they were to meet me in the back room of the *Ararat* restaurant. Furtively we made our way through a back door and into an alley. With Yeranouhi's luggage in either hand I hurried to the familiar little cafe where only that evening I had purchased her birthday cake. The night was uncommonly silent and I could hear Yeranouhi's fading footsteps as she disappeared around the corner.

Inside the "Ararat" I described our predicament to the sympathetic Hurire. He snapped his fingers as an idea flashed in his mind.

"I have a friend," he exclaimed excitedly; "one of us. He's a ship captain. I heard only today that his vessel is taking on stores for a long voyage." He set a pot of so*urge* on the table and scurried out. "I'll be back in an hour," he promised over his shoulder.

When he returned, Yeranouhi, Araxie and I were talking earnestly as we sipped our coffee. Hurire's beaming face told us that he had been successful. Providence? Perhaps. Surely it was a miracle that the ship was sailing that very night.

Araxie ascended the gangplank first. Yeranouhi kissed my cheek. "Good-bye, Soghomon dear. Someday, some way, I'll manage to contact you. Just know that wherever I am I'll be working for our beloved Armenia just as I know that you, too, will be doing your part." She smiled through sudden tears. "I didn't mean to sound so chauvinistic at a time like this. I—I—*Oh, Soghomon!*"

We embraced, weeping.

When the gangplank lifted I turned and walked away knowing a loneliness as empty as the spaces among the planets. I was homeless, not daring to return to my apartment and for the next several days I hid in the back room of the *Ararat* restaurant. The full weight of responsibility was mine alone.

I had not realized how much I had come to depend upon sweet Yeranouhi until now that she was gone. Even as I planned the long search for Talaat I would find my thoughts straying to this girl who had sacrificed so much for our common cause.

I could not know, of course, that the next time we met it would be too late for anything but a tear for Yeranouhi.

IX. THE PATH OF THE HUNTER

Without Yeranouhi's comforting presence I sought to overcome my loneliness by following a myriad of scents that might conceivably lead me to the mass-murderer I was seeking. I combed the main thoroughfares, the back-streets and alleys, searching, prying, asking questions, ever alert for one inadvertent clue. Soon I had traversed the city and wrung it dry of information. Leaving the city proper I made my way to the quays along the Golden Horn where I frequented the waterfront, talking to seamen and visiting the teeming bazaars. But not a sign of Talaat.

My initial confidence ebbed to maddening frustration. Disconsolately I walked toward the offices of the Armenian newspaper, *Jagadamard*, seeking the companionship of my people and also to inquire if any surviving relatives had responded to my announcement that I was in Constantinople. I was within a few blocks of my destination when I came abreast of the *Ararat* Cafe. Ah, here I would find my friend, Hurire, the jolly, rotund proprietor whom I had not seen for several weeks.

The restaurant, usually filled with congenial Armenian patrons, was now strangely quiet, with but two or three people silently sipping coffee. My friend's wife placed a cautious finger to her lips and with a tilt of her head motioned for me to follow her into the back room. Her agitation filled the room like a communicable disease. The few customers left.

She grasped the lapel of my coat. "You must leave at once, Soghomon. Do not return."

An anxious, awesome foreboding hovered about me like an unclean thing. "What happened?" I finally blurted.

"Tekir Pasha and his police—they traced you here. They found out that it was my husband who helped Yeranouhi escape and that he had also given you shelter. They arrested him."

My concern was so evident that she quieted me with a steadying hand on mine.

"Perhaps they'll release him," I said, vainly attempting to sound a note of hope—a hope which I did not feel. "He may return at any moment."

She clasped her hands and it was several moments before I realized that she was praying. When she finally raised her eyes to mine I saw in them the agony of a thousand years of Armenian women who had suffered at the hands of the Turks. This woman had been grievously wounded.

"Tekir Pasha returned my husband the day after the arrest—what was left of him. We sent his body to Tiflis where he could sleep with his loved ones."

I was in a dark mood when I finally arrived at the newspaper office. The overt acts that had led to the punishment of Mugurditchian, and my ill-concealed bumbling in my search for Talaat had resulted in a cruel beating for Yeranouhi, a girl who well merited being called "the Armenian Saint Joan of Arc." My efforts to save Yeranouhi had brought about the death of my dear friend Hurire, who only a month ago had prepared the birthday cake on that fateful January evening.

As I ascended the steps to the newspaper office my feelings of chagrin, remorse and guilt fused into a determination that these sacrifices would be a monument and an inspiration; that the blood they had shed would be sanctified in the hearts and minds of Armenians everywhere. I opened the door, strode to the editor's desk and introduced myself.

He stiffened. "Tehlirian! The police are looking for you."

"I'm aware of that," I said dourly.

"But you don't understand," he insisted. "The chief of police and a squad of men left this very office just an hour ago. They saw your advertisement but I told them you had only left a box number and had never returned."

"Tekir!" I exclaimed, seeing once again Yeranouhi's battered features. "I have a score to settle with him."

The editor shook his head. "You are the rabbit, my friend, not the fox." He reached into a drawer. "I have something for you," he said, handing me a letter.

"But it has no stamp or return address."

He smiled. "It has passed through many friendly hands. Why not read it?"

Within seconds I was staring at the signature: *Yeranouhi!*

I looked up at him, implicit thanks in my every word. "You knew who this was from and you said nothing to the police?"

"I am an Armenian," he said simply, and with deep pride. "Now you must go, Tehlirian; the police may return at any moment. Also, I suggest you leave Turkey. Tekir is only hours behind you." We clasped hands. "Good luck to you and—may you find Talaat."

Outside I hurried to my apartment, anxious to pack my belongings and find another base of operations. I rounded the corner of my street—and stopped dead in my tracks. A Turkish policeman was stationed at my door. I turned and lost myself in another part of the city.

Now I was without funds or change of clothes. Everything that I owned but my Mauser automatic was in my former apartment to which I dared not return. I thanked God that I had had the foresight to burn Anahid's letters so that the Turks could not trace and abuse her as they had Yeranouhi.

In the ensuing weeks I somehow managed to survive, thanks to my countrymen in the Armenian quarter; working when I could, but always searching—searching.

The cryptic letter from Yeranouhi, which was passed on to me by the editor of the *Jagadamard,* was nothing more than a six word message:

"EACH PASSING DAY BRINGS NEW HOPE."

I repeated the words over and over again. Had she referred to the growing strength of our new nation, the Independent Republic of Armenia? Was she getting closer to Talaat?

My quarry, I was convinced by now, had long since fled Constantinople or I would have found him. Utterly discouraged, I decided to visit Archbishop Zaven, risking capture by the police in my need for spiritual comfort. But Patriarch Zaven, I learned, was no longer in Constantinople. He had been assigned a new diocese in France.

What to do! I was tired of my fruitless efforts; sick unto death of the alien Turks who would kill me, as well as any other Armenian, if but for nothing else than that I knelt to the Cross. The war was over but the Turkish mentality lingered on.

The answer came with a rush.

I would go to Paris.

* * * * * * * * * *

Only a poet can describe Paris in the springtime and, alas, I am no poet. It is not so much the function of the tongue, but of the heart, to express the sense of freedom that is the soul of France. Only one who has lived in the Islamic world of Turkey can understand the exhilaration that comes of breathing the air of liberty.

Immediately upon arriving I made my way to the Armenian Church of Paris, hoping that perhaps my old friend and spiritual advisor, Archbishop Zaven, might be there. I also hoped that he might be able to direct me to Yeranouhi—who was somewhere in Paris. He had spoken to her once, he said, but he was unaware of her whereabouts at present. Much to my pleasure, the *Archnourt* (Prelate), Bishop Kibarian, told me that *Arch-Yebiscobos*, Archbishop Zaven, had just arrived from Marseilles. Smiling, he ushered me into his chambers where Archbishop Zaven and I embraced in warm reunion.

Our conversation soon turned to my mission. Again, as I had in Constantinople, I implored his assistance.

Archbishop Zaven was sympathetic but firm. "I can only repeat what I said before. I serve God, not man. Would you have me conspire to take a human life—even Talaat's?"

I could understand the Archbishop's conviction, and deep within me I was proud. Despite my urgent need for help, our church doctrine remained steadfast. It would always be so; a symbol of the highest Christian ethics and standards. How different from the destructive principles of the Islamic Turks.

Archbishop Zaven then suggested that I visit the Armenian National Council which maintained its headquarters in the *Vouillemont Hotel* and which served as the Paris Consulate of the Free Armenian Republic. There, he said, I might at least find temporary employment.

I wasted no time getting to the hotel where I discovered that Avedis Aharonian, the famous Armenian statesman and poet, was one of the functionaries in charge.

I decided to brazen it out. "My name is Soghomon Tehlirian. Archbishop Zaven sent me," I said boldly. "I'd like to see Mr. Aharonian."

The young man shook his head. "I'm sorry, Sir, but that is not possible. Mr. Aharonian is in conference and he leaves immediately for Marseilles. But perhaps I can help you. My name is Terzian." Suddenly he smiled. "Mr. Tehlirian, your exploits have preceded you. We know you are seeking Talaat, the Turk, but we still can do nothing for you—officially."

My face must have fallen for he was quick to reassure me. "Here is the address of a local, Armenian-owned company. A job is waiting for you. At least you'll have an income while you continue your search. In the meantime I suggest that you take your meals at the *Haiastan Cafe*."

"But why?" I asked.

His answer was enigmatic. "Don't ask questions, my friend. Just do as I suggest."

* * * * * * * * *

Armenians are an adaptable people. I laughed when I first saw the *Haiastan*. It had its inside dining room, as all conventional restaurants have, but it was also a typical Parisian sidewalk cafe with its flimsy little tables outside. Here wine-bibbers and passers-by eyed and passed judgment on each other as one sipped contemplatively and the other hurried about his or her business. I was sitting at one of the sidewalk tables with a jigger of *rockhi* before me and wondering why Terzian had been so adamant about my dining here when his reason suddenly became all too clear.

"Hello, Soghomon, I've been expecting you," said a voice as smooth as *halvah*.

I looked up.

Araxie!

She joined me at my table. A hundred questions tumbled from my lips. "Where did you come from? How did you know I was here? Yeranouhi, your sister, is she here?"

Araxie laughed—and it was like the tinkling music of a waterfall. "Not so fast; one question at a time."

"How did you happen to find me here?"

She grinned warmly. "Soghomon, you were told at the Consulate to dine here at the *Haiastan*. Isn't that enough? All of us who work for our Republic meet here daily. They knew we'd meet soon."

A feeling of reassurance diffused me. It was good to know that I had friends, unknown though they may be. "Araxie, take me to your sister."

She shook her head, her curls swaying. "Yeranouhi left Paris for America a month ago. She's working for an Armenian newspaper in Boston."

I was crushed. The only person I had counted on to guide my steps toward Talaat was separated from me by a three-thousand-mile expanse of ocean. Yet it wasn't just patriotism for our beloved Armenia that saturated me with sadness but an inexplicable longing for this young lady who had faced death in my behalf. I wondered . . . ? I deliberately thrust the thought from my mind. No, it was Anahid I adored. But a gnawing hunger persistently nibbled at my mind.

* * * * * * * * *

Araxie Danielian, despite her youth—she was only nineteen—hovered about me like a mother hen. It was she who helped me find a small hotel near the Consulate and not too far from the *Haiastan* restaurant. The cafe was important to my plans because it was there that many Armenians congregated. I could not afford to ignore the off-chance that I might pick up information that would lead me to Talaat.

In the weeks that followed I held a succession of part-time jobs which enabled me to devote my free hours to my quest. A trackdown such as I was conducting can be quite expensive. I needed money to further my search. There were times when I would spend my last *sou* checking out the leads given to me by my new friends at the *Haiastan*. Araxie—bless her—came to my aid during those dark days when I had nothing to eat. More than once she invited me to the hospital where she was employed as a nurse, so that I could still the pangs of hunger.

One dreary evening as I was pouring over a Turkish newspaper, searching for clues, the utter futility of my mission overwhelmed me. I was hungry, alone, without funds and nowhere nearer to Talaat than I had been in Constantinople. I needed contacts, money and official support.

In my despair I saw myself as the sacrificial lamb, while Talaat, the jackal, roamed the hills of Europe, free and probably basking in the memory of the rivers of blood he had spilled. Feverishly I paced the floor, pounding fist into palm. The old recurrent dizziness seized me. My head was a yielding anvil upon which huge hammers crashed. But even as I sank to the floor I heard a knock on the door and Araxie's anxious voice calling me.

I lost consciousness.

The following days were a confused blur of delirious babbling, awesome nightmares and alternating hours of freezing and burning with fever. Vaguely I sensed that Araxie was at my bedside throughout. On the fifth day her cool, professional ministrations brought me to a point where I could sit up and eat a little soup which she spoon-fed to me.

Soghomon Tehlirian at age 24. The Armenian patriot executed the Turkish author of the first Genocide of the 20th Century; that of the Armenians. This original painting by Steven Gaal portrays Tehlirian prior to his trial in Berlin for the execution of the notorious Prime Minister of Turkey, Talaat Pasha. The painting was unveiled by the author, Lindy V. Avakian, keynote speaker at the shrine of Tehlirian, Fresno, California, on Memorial Day, 1965, commemorating the 50th Memorial of the 1915 massacre of 1,500,000 Christian Armenians. (Author's collection)

Yeranouhi Danielian, the "Armenian Joan of Arc," whose loyalty, devotion and ceaseless efforts in behalf of Armenia is now part of its glorious history. She played a major role in the trackdown of Talaat Pasha, often endangering her life to assist Soghomon Tehlirian in his mission. This painting is an original by Girard (Avakian) Aken.

LEFT: This photo of a grinning Talaat Pasha was taken in 1916 on the occasion of his elevation to Prime Minister of Turkey as a reward for his success in the Genocide of the Armenians which he launched in 1915. (Photo: Archives of Avak Z. Avakian)

RIGHT: Talaat Pasha in Germany in 1921, after his features were altered through surgery. Compare with the photo above. The serene, placid face reveals Talaat's confidence that he has successfully eluded pursuit. But his disguise could not save him from ultimate justice. Two weeks later he was executed by Soghomon Tehlirian. To gain an insight into this man's nature, cover the lower half of his face with a piece of paper and see the remorseless fury that was his.
(Photo: United Press International)

One of the dispatches signed and sent by Talaat Pasha to all commanders, ordering the Genocide of the Armenians living within the borders of the Turkish Empire. The order was sent from Constantinople (Istanbul) in September, 1915. (Photo: Archives of Avak Z. Avakian)

Enver Pasha, Turkish Minister of War under Prime Minister Talaat Pasha. Photo catches the icy hauteur and Prussian arrogance which he assumed as Turkish Military Emissary to Germany where he also graduated from the Prussian Military Academy. Together with Talaat and Djemal, this triumvirate ruled Turkey with an iron (and bloody) hand.
(Photo: United Press International)

This comic-opera pose by Djemal Pasha, Turkish Naval Minister, was taken after his participation in the slaughter of hundreds of thousands of innocent Armenians. One of the top three Turkish war criminals, he was executed by an Armenian patriot for his many crimes against the Armenian people.
(Photo: United Press International)

This photo was taken in 1918 during a reunion of the Supreme (Young Turk) *Ittihad-Terraki* Council. Talaat Pasha is seated, third from left, front row. Directly to Talaat's left is Said Halim Pasha, and to Said Halim's left is Djemal Pasha. (Photo: Archives of Avak Z. Avakian)

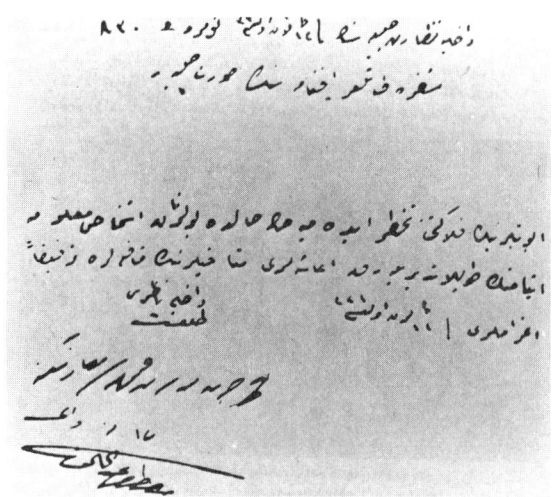

Khalil Bey, one of Talaat's underlings, in a photo taken secretly in Berlin.
(Photo: Archives of Avak Z. Avakian)

Another official order by Talaat Pasha, then Minister of Interior, was sent on December 12, 1915. Here he orders the death of children who might remember their parents, temporarily sparing those under five years old. (Photo: Archives of Avak Z. Avakian)

Turkish Army Cavalry with artillery, going into action. Many of their weapons were furnished by Turkey's World War I military ally, Germany.
(Photo: United Press International)

Part of over 13,000 Turkish troops who assaulted the 5,000 peaceful Armenian inhabitants of Shabin Karahissar who took refuge a thousand feet above the city in an ancient fort. All but a few were slaughtered in the ensuing "Battle of the Aerie," or "Eagle's Nest." See Chapter Three. (Photo: United Press International)

Atop this lofty mountain was the hitherto impregnable fortress built by the conquering Romans, called the "Eagle's Nest," the fort of Shabin Karahissar (summit). Nestled in the foothills at the base of the mountain was the town. 5,000 Armenian men, women and children retreated to the summit and fought for 26 days in June, 1915. Only a pitiful few survived. (Photo: Archives of Avak Z. Avakian)

The historic humanitarian and military figure, General Antranik, Supreme Commander of the 10,000-man Armenian Volunteer Regiment, who decorated Soghomon Tehlirian for valor under fire.
(Photo: Archives of Avak Z. Avakian)

Turkish troops rendezvous in the bitter cold. Such lulls only served to anger the Moslem troops, many who believed that for every Christian murdered, Allah would hold in reserve one beautiful Armenian girl in Valhalla.
(Photo: United Press International)

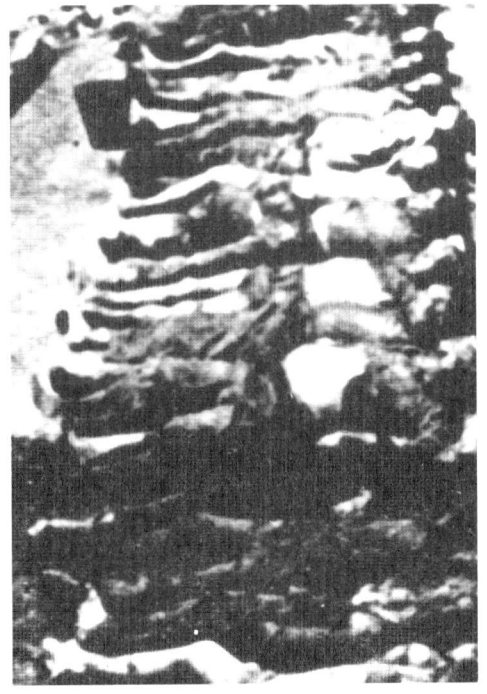

In April, 1915, 300 of the civic, spiritual and intellectual Armenian leaders of Constantinople (Istanbul) were arrested and murdered by the Turks. The atrocities were ordered by Talaat Pasha. A list of the 300 names was given to Talaat by the Armenian "Judas" Mugurditchian. Only one of the 300 survived: Bishop Krikorees Balakian. The victims shown include many of Armenia's beloved poets, writers and clergymen: Varoujan, Siamanto, Zartarian, to name a few. Mugurditchian paid for his crimes at the hands of Tehlirian in Constantinople. See Chapter Six.
(Photo: Archives of Avak Z. Avakian)

The city of Trebizond, Armenia just prior to the 1915 Genocide. Here, 15,000 innocent Armenians were massacred. Men, women and children were packaged into huge wooden boxes which were then nailed shut. Most of the victims were placed aboard boats and then drowned. This seaport was nearly destroyed by the rampaging Turks, who drove the survivors into the Black Sea. (Photo: Archives of Avak Z. Avakian)

Armenian leaders of the city of Aleppo: "Death by hanging," ordered by Talaat Pasha, "in the public square." Although the order was directed towards "leaders," the underlying hatred for Christians was evident: three of five victims were clergymen. (Photo: Archives of Avak Z. Avakian)

Christians massacred by the Turks on the plains of Moush in July, 1915. This scene was repeated thousands of times throughout Armenia. Notice the mark of the killers: hacked off arms, legs and heads; a grim reminder of the intensity of the Islamic hatred towards Christianity.
(Photo: United Press International)

"Kuzlurmach," The Bridge of Death. Shown is the river Alice. The bridge is located halfway between the cities of Sebastia and Yevtogia, south of the Black Sea. It was turned into a watery cemetery for Armenian victims who were shot or axed and then thrown off the bridge because they could not continue the death march to the deserts. Deran Kelegian, one of Armenia's literary giants, was murdered here by Turkish guards.
(Photo: Archives of Avak Z. Avakian)

Just before this scene occurred, Turks laughed as they watched nearly 800 women fighting over bits of meat from a dead horse. The ugly game got out of control and the Turks shot a dozen women. Here, a few stragglers pick up tiny pieces of leftovers. Within days, on the outskirts of the city of Busarah, all 800 were murdered, raped or died of starvation.
(Photo: Archives of Avak Z. Avakian)

EIGHT COMMANDMENTS OF THE KORAN
CONCERNING CHRISTIANS.

(THE ARABIC INSCRIPTION ON THE NEXT PAGE.)

(1.) "They are surely infidels, who say, Verily God is Christ the son of Mary." (Koran, Chap. V.)
(2.) "O true believers, take not the Jews or Christians for your friends: they are friends the one to the other; but whoso among you taketh them for his friends, he is surely one of them." (Chap. V.)
(3.) "War is enjoined you against the infidels; but this is hateful unto you; yet perchance ye hate a thing which is better for you, and perchance you love a thing which is worse for you; but God knoweth, and ye know not." (Chap. II.)
(4.) "Fight therefore against them, until there be no temptation to idolatry, and the religion be God's." (Chap. II.)
(5.) "Fight against the friends of Satan, for the stratagem of Satan is weak." (Chap. IV.)
(6.) "And when the months wherein ye are not allowed to attack them shall be past, kill the idolaters wheresoever ye shall find them, and take them prisoners, and besiege them, and lay wait for them in every convenient place." (Chap. IX.)
(7.) "When ye encounter the unbelievers, strike off their heads, until ye have made a great slaughter among them." (Chap. XLVII.)
(8.) "Ye are also forbidden to take to wife free women who are married, except those women whom your right hand shall possess as slaves. This is ordained you from God." (Chap. IV.)

THE ARABIC FORMULA OF THE MOHAMETAN CREED.
"There is no Deity but Allah and Mohamet is the apostle of Allah."

EIGHT COMMANDMENTS OF THE KORAN
CONCERNING THE CHRISTIANS.
(IN ARABIC.)

For the translation see the reverse page.

Eight commandments of the Koran concerning Christians: English translation on the left was translated from the Arabic on the right.

Talaat's "enemies of Pan-Islamism" are shown at their destination: the cruel desert of Der el Zor. This scene in 1916 shows an Armenian mother and her two emaciated children. Nearly a million corpses, in surface graves (they were denied burial according to Talaat's interpretation of the Koran and his direct order), were strewn across this blistering, sandy graveyard.
(Photo: Archives of Avak Z. Avakian)

Incontestable evidence of Turk savagery. This photo was taken by German soldiers near the Armenian city of Erzeroum in 1915.
(Photo: Archives of Avak Z. Avakian)

Armenian Volunteer soldiers entering the city of Kharpert saved these children, "enemies of the Turkish Empire and Islam," from certain death.
(Photo: Archives of Avak Z. Avakian)

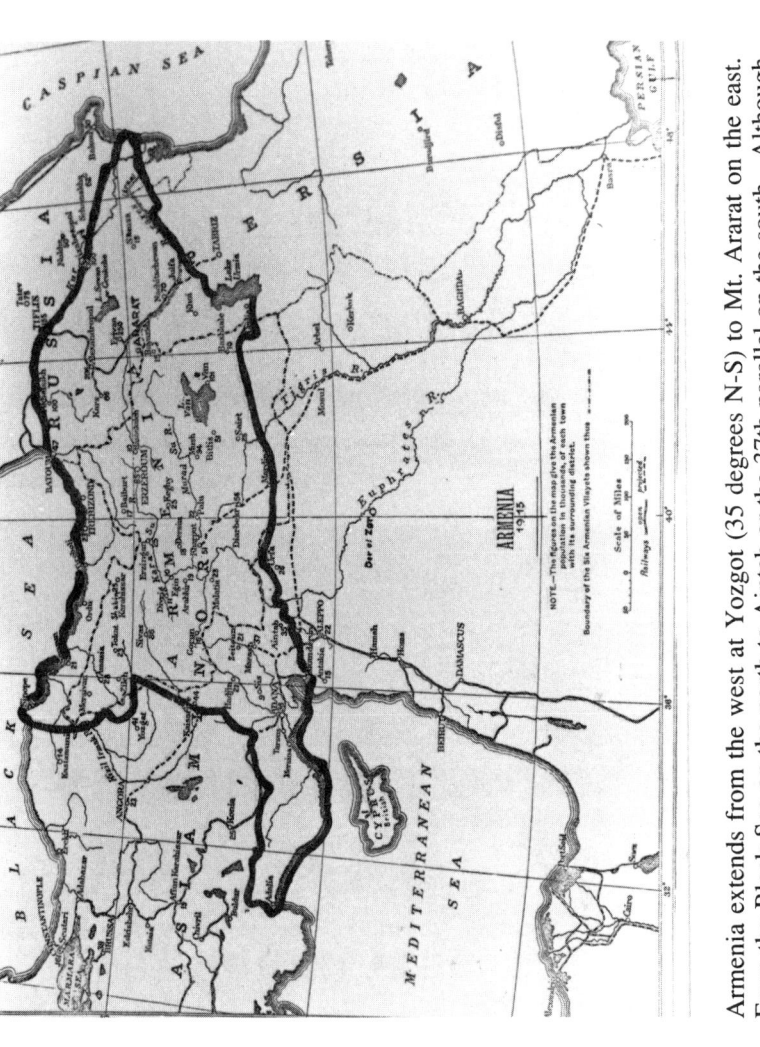

Armenia extends from the west at Yozgot (35 degrees N-S) to Mt. Ararat on the east. From the Black Sea on the north to Aintab or the 37th parallel on the south. Although the Turkish Empire covered all of Asia Minor, including Armenia, Turkey is actually situated in the area where the word Asia is seen. (Map: Archives of Avak Z. Avakian)

Top: Christian Armenians outside Jerusalem after marching hundreds of miles over the mountains. Starved, beaten and robbed, many died on the way. Center: A few hours later the refugees were set upon and murdered. Bottom: A group of little Armenian children, picked up at the wayside; all that was left. (New York American)

Her husband among the slain, this woman holds on to her only surviving child and a deep faith in a living Christ. Notice the gripping expression of grief as her hand suppresses the sobs from her lips.
(Photo: Archives of Avak Z. Avakian)

In a field on the outskirts of the city of Kharpert, the Turks pause for a brief rest. One official report quotes a Turkish civilian: "Killing *Giavours* (Christians) is difficult work." (Photo: Archives of Avak Z. Avakian)

Survivors of the death marches, these two mothers and their children were driven into streets of Bitlis, Armenia by Turk soldiers on order of Talaat Pasha; their homes confiscated and locked after an officer affixed the black seal. The houses were then given to Turkish families. Two months after this photo was taken in 1915, after surviving the blistering marches into the Syrian desert of Der el Zor, the children were bayoneted and drowned; their mothers murdered. (Photo: Archives of Avak Z. Avakian)

A parade of baby orphans in Armenia's "orphan city." The name was given to this group of former army barracks at Alexandropol, a Near East Relief Orphanage established on December 11, 1922. This handful of survivors were spared the fate that met thousands of their tiny brothers and sisters. (Photo: United Press International)

In 1926, the *Chicago Tribune* republished these photographs of Armenian girls rescued from the Turks by officials of the Near East Relief Association at the cost of five dollars per slave girl. Center: Arabian sheiks. Bottom: Turk soldier abducting an Armenian girl (slung over his shoulders).

Three Moslem warriors: A Turk on the left, with two Kurd chieftains, near the city of Malatia. Slave girls were their prize possessions: they were too impatient to kill a Christian and wait for their Armenian slave girl in Paradise. (Photo: Archives of Avak Z. Avakian)

RIGHT: Rescued Armenian girl, slave to Turkish Moslems. Tattoo marks show names of previous "owners." (Photo: American Near East Relief Association)

True, my body was mending, but the spirit within me had not responded. My depression was an abyss whose walls were sheer and high. "Go back to the Caucasus," I told myself. "Go back and claim Anahid. Settle down."

But I knew I would not—*could* not! Not yet!

Araxie's cheerful voice awakened me when she arrived early the following day. "Two soft-boiled eggs for you this morning, young man," she grinned.

"Not hungry," I grumbled.

"You will be when you hear the good news," she said, plumping up my pillows and spreading the breakfast before me.

I was at the point of asking her what she meant by "good news" when I noticed the envelope she had placed on the tray. I stared at it a moment, my pulse racing. It was from Yeranouhi. My eager fingers tore the envelope open. I read:

Boston, Massachusetts
April 21, 1920

"My Dearest Soghomon:

"America is a wonderful and pleasant country and I am so glad to be here. I write for the Armenian press but as always I am immersed in the struggles of our people and am quite active in Federation matters.

"You will be glad to know that the official help you need to complete your mission has been approved. Please come to America—to Boston, at once.

"You will soon receive instructions from Boston headquarters of the Federation.

"It will be good to see you again.

Devotedly,
Yeranouhi"

It is truly amazing how quickly one's health responds to good news. Had not Araxie restrained me I would have leaped from my bed and danced for joy. "It finally happened!" I shouted exultantly. "The Federation will back me."

Araxie's pleasure almost equalled mine. "Eat your breakfast," she said firmly. "You must be well and strong for the days ahead."

Suddenly famished, I devoured the food and finished the last of the coffee. Araxie reached into her purse and handed me a note. "Mr. Terzian gave this to me last night," Araxie explained. "It says you are to report to the Armenian Consulate here in Paris as soon as possible."

* * * * * * * * * *

My illness had taken a week to run its course and I was still somewhat shaky when I presented myself at the Consul's office. Terzian wasted few words, although those that he did employ were as formal as a State document:

"We have a letter from the Central Executive of the Federation in America. Our instructions are to furnish you with money and a passport so that you can complete a certain task which is important to you and to the Armenian people." Solemnly he shook my hand. "As a government official, Mr. Tehlirian, I cannot openly acknowledge my participation in this matter but, as an Armenian—*good luck!*"

My ship sailed within a week. Araxie accompanied me to the pier and promised that she, too, would follow to America shortly.

I was on my way, with the support of a world-wide organization behind me.

* * * * * * * * * *

The voyage did much to improve my health. For the first time in years I could relax. My former depression had entirely disappeared and I was now confident that the monster, Talaat, would meet his fate. As the ship entered New York harbor, I thrilled to the glorious sight of the Statue of Liberty and, like all newcomers, was awestruck by the towering skyscrapers of lower Manhattan and the dramatic pulse of the city.

At the New York offices of the Federation I was immediately assigned to a guide who escorted me to the immense cavern that is Grand Central Station. There I boarded a train to my final destination.

In Boston a police officer directed me to the Hairenik Building where the Federation maintained its headquarters. Somewhat diffidently I introduced myself, but whatever shyness I may have felt was quickly dissolved under the warm welcome given me by the Federation officers.

A stately figure approached me. There was about him that

aloofness usually associated with the scholar, the idealist, the thinker. Yet he radiated integrity, strength, character and a wisdom far more perceptive than mine. He extended his hand. "I am Ambassador Armen Garo."

So this was the great Garo—Armen Garo Pasdermajian—the man who led the Armenian Expeditionary Forces against the Turks at Khanasor; the regional commander of the Armeno-Tartar Wars; the first Armenian member of the Ottoman Parliament in 1914 and the Ambassador to America of Free Armenia. But perhaps he was best known for his daring capture of the British and French owned Bank of Ottoman in Constantinople where, on August 26, 1896, he led the Armenian Revolutionaries against the Turkish financial institution. It was Garo's intention to focus world-wide attention on the plight of the subjugated Armenians. The maneuver succeeded as planned but the Turkish Sultan, Hamid, retaliated with a brutality reminiscent of the Dark Ages. He selected six thousand Armenians at random and put them to death. For three years (1894-1896) the monstrous Abdul Hamid II continued his wholesale murders until some 325,000 Armenians had been slaughtered. All these things flashed through my mind as we shook hands.

"I am proud to meet you, *Hebados* (Ambassador) Garo," I said humbly.

His smile was engaging. "You are younger than I thought. How old are you, Soghomon?"

"Twenty-three, Sir."

"You are the lad who punished the traitor, Mugurditchian?"

"*Aiyoe, Vesemashook* —Yes, your Excellency."

"You seek Talaat, the Turk, I am told."

"That is true."

Ambassador Garo was suddenly all business, his speech precise. "My son, you will meet me tonight in the banquet room of *Koko's* restaurant, a few blocks from here. We are holding a special Federation meeting and I think you'll find it interesting. Our agents are even now warm on the trail of Talaat and his henchmen."

His words fell like drops of water on a thirsty tongue. Was this actually happening to me? Was this really Armenia's ambassador to the United States telling me that the Federation was closing in on Talaat's lair?

At the meeting that night, Garo delivered an inspiring, almost intoxicating speech. He introduced me to the Assembly and I tried, miserably, to equal his introductory speech. Afterward, the statesman took me aside and presented me with a sheaf of Turkish documents and photographs. He placed them carefully on the table between us and handed me one of the pictures. "This," he said quietly, "is a photo of Talaat. But bear in mind, Soghomon, it is quite possible that he has altered his features."

I leaned forward, studying the dog-eared, cracked photograph. It was the first time I had ever seen Talaat's face. So this is my target!

I studied the criss-crossed details of the fiend's face until each suety fold was etched deeply in my mind. "I have never before known what he looked like," I murmured.

"But I knew, and I haven't forgotten," said Garo, his voice clipped. "I can still remember our last meeting with the Turkish leaders at the Parliament Building in Constantinople. I was Armenia's representative in the Turkish Parliament, if in name only. Talaat and I were debating the Armenian question when suddenly, without reason, he banged his beefy fist on the table and roared, 'I have my own way of solving Armenia's problem!'"

The ambassador paused for a moment, his face bitter. "Talaat's fiery exit marked the beginning of the mass slaughter of our people. That evil man is still alive. You need no further instructions, Soghomon."

The meeting lasted until the early hours of the next morning. I could almost taste the spirit of cooperation and comradeship that surrounded me and it was like nectar on the lips—sweet and satisfying.

It was almost dawn and the flowing *rockhi* coursed warmly through our veins. Ambassador Garo put an arm around my shoulder. "You have an important task ahead, Soghomon, but you are not alone. A million-and-a-half Christian Armenian dead march with you. Their voices cannot be heard; their bones are scattered in the hills and plains of our Motherland and their blood is mingled with the waters of the Euphrates. When you meet Talaat, it will not be you alone who metes out punishment. You will have with you the souls of one-and-a half million men, women and children who were murdered by him and it is their fingers that will point to Talaat and say, 'Soghomon, that man robbed us of our lives.'"

Garo's impassioned speech—for it was no less than that—left me breathless. It was easy to see how he had become a member of the Turkish Parliament; a lone, eloquent fighter in the enemy camp.

Suddenly Ambassador Garo's attention was requested by an out-of-breath, important-looking gentleman who had just moments before rushed into the room. "Stay here, Soghomon," he ordered. "I will be right back."

He strode purposely over to the other man and they exchanged words rapidly. As they ended their conversation and Garo turned and began briskly walking back toward me, I could see grave concern in his face. In moments I knew the reason why.

"I must return to Washington, D.C. at once," Garo announced gravely. "I've just received word from Attorney General Darbinian (Reuben Darbinian, Attorney General of the Independent Republic of Armenia, a leading officer of the Federation, and later Editor-in-Chief of the *Hairenik, The Armenian Review* and other Armenian language publications in America, with headquarters in Boston.). He informed me that our Armenian Republic is in deadly peril."

"From whom?" I gasped. "The Turks again?"

"I'm afraid it is more serious than that. Quite unofficially, you understand, our agents report that the top military leaders of the Soviet Union and Kemal's Turkey have been holding secret conferences. There is strong reason to believe they are planning a combined military aggression against us."

"But we have a treaty with Russia and Turkey," I protested inanely. "The rest of the world would never let them invade a peaceful country."

Garo's voice was bitter. "The rest of the world did nothing, other than to lodge a few protests when the Turks spilled Armenian blood like water. All we can do now, Soghomon, is pray. I will be doing what I can in Washington, D.C., but meanwhile, you are to await your orders from our agents in Geneva, Switzerland."

Despite the somber prediction, I could not in my youthful naivete believe that Russia and Turkey would combine forces and attack our little Republic. Therefore, it was with scarcely concealed jubilation that I mentally marked *fini* to the long, lonely months of solitary searching for Talaat. But there was one other person whom I knew would want to share my pleasure; *Yeranouhi* —my faithful partner who had made all this possible.

"Mr. Ambassador," I began, "if it weren't for Yeranouhi Danielian I would not be here in Boston, nor might I ever have won your support. I haven't seen her since she left Constantinople for this city. If you would give me her address, Sir, I would be grateful to you."

Armen Garo shook his head, his voice tinged with regret. "I'm sorry, Soghomon, but I found it necessary to send her to California."

My heart sank. "California?" I repeated vapidly.

"She's writing for an Armenian newspaper there," he continued gently. "But more important, she is lecturing to build additional support for our Armenian Republic. A very talented young woman, Miss Danielian."

Sadly, though proudly, I listened to Ambassador Garo's account of Yeranouhi's activities in America. I learned that she was now in Fresno with Avak Zakar Avakian (the author's father), a founding officer of the Federation in the United States. Avakian had recently launched a West Coast branch and Yeranouhi, always true to form, was busily engaged in the organizational work. Further, she was occupied with securing financial aid for the victims of the Turkish atrocities back home.

"I know you would like to see Miss Danielian again," Garo went on as though reading my thoughts, "but I cannot permit you to leave for California. We have no idea when your instructions from Geneva will arrive. It may be today, tomorrow, or next week. But whatever the day, you must be prepared to leave at once."

There was no question as to his logic; he was right, of course. If I was to find Talaat I must keep pace with the leads supplied to me by the Federation's undercover agents who, thank Heaven, were now working with me.

The days stretched into weeks, my impatience mounting with every visit of the empty-handed postman. Finally the long-awaited summons was in my hand. The directive was curt:

"Further orders await your arrival in Switzerland.
Report to our office in Geneva.
Ayvazian"

* * * * * * * * *

The voyage seemed agonizingly slow. I secluded myself in my cabin in an effort to avoid contact with fellow passengers who might question too deeply into the reasons for the journey. My every thought was now as undeviating as a bullet on target.

In Geneva I went directly to the Federation office as instructed. I was somewhat disappointed by the air of abandonment that pervaded the Swiss office for this had once been World headquarters, proudly called *Droshag* (Flag) by freedom-loving Armenians everywhere. But, with the founding of the Republic of Armenia, the need for an international headquarters in a neutral country no longer existed and most of its functions outside of Armenia had been transferred to Boston.

A grizzled occupant, his face weather-beaten and battle-scarred, greeted me and I extended my hand. "My name is Soghomon Tehlirian. I am supposed to . . ."

He snorted an interruption. "*Gedehm! Gedehm!* —I know! I know!" he interjected petulantly, making full use of an old man's prerogative to scold youth. "*Hi gah vor Teallairiayanee anoun chugeedair?* —Is there an Armenian who does not know of the name Tehlirian?" He withdrew an envelope from a metal box and handed it to me, still grumbling between his toothless gums. "Just because you got Mugurditchian first, don't think you can come in here and lord it over me. I would have caught Mugurditchian and his Turk friend, Talaat, myself, only I didn't have time. I could have taken them with one hand tied behind my back."

I grinned widely. "*Bahbig* —grandpa, I believe you."

The letter which my pugnacious old countryman had given me had been carefully coded, but to me it was self-explanatory. I now understood why Ayvazian wasn't here to greet me. My so-called cousin was now in Berlin. I read the letter line by line, word by word and syllable by syllable:

November 26, 1920

"Dear Cousin Soghomon,

"It is with pleasure that I learn of your desire to study mechanical engineering in Berlin. Undoubtedly you will have little difficulty securing a student's visa from the German Embassy in Geneva so that you can attend school here.

"Do not be overly concerned with the language barrier. My friends and I will assist you so that ultimately you can get your diploma—an occasion which will please us all.

"Knowing your liking for fine cuisine, I look forward to dining with you at such excellent restaurants as *Maxl's* in Tiergarten Square.

"Our family joins me in sending you the best of wishes.

> Sincerely,
> Your cousin,
> *Ayvazian*"

I let out a joyous yelp, grabbed the astonished old man in my arms and gave him a bear hug. "*Bahbig,* I'm going to buy you the best *shish kebab* dinner you ever tasted. Get your hat and coat."

There was good reason to rejoice. Later that evening in my hotel room I studied the letter for the dozenth time. My "cousin" Ayvazian had obviously taken precautions so that neither of us might be endangered should the letter fall into unfriendly hands. Again I realized that there was very little the Federation did not know about me. But how, I wondered, had they learned of my interest in mechanical engineering? Probably from Yeranouhi. The passage that suggested I secure a student's visa so that I could attend a school in Berlin needed no elaboration. I grinned at Ayvazian's audacity when I re-read his promise to assist me in getting my "diploma"—Talaat! So I was to meet him at *Maxl's* restaurant in Tiergarten Square. Good! As I read his closing sentence I laughed aloud—"Our family joins me in sending you the best of wishes." Apparently he was working with other Armenian secret agents in Germany. From the depths of my being I returned silent greetings to my "family."

It required six days to obtain a visa. On December 3, 1920, I left for Berlin, my visa stamped:

STUDENT: MECHANICAL ENGINEERING

Just before I boarded the train, I heard a newsboy calling an "Extra." The only word I could distinguish was "Armenia."

X. REQUIEM FOR ARMENIA

For three consecutive nights I had dinner at *Maxl's,* lingering over countless cups of coffee, wondering how I would recognize Ayvazian when and if we met. One thing I was sure of: the Germans may be famous for knackwurst, but their coffee is only distantly related to the aromatic, full-bodied Armenian *sourge.* On the fourth night my attention was drawn to a nearby table where a young man, not much older than I, was reading an Armenian newspaper. Not once did he glance toward me. My eyes strayed to the headline and then riveted on the bold characters:

ARMENIA FALLS
Turko-Soviet Invasion Crushes Republic

I walked over to his table. "It has been a long time since I've seen a paper in my own language," I began tensely. "The headline: it's—it's tragic!"

"*Koor anouneht eencheh* —What's your name?" the stranger asked without raising his head.

"Tehlirian. Soghomon Tehlirian."

"When and where were you born?"

"April 15, 1896, in Erzinga, Armenia."

"What is your fiance's name?"

"Anahid Tatigian," I answered.

The stranger looked up, grinned and shook my hand warmly. "Just wanted to be sure, Soghomon. I'm Ayvazian, your self-appointed 'cousin.' Shall we go to my place?" His voice was light with amusement but I was soon to learn how serious he could be. He was one of the most dedicated Federation agents I've ever known.

In his apartment that evening, Ayvazian told me of the rape of Armenia. I could not read German well, nor had I seen an Armenian newspaper since my arrival in Berlin. Therefore I was unaware of the catastrophe that had again overwhelmed my people.

Over cigarettes and coffee Ayvazian described the circumstances that led to the conquest of Armenia. Here is what he told me:

"Soon after the Armistice of World War I, on January 16, 1919, the Allies sent its representative to help secure peace in Eastern Turkey. While the Allies drowsed, confident they had made a proper choice, the Turkish official, Demad, appointed Mustafa Kemal to 'secure the peace.' Kemal, who was widely known as Enver's shadow during the massacres, promptly began to exploit his appointed position. (COMMENT: Mustafa "Kemal Pasha" Kemal was born in 1880 and died in 1938. After 1934 he was known as Kemal Ataturk. An Army officer, he took part in the Young Turk Revolution in 1908 and, in association with Talaat, he also fought against the Western Allies in the 1st World War. After Turkey's collapse he organized the Nationalist Party and Army in Eastern Turkey. Later, as virtual dictator, he was to serve five terms as "president" of Turkey.)

"On May 15, 1919, Kemal boarded a steamer to Smyrna and traveled to Anatolia, a province of Turkey. Within weeks he made his way to the eastern border where he cast a covetous eye on the growing assets of the newly established Republic of Armenia—information which he was to later use in open warfare against the infant democracy. Soon, his political intrigues gained wide notoriety. Before long, reports reached the Allied High Command of Kemal's wily activities. An immediate directive to Demad to recall Kemal met with insolent delay. But Kemal no longer needed the prestige of his Allied sponsors; he had already used his position to gain support from three cunning, ambitious officials with an unholy lust for power: pashas Ismet, Fevi and Kiazim. (COMMENT: Ismet Inonu, who again became premier of Turkey in 1962, was Kemal's military chief of staff, 1919-1922, in the aggression against the Greeks. With fanatical zeal he massacred 30,000 non-combatant Greeks at the city of Inonu. So perverted was his pride that he adopted the name of the city as his own; thus his name: Ismet Inonu. Under Kemal he was responsible for the massacre of 250,000 Armenians, Greeks and some Jews. He last left the helm in Turkey as its premier in February, 1965. Ironically, Inonu was a candidate for the 1965 Nobel Peace Prize, despite his disgraceful past.)

"Mustafa Kemal, now president, proclaimed a coup and vowed, in the name of Allah, to drive the *giavours* —infidel

Christians—from Turkey and to expand his empire. The crafty Grand Vizier Demad stalled all negotiations until the Allied-held province of Anatolia was returned to Turkish rule. By the summer of 1920, Mustafa 'Ataturk' Kemal's regime was in full sway. Under the banner of the Grand National Assembly he attacked the French at Marash. Two weeks later he unleashed his Islamic hordes against the British at Ismid. In the meantime, Kemal ordered the massacre of 50,000 innocent Armenians who were still living in Turkey and who had not yet fled to the sanctuary of their newly born Republic. The only reason for this national crime was to appropriate the property of the murdered victims. Inflamed by the cry of 'Allah' or 'Christ,' Kemal's ignorant, easily persuaded forces, incited by the carefully revived injunctions to kill Christians, slaughtered the Armenian minority, as well as thousands of Greek men, women and children. (COMMENT: Thus, the policy of Kemalist Turkey was full genocide, as were the policies of Sultanic and *Ittihadist* Turkey. Kemal's order, which resulted in the deaths of 50,000 Armenian men, women and children—in the Kars and Ardahan district—was furthered and intensified when, in 1922, he massacred 200,000 Greeks, Armenians and Jews in Smyrna. Ismet Inonu was then Kemal's chief military advisor.)

"In December of 1920, the Soviet Union and Turkey invaded and throttled the two-year-old Republic of Armenia. In a gigantic pincer movement, three separate Red armies, under Lenin's direct orders, swooped down from the north. Simultaneously, the Turks, under Mustafa 'Ataturk' Kemal, in callous violation of the Armistice of World War I, invaded from the west and southwest. Defenseless in the face of this overpowering military aggression, abandoned by the then isolationist Allies, the Armenian Republic lost its independence, its culture—its all."

(COMMENT: The Republic of Armenia was the first nation to be invaded and enslaved by the Soviet Union. To this very day, Turkey and the Soviet Union hold Armenia captive.)

It was quite dark when Ayvazian finished his detailed account of the events leading to the fall of Armenia. Outside the window of his Berlin apartment the lamps were flickering beacons in the night. I lit another cigarette and turned to him. "Ayvazian," I asked, "what happens to us who were not in the Mother Country when she was conquered?"

"We go right on fighting all over the world. Not with bullets perhaps, but with propaganda; with appeals to the world's conscience. And," he concluded grimly, "we'll not stop until we've won our country back."

We clasped hands in mutual respect and determination. Elsewhere, I sensed, Armenians in every city in Europe and the United States were likewise pledging their loyalty to our ravished Motherland. Somewhere in California, Yeranouhi undoubtedly was working in behalf of our enslaved country. In the Caucasus, now overrun by the Russians, my blessed Anahid, together with thousands of other patriots were, I was sure, praying that the Federation would again assert itself. I shuddered to think of Anahid held captive by the Communists. If they were to learn that I was working with the Federation for the liberation of my people, it would surely go hard with her.

"What of my mission?" I finally asked Ayvazian, when the raw shock had somewhat abated.

"You are to continue exactly as planned. If we let Talaat and the others go unpunished, what can we expect of future assassins now that we do not even have a country behind us?"

"And that means . . .?"

"*. . . Execute him!*"

XI. THE LAIR

Weeping would not restore the Motherland. If we were again to fight for our enslaved Armenia it would have to be with confidence in the integrity of our erstwhile, democratic allies and the knowledge that eventual justice was on our side. Yet we were not ashamed of our tears for they helped cool the hot anguish that any man knows when he loses a loved one or a precious ideal; his sweetheart, his mate, his country. But now we were done with tears. This was the time to bare our knuckles.

Ayvazian placed cups and saucers on the table. It was a relief to sip real Armenian coffee after the substitutes I had been drinking since my arrival in Germany. "Tell me," I asked, at length, "do I get my diploma here or am I to go to still another part of the world?"

He smiled broadly, "You graduate here in Berlin—*Sigma cum laude,* I hope. We suspect Talaat is in the city, although we don't know exactly where. But we'll find him; you can be sure of that." He leaned back, lit a cigarette and for a few moments admired the smoke rings that spiralled lazily to the ceiling. "You'll be interested to know that a whole tribe of Turkish killers now live right here in Berlin."

"For instance . . . ?"

"Bedri, Hakka, Shekir, Halim and Djemal, to name a few."

"With the exception of Halim and Djemal, they're only small fry," I complained, vexed.

"They're not so small as you think," Ayvazian insisted. "Bedri, as chief of the Constantinople police, butchered hundreds of our Armenian leaders, on Talaat's orders. Hakka and Shekir were no better. They plundered and deported our people, sending them to certain death in the deserts. Halim was Prime Minister before Talaat was promoted to that position. Djemal, as Naval Minister, made many high level decisions that inevitably sent thousands of innocents to their graves." (COMMENT: Djemal Pasha, Naval Minister and commander of the Turkish Army in Syria and Palestine during the Massacres, was later executed in the Soviet Union while talking to the notorious Communist chief of the Soviet secret police, Lavrentia Beria. Beria and his men failed to apprehend the executioner. He later commented: "He had to be an Armenian.")

Angrily Ayvazian jabbed his cigarette into the midst of a pile of butts in the ash tray. "That scoundrel Djemal drove hundreds of our girls into Turkish military barracks where they were violated. Within days, those who hadn't already died were axed to death and thrown into the streets."

Involuntarily my hand crept to my coat pocket, my fingers tracing the outline of the gun inside. "I agree they should be punished, Ayvazian. I hope they get what they deserve. But they were all under the direction of one man, Talaat. That's the man I want. But these local Turks might give us some clues. Tell me more about them."

"Djemal operates a tobacco store right here, not too far from the *Brandenburg Gate*. The shop also serves as headquarters for the *Ittihad*—the Young Turk Party." Ayvazian lit another cigarette and inhaled deeply. "As to the Turk, Enver," he concluded, "he is in Moscow. No need to tell you it was he who helped the Communists plan their sneak takeover of Armenia. Evidently he thought that the Soviets, out of gratitude, would back him so that he could seize control of Turkey. He didn't achieve that goal because, although the Reds may have promised him the whole Ottoman Empire, he forgot one primary fact of life: A Communist is just as big a liar as a Turk."

A sharp knock sounded on the door. "Ah! That must be Hazor," Ayvazian exclaimed, interrupting his story. "I've been expecting him. Just the fellow I want you to meet."

He admitted a swarthy young man wearing a fez who, at first glance, was unmistakingly Turkish. I knew a moment of panic. Had I been betrayed? I had given Ayvazian my credentials but he had not offered his. What was a Turk doing here? My suspicion seemed to be confirmed when he greeted Ayvazian in Turkish: "*Nausoosome* —How are you?" he asked.

"*Ayehm!*—Fine!" Ayvazian replied cheerfully, also in the hated language.

Had I been trapped by two armed Turks who knew my every plan? Ayvazian's face-splitting grin arrested me just as I was thinking of reaching for my gun or bolting for the door.

"Relax, Soghomon, he's one of us." Ayvazian introduced me, making a great show of concealing his mirth. "Soghomon, I want you to meet Hazor, sometimes called Hazor Bey—as loyal an Armenian as you'll ever meet, despite that map of Turkey he calls a face." (COMMENT: "Hazor" was the pseudonym adopted by undercover agent Hrach Papazian, who moved to Lebanon after the trial of Soghomon Tehlirian.)

Hazor fascinated me. He not only was indistinguishable from a Turk, but he spoke that language fluently. What impressed me most was that he had long since gained the confidence of a group of young Turkish students in Berlin. Hazor's impudence knew no bounds. He moved in with them as a fellow boarder where, together, they studied and fraternized. He made friends easily. He was fun-loving and not above an occasional nocturnal escapade with his alien "friends." But that amiable exterior concealed a dedicated, diamond-hard Armenian—a veritable river of enemy information which he relayed to Ayvazian and thence to the Headquarters. Hazor was a valuable agent indeed.

"Soghomon, how would you like to take a tour of the city with us; I'll show you the sights," Hazor suggested slyly.

I was no tourist and he knew it, but Ayvazian's knowing wink hinted at a purpose behind the levity. "Just the thing," I agreed heartily; "a nice, idle walk in Berlin's fresh air."

Outside there was no semblance of the tourist in their purposeful strides and within a few minutes we had reached our destination. Silently Hazor pointed to a small store across the street. I looked and then turned to him perplexed.

Ayvazian gave me the answer. "That's Djemal's tobacco shop," he explained quietly.

We entered a small cafe directly across the street from Djemal's shop where, over coffee, we watched the tobacco store. For some time the shop did very little business. Now a somberly-dressed woman approached the tobacconist, looked first to one side, then the other, and entered.

Hazor clutched my sleeve. "The woman in black!" he hissed. "I've heard of her."

"Who is she?"

"I don't know. But she's important; that's certain."

We held a hurried conference. Ayvazian was to keep the shop under surveillance from his present vantage point in the restaurant. Hazor was to casually saunter into the shop in an effort to overhear the suspect's conversation. I, in turn, was to follow the woman in black when she left the store. Perhaps this was the queen bee who might lead me to the Turkish hive.

Ayvazian and I watched Hazor cross the street and enter the shop. Had the moment not been so charged with drama, I would have grinned at his suddenly-assumed air of Turkish arrogance. He would have fooled Mustafa Kemal himself.

Presently the woman in black emerged and walked briskly to the corner, her fur collar turned high against the bitter December cold. It had begun to snow and I was thankful for the extra shield as I followed her for several blocks. Suddenly she paused before a spacious, iron-fenced home, fumbled in her purse for a key, unlocked the gate and entered the house.

I scribbled the address on the back of an envelope:

#4 *Hardenburgstrasse*.

For an hour I lurked in the vicinity until the near-zero weather penetrated my overcoat. There was nothing further to be gained here, so, teeth chattering, I returned to Ayvazian's place.

They were both drinking *sourge* when I arrived. Gratefully I accepted a cup of the steaming coffee while my companions talked, ostensibly ignoring me, but actually considerate enough to allow me a chance to thaw out. At length I lit a cigarette. I seldom smoked but this was something of an occasion: my first concrete association with these two professionals. It had been my intention to give them a resume of my activities but Ayvazian and Hazor would have none of generalities and I ended up with a detailed accounting of my every step and observation as I shadowed the woman in black.

Now it was my turn to ask questions. "What did you two find out?"

Ayvazian elevated his palm and shoulders, an eloquent gesture denoting that he had learned nothing.

"How about you?" I asked Hazor.

His report was disappointing. "I heard very little. All Djemal said was that he hoped she would let him know."

"Know *what?*" I asked sharply.

Hazor shrugged. "Your guess is as good as mine."

"What did the woman in black say?"

"I remember her exact words. She answered, 'Of course, if he approves.' They both talked in Turkish."

We tried to make sense out of the brief conversation. "You're sure she was no ordinary customer? She made no attempt to buy anything?" I asked.

"Positive! And this was no clandestine lover's meeting either," Hazor reflected. His Turkish face split in a wide grin. "I've been in lots of those—I *know!*"

Ayvazian said thoughtfully, "We do know that the woman in black has information Djemal wants. We also know that there is another—someone important—who must give approval before he can get that information. Our course then is clear. We must find out what he wants and who it is that is so important he can give approval to a man such as Djemal."

I agreed. "Djemal was one of the three Turkish assassins cited by Serkoyan at the Congress in Constantinople over a year ago. Whatever this intrigue going on here in Berlin among the Turks, there is only one man who would dare to presume to give Djemal orders, and the woman in black knows who he is—and, Gentlemen, so do you."

We exchanged quick glances. *Talaat!*

Ayvazian, who apparently was in charge of the intelligence operation in Berlin, assigned another agent, known only as Sumpat (Not to be confused with the heroic Armenian General Sumpat—Gotoyan—who, with a tiny army of civilian volunteers, vainly defended the city of Moush against overwhelmingly superior Turkish Armed Forces.), who was to keep #4 *Hardenburgstrasse* under close observation throughout the night. It was still snowing on that afternoon of the next day when I replaced Sumpat and focused my attention on the mansion across the street. Hours passed. Suddenly a figure alighted from a car, scurried up the stairs and into the house. Vainly I tried to get a close look at his face.

At that moment Hazor appeared out of the swirling snow. "Soghomon, I saw that man who just went inside."

"Who is he?"

"One of Talaat's underlings, Hakka Bey. Ayvazian told you about him yesterday. He's one of the Turks responsible for the massacres—not as bloodthirsty as Talaat perhaps, but bad enough."

"Have you heard anything about the woman in black?"

"I think she's Enver's wife, but I'm not sure."

Now the pieces of the puzzle gradually began to fit together. We had identified Hakka and possibly the woman in black. That could only mean we were nearing the hour when either Talaat or Enver would make his appearance. But I was plagued by one thought: Ayvazian had said Enver was in Moscow conniving with the Reds to overthrow his own government. If the mysterious woman was really Enver's wife, could that mean that he was now in Berlin? I proposed to find out.

I had been lurking near the big house for the better part of an hour when the front door quickly opened and the man known as Hakka reappeared. Cautiously I followed until he entered a two-story, frame house. Again I jotted down the address: #47 *Ouhlandstrasse*. We had uncovered still another nest of Turkish plotters. It was the kind of house one might expect to find in the pages of an overly melodramatic spy story. But there was nothing fictitious about this. Here was cold, grim reality: a house that could result in death—mine, or . . . ?

The snowfall was reaching blizzard proportions. Thoroughly chilled I made my way to *Maxl's* restaurant where, as I expected, Ayvazian and Hazor were awaiting me.

After a meat-and-sauerkraut dinner with an unpronounceable name, and "coffee" of equally mysterious origin, Ayvazian, through his ever present pall of cigarette smoke, flicked a thumb towards Hazor: "Our friend seems to have uncovered an interesting bit of news."

I questioned him with an upraised eyebrow.

"That tobacco shop of Djemal's is evidently a clearing house of information for the fugitive *Ittihadists*—the Young Turks. Today I spotted another of Talaat's men—this time Shekir."

We were getting close. "The woman in black; is she really Mrs. Enver?" I asked.

"All I have to go on is an old tintype," Hazor said. "It doesn't look like her but there's a slight resemblance. We'll find out soon," he promised, with more confidence than I believe he felt.

Ayvazian spoke, for the first time in several minutes. "We'll all have to be more cautious than usual from now on. Something's in the wind, Gentlemen. They're probably planning a coup of some kind. In any case the Turks are sure nervous—and suspicious."

"You're right," Hazor agreed. "They seldom leave their homes. It must be something that concerns the top echelon only: the Turkish students seem to know nothing about it."

Yes, it was the high brass all right. How high, I was soon to learn.

* * * * * * * * *

Events were now moving forward as inexorably as the hands on a clock. Ayvazian visited me in my room, his manner brisk and businesslike. "Soghomon," he said, "the Berlin Headquarters is holding a special meeting tonight."

"What for?"

"We're expecting an important guest: Dr. Libarid Nazariantz."

"Why, I've heard of him!" I exclaimed, impressed. "He's one of our outstanding intellectuals and statesmen."

"That's the man," Ayvazian nodded. "He was attached to the Armenian Embassy here in Germany—when we had a country. He's now with us in the Federation."

It was an interesting group of patriots who assembled to hear the visitor. Dr. Nazariantz was the least likely figure one would have expected of a diplomat. A typical revolutionary, he lacked the suave manners and deliberately nurtured polish usually associated with emissaries. A fire-brand and an extraordinarily effective speaker perhaps, but he was endowed with a heart-warming depth of simple compassion—a strange, paradoxical man. There was not one among us who did not know that his love of national liberty was equalled only by his hatred of tyranny.

"My fellow Armenians," he began, "I will mince no words. We have lost our country, but not our self-respect. Again we have been deceived by those who claimed to be our friends. The Godless Bolsheviks, on one hand, and the Islamic persecutors of the Christians on the other, combined forces to conquer us. But what they accomplished is only a geographical victory. Our sovereignty may have been destroyed but the Armenian spirit lives on."

We were on our feet, cheering wildly, laughing and sobbing at the same time.

"I now call upon that living spirit to strike back at those who have trampled underfoot everything that we, a peaceful people, have always cherished. We no longer have an army, but—by God!—we have fighting hearts. We must—we *will* continue the fight against the criminals who robbed us of our birthright!"

I recall little of the next few moments. We cheered until our voices grew hoarse. All of us were shouting and weeping, knowing that as long as we had inspired leaders like this, the Armenian heart would beat forever.

Dr. Nazariantz pointed a finger at me. "Through my dear friend Avak Zakar Avakian of the Federation in America, I learned of the crusade upon which Soghomon Tehlirian, one of our patriots, has embarked. This man already brought to justice one of our own people—a man named Mugurditchian, through whose veins flowed the blood of a serpent."

Again there was an enthusiastic burst of applause. I marveled. Here in Germany the name of Tehlirian had become a symbol of unity, kinship and—justice. Embarrassed, I rose to my feet and acknowledged the heartwarming response. I have never been one to bask in the limelight. Mutely I pleaded with Dr. Nazariantz to resume his inspiring message.

Our guest continued, the shade of a grin on his face. "Knowing the speed with which rumors fly on Armenian tongues, I'm sure that you all know the reason for brother Tehlirian's visit to Berlin." A knowing murmur filled the hall. "He is here to find the arch-killer Talaat, and my brothers, it is our duty to help him. We, too, have an obligation to seek out and punish, not only Talaat, but the other Turks who were instrumental in the murder and plunder of nearly all of our people.

"It has been reported to me by our countrymen, Ayvazian and Hazor, that the Young Turk Party has concentrated many of its leaders here in Berlin, and I am further informed that they are growing apprehensive. It is only a matter of time when they discover our program for retribution. I ask you, therefore, to proceed with increased precaution." Dr. Nazariantz then asked if there were any questions.

Ayvazian rose to his feet. "*Doktore* Nazariantz, we have been watching someone we call the woman in black. We cannot be sure but we think she is Enver's wife. Can you tell us whether Enver is here in Berlin?"

Dr. Nazariantz paced the platform for a few moments. "No," he said at length, "I don't think so. Judging from the information we have, he has no reason to be here in Berlin at this time. In fact," he went on, confirming our earlier reports, "we are confident that he is in Moscow fomenting a new Turkish revolution which he hopes will seat him as the new dictator. But," he concluded thoughtfully, "it seems to me that his wife would be at his side. I do not believe that the woman in black is Mrs. Enver. I agree, though, that she is apparently a woman of consequence in Turkish circles."

I raised my hand and Dr. Nazariantz gave me the floor. "Sir, what of Talaat?" I asked.

"He may well be here, brother Tehlirian. You may be sure he is our main target. We do know he has been active here in Berlin, just as we know that Enver is equally busy with his plots in the Soviet Union." The meeting was concluded with the inevitable piping-hot *sourge.*

(COMMENT: Dr. Nazariantz's assumptions had been correct. Enver Pasha had indeed been in Moscow and with Communist support had been organizing troops for an attack on Armenian provinces. He was later killed in the partisan resistance, where his death earned him a unique distinction: Enver Pasha was the only one of the Turkish mass-murderers marked for execution who died in combat. He alone, of the dozen leading war criminals, did not meet death at the hands of Armenian patriots.)

My mission suffered another setback in the weeks that followed, what with the recurrence of that typhus infection I had picked up in the guerrilla war against the Turks, and another of those infernal mental depressions. Strange, is it not, that such problems would affect me now when I was evidently near to closing in on the kill? Yet, that is the way it was.

Fortunately I had struck up an acquaintance with a Federation official, Yervant Apelian, that quickly ripened into a warm friendship. The twenty-five-year-old Apelian was also the First Secretary of the Armenian Embassy until the conquest of our Republic. His companionship during my illness was a godsend. But male companionship was not enough. Once again I was tormented by visions of my beautiful Anahid; longing for her, needing her. And again I saw Yeranouhi's smiling face; glorified in her repeated acts of courage. I wondered if she were not really my heart's choice, but always I was confronted with the same answer: a valiant lady, indeed. For the countless time . . . ? Always the same answer. I longed only to have my lovely Anahid in my arms; she was my life—my all!

It was Apelian's opinion that a change to a more congenial environment would help restore my health; the physical and emotional exhaustion had worn me down. Within a few days I had moved to an apartment adjacent to Apelian's. My new address: #51 *Augsburgstrasse,* was truly a change for the better. There, Apelian, whom I called by his Christian name, Yervant, introduced me to Levon Eftian, an Armenian student who lived with his relatives while studying in Berlin. Yervant and Levon not only proved to be close friends but it was the effervescent Levon Eftian who, for the next several weeks, was my guide on a series of adventures that led from the tragic-comic to the outer strands of a spider's web.

It was impossible to rebuke Levon, although at times, he should have been spanked like a small boy. His spirits were as bubbly as a goblet of rhine and seltzer. But since my mission called for a serious appraisal of every move I made, I often found Levon's zesty behavior quite uncomfortable. There were times when I wanted to confide in him; to tell him truthfully why I was in Berlin. But he was not a member of the Federation and to do so would have placed him in jeopardy as an accessory before the fact—the fact of Talaat's certain death at my hands. Yet there was no restraining this exuberant young man.

One evening Levon burst into my room unannounced. "Soghomon, get your coat, we're going out tonight. I want you to meet someone special."

"Who?" I asked suspiciously.

"Leona Bailunzon, my German language teacher."

I hesitated. "I'm kind of tired tonight."

"Aw, c'mon!" he insisted, reaching for my overcoat and handing it to me. "I don't know what it is you find so interesting in all these maps and books you're always studying, but you're becoming a regular hermit."

There was no arguing with the impish Levon. "All right," I said resignedly.

"You'll like her, Soghomon. She's a doll."

He was right. "Doll" is not a word I ordinarily use, but there was no denying she was a charming young lady. Her apartment was a postcard of femininity, except for an austere parlor which she used as a studio. It was a fortunate meeting. We had scarcely finished our coffee and *streizelkuchen* when I was talked into becoming her student. According to the buoyant, persuasive Levon, who spoke through a mouth crammed with pastry, I could not have found a better German-language teacher. I made no claim of clairvoyance or even unusual perception, but it required no soothsayer to recognize that Levon's interest was not so much in obtaining a German teacher for me as it was in winning a German girl for himself. The rascal was using me. I couldn't help but grin.

My tutelage, under the patient guidance of Leona Bailunzon, began a few days later. It was a momentous first lesson; one that was to be recalled during the trial that followed.

Soon I began to conjugate those impossible German verbs; slowly they were beginning to make sense to me.

"Is there anyone in your family who understands German—who might help you in your lessons?" Leona asked.

For a moment I had no reaction. And then her question

triggered something inside. A sudden picture flashed through my mind. My twelve-year-old niece had once studied these very same German words. Who would pay for her lessons now? Who would help her? *No one!*

The old dizziness returned—overwhelming, agonizing—again I was gripped with that sudden fever.

Leona, her eyes wide with concern, hurriedly brought me a small glass of brandy. "What is it?" she cried. "Why are you shaking so?" she asked. "Here, let me wipe the perspiration from your forehead."

Leona's startled features swam before me. I was slumped in my chair, mumbling. "Someone in my family to help me, you ask? No, there is no one. Somewhere, perhaps a few of my family are still alive; but only *perhaps!* Only a little girl remains. They killed eighty-four . . . Have they all gone but one?" I tried to rally my thoughts, to force myself back into a semblance of normalcy. But I was again sinking into the quicksands of my private recurring nightmares. Down—*down!* I made a last attempt to clutch at a straw of reality, caught hold for a moment, and then lost my grip. Vaguely I remember ranting: "Home? Family? I have no home—I haven't even a homeland." My hoarse voice must have been frightening to the young teacher. "Everyone... gone. I *must* ...find . . ."

Later they told me I wept before I lapsed into unconsciousness.

* * * * * * * * * *

Levon Eftian's voice awakened me the following morning. Inexplicably, I was once again in my own apartment. "Soghomon," he called softly through the door, "there's a gentleman here to see you."

Unsteadily I rose to my feet, slipped into a robe and admitted Levon and Hazor. Concern showed plainly in their faces. I sat on the edge of my bed, dully aware that I was back in my own rooms. Levon opened the window a crack, the fresh winter air helping to clear the cobwebs in my mind. Without a word Hazor lit the one-burner gas stove and started a pot of *sourge,* the aroma of the coffee soon filling the room. Belatedly I realized that my two friends had not been introduced; that they had undoubtedly just met in the hallway outside my door. I was too sick for grandiloquent introductions. "Hazor," I said, "meet Levon. Levon—

Hazor."

The two shook hands. Ill as I was, however, I could not help but be amused by Levon's look of suspicion. If I had not been feeling so poorly, I would have smiled. "Pay no attention to that Turkish face, Levon," I assured him. "Hazor was just born unlucky."

Hazor, for his part, spoke to Levon in Armenian. "Our friend, Tehlirian here, seems to be a little under the weather."

"He got sick last night," Levon answered, also in the Mother tongue. "I brought him home and put him to bed." The irrepressible Levon Eftian grinned broadly. "He was studying German. Believe me, it's enough to make anyone ill."

"How did you know I was there?" I asked.

"I didn't. I just went calling on Leona—pardon—your teacher, Miss Bailunzon. But don't worry," he commiserated, "I'll take your place hereafter."

Hazor started to set out three cups and saucers. "No time for coffee now," Levon protested gaily. "I have a luncheon date with Leona." I thanked him for bringing me home last night, and as he went through the door he took a parting shot at Hazor's Turkish-looking face. "If ever you meet me on a dark night, be sure you're wearing a mask," was his genial parting remark.

Hazor laughed good-naturedly, thoroughly accustomed to comments about his alien features. "I sometimes think," he chuckled, "that way back in my family somewhere, one of my ancestors got naughty one moonlit June night in Constantinople."

We could hear Levon's laughter echoing outside in the hall. With Levon's departure, Hazor now grew serious. "When you didn't show up on the watch this morning, I figured something was wrong so I dropped over to see you. Something big is developing, Soghomon. Headquarters told me that 47 *Ouhlandstrasse*` is a key *Ittihadist* point and that the enemy has important events planned. It could happen any day."

I started to rise but he gently pushed me back on the bed. "No, you don't," he admonished. "Sumpat or Ayvazian or another agent will stand your watch. You're too sick to go out."

I brushed his hand aside. "Sick or not, I'm standing my own watch. Nothing—not anything, is going to prevent me from being in on the execution."

Hazor shrugged, knowing that the very thought of closing in on Talaat was all the medicine I needed. Despite his further objections we were soon posted within twenty yards of the mysteri-

ous house on *Ouhlandstrasse.*
An hour passed, and then another. I said nothing to the anxious Hazor about my alternating periods of chills and fever. Once I had to grasp a rail to keep from falling in a faint. Hazor was just about to say something when two men suddenly approached, unlocked the gates and entered the house. We retreated back into the shadows. "Did you recognize them?" I whispered.
He nodded. "The Turks—Dr. Behaeddin Shekir and a Dr. Nazim. I don't know too much about Dr. Nazim, but he's another of the wanted killers. I didn't know he was in Berlin." We waited silently for another half-hour until Shekir came out, alone.
"Hazor," I said urgently, "I'm going to follow him. You stay and keep an eye on this Dr. Nazim."
"Good luck, Soghomon." Hazor patted my shoulder and I set off down the street to *Wilhelmstrasse,* trailing Shekir to the British Embassy. I learned later that Shekir attempted to get English support for the Young Turks in their plot to impose their own brand of government in Turkey—not an administration which would have granted a measure of freedom to the Turkish masses and their satellite states but, rather, one which would line their own pockets.
The weather was bitterly cold and I reflected ruefully on Hazor's advice to remain in bed. He was right, for I was again alternately shivering and burning. Desperately I fought to suppress the mounting giddiness, as ill now as I had been last night. The faintness engulfed me and I sank to my knees. I tried unsuccessfully to regain my feet and then rolled over onto the sidewalk, unconscious. It could not have been much more than a few minutes when I opened my eyes to find a crowd of curious bystanders milling about. "We'd better call an ambulance," somebody suggested.
The comment penetrated my benumbed brain. I certainly could not afford to reveal my identity to the authorities or answer any questions about the gun I was carrying. The only way to insure privacy was to leave—at once! A young Samaritan helped me to my feet and I assured the sympathetic onlookers that I could make my way home unattended.
How I made it to my apartment will forever remain one of those unsolved mysteries. I recall sinking to the pavement once or twice, rising drunkenly and then struggling to my room. Once there I threw myself across the bed, veering from insensibility to semi-consciousness until that evening when I awoke to find

Hazor, accompanied by a Dr. Kassirer, bending over me. A sedative was administered and I was firmly ordered to remain inside until my health returned.

"Exhaustion," the doctor pronounced, "and a touch of typhus. You'll be all right in a month or so, provided you get enough rest."

There was no alternative to the doctor's ultimatum. Either I would follow his orders or else allow my resistance to become even further weakened, thus jeopardizing my entire mission.

But the thought of allowing the Turkish murderers to continue their plots for still more killings brought me to a decision. Within a week I asked Ayvazian and Hazor, my constant visitors, to call an immediate conference of all Armenian agents in Berlin, the meeting to be held in my apartment.

They arrived that evening: Ayvazian, Hazor, Sumpat, Hrap and Norire and a few others I had already met. Also attending were two agents who were not familiar to me. Ayvazian introduced the newcomers:

"Soghomon, say hello to Vaza and Hago. Headquarters thought it best to send along a couple of new faces not familiar to the Turks. They'll be working with us until . . . "

". . . until we find Talaat and the rest of his assassins," Vaza finished, Hago nodding his assent.

It had been my purpose to ask them to keep a sharp eye on Djemal's tobacco shop and the houses on *Hardenburgstrasse* and *Ouhlandstrasse*. They were then to report to me any significant activity which might lead me to Talaat. But I could have spared myself the trouble. They had all agreed, among themselves, to keep the suspects under 'round-the-clock surveillance while I was convalescing. I experienced only one disturbing thought: there was not a man present who had not suffered because of Talaat's campaign of terror, or lost one or more of his loved ones during the massacres of their people. If any of them encountered the chief killer before I did, there was little question but that Talaat would be in the arms of his Allah long before I recovered. Even at that, the thought was good medicine.

* * * * * * * * *

In February, 1921, when I had been confined to my bed for about a month, Sumpat brought me news that so enthused me I could feel a new vitality surging through my veins. The Federation had notified us that the *Ittihadists* were to hold their "Young

Turk" Party Congress in Rome. There was also a good possibility, reported the Armenian intelligence agents, that several of the prominent Turkish assassins would attend.

It was this event that led the *Ittihadists* to their first serious error: they allowed a news release to be published which gave the exact time and place of the meeting. That same night we held an emergency session. It was unanimously concluded that Talaat, if he were in Berlin, would be forced to reveal himself en route to the convention in Rome. It was also agreed that one of us should leave for Rome on the same train, not only to observe the Turks, but to gather additional information from the Armenian community in the Italian capital.

We had already learned from Hazor, who still lived with the Turkish students, that most of the *Ittihad* followers were concentrated in the *Charlottenburg* section of Berlin, near the railroad station, so it was no difficult matter to keep them under constant watch.

Our vigilance paid off on the fourth day. Hazor and agent Hago, the newcomer to whom I had recently been introduced, were with me at the railroad depot when suddenly we spotted Shekir and three of his cronies entering the station.

"The train is about ready to leave for Rome," I said to Hazor and Hago. "If Talaat is really here in Berlin he'll have to make an appearance soon." We waited tensely for fifteen, hour-long minutes. Hago nudged me and pointed. A beefy, well-dressed, cane-carrying man swaggered into sight, entered the station, and was quickly surrounded by a group of fawning Turkish students. One of them addressed the arrogant figure: "They are awaiting you inside the train, *Pasha*," he said, pointing to the window of the "Class A" car.

"They? Pasha?" We looked at each other. Who was this brutish-looking man for whom the leading Young Turks waited like so many young lackeys?

The obese stranger strode to the train and imperiously rapped his cane against the pane of glass. A quartet of faces appeared at the window. We were too far away to hear what he said, but inside the railroad car, Sumpat—bless his heart—had managed to get a seat within hearing distance. He told us later that the swinish one had ordered his henchmen to use whatever means necessary to persuade the British to back them in their plot to undermine their own country. In return they would grant England a favorable trade treaty. As for the capital needed to finance the overthrow of

Turkey, Sumpat reported, they could always murder or deport whatever Armenians were left and transfer the property of their victims to their own war chest. It was the same old vicious story.

The train was pulling out of the station when the lumpish *Pasha* and his admiring friends emerged into the street. I rounded the corner and saw Hazor and Hago unobtrusively mingling with the crowd. I joined them.

"I think that's your man, Soghomon," Hazor said tersely.

I whipped out the dog-eared photograph of Talaat that Ambassador Armen Garo had given me in Boston. "It looks like him," I confessed, "and then again it doesn't. The features are somewhat different. He could be a relative—a brother, maybe." Our quarry was now some distance away.

I said a hasty good-bye to my two friends and followed the stranger and his student-admirers to the Zoological Gardens where they finally stopped. The youths bowed ceremoniously as they departed, executing a *tamenah* —a courtly Turkish bow. Whoever he was, the portly one commanded the respect accorded only to officials of high status. He *must* be Talaat, I thought—but no, the shape of the nose, the slant of the eyes, the meticulously razored face, they were different from the mustached stranger who glowered in the yellowed photograph.

There was a compelling familiarity about the foppish Turk as he walked on alone, strutting militarily despite his gross weight. I trailed him to #4 *Hardenburgstrasse* where he entered the house not to emerge again that day.

The following morning Hazor, Hago and I conferred briefly. Hazor agreed to stand watch at #47 *Ouhlandstrasse*; Hago would keep an eye on Djemal's tobacco shop and I was to keep #4 *Hardenburgstrasse* under observation.

It was ten a.m., not long after I had taken up my position, when the pudgy Turk appeared at his front door and glanced cautiously in both directions while I lurked in the shadows of an alley. He started walking purposefully and I hurried in pursuit, following at a safe distance until he reached #47 *Ouhlandstrasse,* the hideout of Shekir, the shifty-eyed Dr. Nazim and their fellow conspirators. I exchanged information with Hazor, whose post this was, until precisely eleven o'clock when my quarry left and returned to his own home.

We were making progress, but slowly, it was agreed at a meeting that night in my apartment. To speed our work it was proposed that Hazor visit the Berlin police department where he was acquainted with an Armenian officer who might permit him to examine the alien visa files. Vaza announced that he would contact the landlady of the house on *Hardenburgstrasse* to determine the obese Turk's identity. We were again examining the photograph of the man we believed might be Talaat when an overseas cablegram arrived. I could feel my temples pounding as I read the cable.

"What's the matter?" Hazor asked, seeing my face go white. "Who's the telegram from?"

"It's from Federation Headquarters in Boston. They've learned the name of the heavy-set Turk we've been following."

"Who is he?" Hazor and Vaza asked in the same breath.

"*Talaat!*"

If my voice sounded icy, it was but a vague indication of the inner coldness that chilled the blood in my veins. I had found the monster at last!

Hazor, who had been carefully examining the crumpled photo, nodded. "We were on the right track, Soghomon. It's just as we thought. Talaat had his face altered somehow. Draw a thicker mustache on that face and a fez in place of that fedora and you've got your man."

When I answered, it was scarcely above a whisper. "It's time I oiled my gun."

XII. A BULLET FOR TALAAT

The moment of retribution was almost at hand. I would soon be twenty-five, yet it seemed I had spent half of my lifetime pursuing the man who was known as the "Monster" to thousands of surviving Armenians whom he tired to exterminate. It was hard to believe that I had already given three years of my life searching for Talaat.

Vaza had made good his promise to invade Talaat's house. Posing as a Swiss insurance salesman in need of a combination office and apartment, he told the landlady he had learned that she might have a vacancy. He managed to gain admittance and studied the arrangement of the rooms and halls. His invasion of #4 *Hardenburgstrasse* was carried out with military precision. He learned, among other things, that Talaat and his wife were registered as Mr. and Mrs. Ali Salieh. Another interesting fact that agent Vaza uncovered was that the mysterious woman in black was none other than—Mrs. Talaat. The air of intrigue heightened when Vaza found that the house was leased by Shia Bey, Secretary of the Turkish Embassy. Here was further proof that the government of Kemal Ataturk had not only lied about seeking Talaat for "crimes against his own government" but that they were officially supporting him in his sumptuous quarters.

(COMMENT: Shia Bey, scheduled to appear as a witness against Tehlirian during his trial, became enmeshed in a Turkish web of intrigue that reached all the way to Kemal Ataturk in Constantinople. To this very day the Turks evade all questions concerning their peculiar actions during the trial.)

There could be no doubt now that if the beast was to be brought to bay it would have to be done by an Armenian. Could it be that Kemal was maintaining Talaat in exile for the purpose of using his unique talents for still another massacre? If so, the present Turkish Government would do well to find another candidate. I was now measuring Talaat's life in hours. Our constant surveillance had revealed another essential fact—Talaat seldom deviated from his daily routine. He usually left his house at 10 a.m. to return at 11.

Then and there I made my decision.

That time schedule would cost him his life. Between 10 and 11 a.m. I was going to execute Talaat.

I moved in for the kill. First, I secured an apartment at 37 *Hardenburgstrasse,* across the street from the Turk's residence; one which afforded me an opportunity to observe his every move.

Fate has a way of unfolding in an unpredictable manner, sometimes tragic, sometimes ironically humorous. The next two weeks combined both of these elements. First, Talaat, for reasons of his own, selected to change the time of his daily visits to his henchmen. His hours were now erratic. Secondly, the one time I might have cornered him I was prevented from doing so by a minor circumstance which, reflectively, was ludicrous to the extreme, but nonetheless nerve-wracking when it occurred. To compound my problems I almost forewarned Talaat through an incipient impulse to punish Djemal for his part in the Armenian massacres, an act which would surely have frightened Talaat into anonymity. Talaat's subordinate, Djemal, and a stripped screw helped to complete the comedy of errors.

Comical? Tragic? Perhaps! One morning as I was watching from my window, Talaat entered the street, a brief case pressed closely against his side. I reached for my Mauser and hurried down the stairway to the front door. I grasped the knob.

It spun loosely in my hands.

Frantically I twisted, tugged, turned and rattled that damned knob, but it just wouldn't catch. Despairingly I saw Talaat's vast hulk through the glass portion of the door as he disappeared down the street. I was aflame with frustration when the landlady finally appeared with a box of tools, but it was another five minutes before we were able to open the door.

Where to search for him? After a few false starts I concluded that he might have gone to visit his co-conspirator, Djemal, at the tobacco shop. Talaat was nowhere in sight. Inside, however, was Djemal, the second of the three greatest assassins alive. I could have killed him on the spot. Indeed, my finger curled around the trigger of my Mauser but my common sense prevailed and I quelled the impulse. I was after one man: Talaat. An impulsive act at this time would mark failure for my mission. As for Djemal, what with so many other dedicated Armenians seeking him, that man's days were numbered anyway.

One would think that after years of searching for the Turkish devil and having found him, punishment would have been swift.

But I had not taken into account that if we Armenians with our worldwide Revolutionary Federation and numerous agents had formed a network of closely knit activity, so, too, had Talaat and his "Young Turk Party" established a defensive organization. He, too, had his agents.

It is not without a certain pride—indeed history has proven it in almost every case—that when Turkish intelligence is pitted against Armenian intelligence, the Turks fare a very poor second. So it happened in this case. Our agents infiltrated every one of their important hideouts in Berlin. As for the enemy, we can imagine what chagrin they might have felt had they known that Hazor, one of the most popular "Turks" in Berlin was, in fact, an undercover officer; our agent Sumpat had accompanied them to Rome on their ultra-secret mission; that Vaza had penetrated Talaat's home. The one-sidedness of this battle of Turkish vs. Armenian intelligence can best be understood when it is realized that they did not even know of the restaurant we frequented. Even today there is not an Armenian in the world who is familiar with this case who cannot help but laugh at the spectacle of homage paid by the Turks when they presented a citation of honor to Hazor of the unfortunate Turkish face, the darling of the Turkish student body, who was elected by them as the outstanding *Turkish Student of The Year*. As for the citation, one evening when in our cups, we pinned it in a place of honor on the wall of the gentleman's room at *Maxl's* Restaurant. For once in our lives we agreed with the Turks. We, too, were proud of Hazor—one of the greatest and most likeable Armenian agents in the Federation.

I have already explained what happened on that fateful morning of March 15, 1921 (Chapter One). The night had been long and I spent most of my sleepless hours anticipating Talaat's next move. It was then I remembered that Ayvazian had given me an Armenian newspaper and insisted that I read an excerpt from a book written by a Mrs. Bertha Papazian. (COMMENT: Mrs. Papazian's reports are now part of the archives of the Armenian Chair at the University of California at Los Angeles, and Harvard University.) I started to sip a cup of coffee but I had not read more than two or three lines before the *sourge* was forgotten. The account, grisly in its content but poetically beautiful in its conception, held me enthralled.

I read:

"While the funeral pyre of Armenia was being kindled;

while humanity, which had flowered nobly in spite of insuperable difficulties was being thrown as dross into the flames by barbaric and sacrilegious hands; while white-haired men and women maintained their simple faith in a Divine justice; while fathers, mothers, brides, youths, maidens and infants who had just opened their innocent eyes upon this world were being sent to swell the hosts of martyrs to Christianity and to freedom; the old frenzied cry of *'Christ or Mohammed'* ringing in their ears; upon the heights of Zeitoun, amid the cliffs of Sassoun where the race had preserved a scant immunity from Turkish powers; there thundered forth the defiant voices of the ancient heroes—the shouts of the brave mountaineers, who, although scantily armed, held the foe at bay for months—to the marvel of the world.

"Zeitoun, a hill town of the Rhupenian Dynasty (Kingdom of Armenia which flourished from 1080 A.D. to 1095 A.D. under Prince Rhupen, and which marked early Armenian resistance to alien aggression against its Christian principles), refused to surrender until former peace terms had been entered into with Turkey. And when in Sassoun the inevitable happened and the Turks, outnumbering the Armenians twenty to one, came rushing up the heights, the women of the villages, with their babes in their arms and calling upon God to help them, fought side by side with their husbands, fathers and brothers until death, inflicted by hordes of Moslems, overcame them all. It is no longer possible to summon up the inhuman acts that crowd the stage. The drama has burst its national bounds and has become worldwide. We see two worlds, one in darkness and one in light, struggling for birth in the hearts and minds of men. The gigantic evils embodied in a succession of depraved sultans and temporizing world policies, made manifest by this great crisis, prevent issues and opportunities which call for potent and colossal heroes. We see none. The prophetic, Cassandra-like warning from Sir Gladstone, 'To serve Armenia is to serve civilization,' evokes no world response. And the few who do respond, now they even cease to perceive.

"We see Armenia rise with all her glorious past upon her. We see her turn horrified, dumbfounded and appealing eyes upon the six mighty Western Powers. Armenia, the Apostle of Christianity, its servant and defender, she who held back the Saracens in the days of her power, she who had given her sons to the cause of the Crusades, the Mother of Democracy, now stands bare, bleeding, her arms outstretched to the Christian West, to the Six Great Knights who are armed to the teeth, whose Navies ride the oceans of the world, whose Armies patrol the earth, asking for their help. We see her standing thus. But the great forms have been dwarfed, their eyes are averted, their ears deaf.

"Germany, capitalizing every element of the situation, even the blood of the victim, openly declares herself the protector of the Islamic world and furthers her *Drang Nach Osten* scheme; so well termed the spine of the present war. Germany reaches out for the acquisition of land for her Berlin to Baghdad Railway and the road to world conquest. She clasps hands with the Turks. Heed the cry of your Christian brothers and sisters in Armenia, Mankind, less they be completely destroyed by the Islamic persecutors."

The superlative report inspired me, uplifted me, nourished my spark of life. I did not know the gifted author but I did know I would never let her down. The instigator of all the sorrows she had described was now focused in the composite of one man. Grimly I sat before the window concentrating my attention on the house across the street.

* * * * * * * * *

It was nearing ten a.m. on that dreary Tuesday morning of March 15, 1921, when Talaat appeared on his front steps. Soft-falling snowflakes were quickly turning into slush. As usual, the huge Turk glanced cautiously in both directions and then continued toward the *Ouhlandstrasse* address where his confederates were gathered. Once again I shoved my short-barreled Mauser automatic in my pocket and leaped down the stairs and into the street.

Minutes later I stood over Talaat, a smoking gun in my hand. One single bullet ended his gory career—a death far more merciful than he had ever accorded to the million-and-a-half people he had murdered by sword, axe, bullet, starvation and drowning.

He died instantly, with neither sound nor quiver. Numb, I looked down at Talaat's body, making no attempt to flee. A crowd of horrified citizens gathered about me and the prostrate figure of Talaat hanging over the curb at the sewer. Several men among the spectators pounced upon me, threw me to the ground and beat me viciously until a police officer arrived. It was well that he appeared when he did. The mob of Germans were in an angry mood. "He's a cold-blooded killer!" someone shouted. "He shot that man—I saw him!" cried another.

I rose to my feet and surrendered my pistol to the policeman. "My name is Tehlirian," I said quietly. "I'm an Armenian. And that," I said, pointing to Talaat's body, "was a Turk."

XIII. PORTRAIT OF A PRISONER

The forenoon sun had not yet entirely dispelled the chill of the morning when I was hustled into Charlottenburg Police Station. There, after some preliminary questioning by a stereotyped sergeant, I was led to a cell where a doctor attended the head wounds I had suffered at the hands of the infuriated mob. After an all-too-brief rest, I was manacled and then taken to a Secret Service bureau where I was again interrogated. But try as I would, I was unable to offer coherent answers.

It was as though I was encased in a mental suit of armor which no amount of questioning could pierce. A feeling of exultation permeated my every fiber. My mission had been accomplished. Over and over again, the phrase kept repeating itself.

Imprisonment? Death by hanging? Strangely, I felt a peculiar sense of detachment. If it was my destiny to be the instrument of retribution, then that same destiny would protect me in the future. If not, I would meet it with head high, in the knowledge that I had done what I believed was morally right.

A succession of interrogations followed, all of them futile until the police realized that my knowledge of German was much too inadequate to understand them or to express myself with any degree of clarity. Belatedly, they decided to employ an interpreter and again I was led back to my familiar cell. My cubicle was not much bigger than a piano packing-box. A pale shaft of light struggling through a heavily-barred window was the only evidence that dusk was approaching. I stretched out on the wooden bunk and tried to rest. Oddly enough, despite the hard planks that served as a bed, I was almost comfortable except for my injured head which still throbbed with pain. Blessed sleep had just eased my hurting when I was awakened by a guard and again taken to the interrogation room. There were six officers awaiting me this time, including a goateed official seated behind the desk. It was with difficulty that I suppressed a gasp at the objects arrayed before him on the desk. A copy of *Der Morgen Poste* emblazoned the execution in 96 point, extra bold headlines:

ARMENIAN STUDENT SLAYS TURKISH OFFICIAL
Police Suspect Political Motive

While the headline was disconcerting enough I looked askance at the other items flanking the newspaper. One was a fedora hat, its lining protruding and blood-stained. Talaat's cane lay across his brief case. Standing nearby was an officious-looking detective who was making a great pretense of examining my pistol as though it were a cannon in disguise.

The goateed official addressed me. "I'm Chief of Police Heinz Gnass. We have some questions to ask you, young man, and this time we have an interpreter so we'll be expecting some direct answers."

For the first time since my arrest I experienced a sense of relief. There were many things I could express to a fellow Armenian who would not only understand me, but with whom I could establish an emotional rapport. But my elation died when the young interpreter entered the room. I boiled inwardly in a surge of outraged indignation. He spoke to me in Turkish.

I glared at him in stony silence.

There was no question as to the Turk's sympathies. "Scoundrel!" he hissed. "How could you murder such a humanitarian as Talaat Pasha?"

"In the same way he butchered my mother, brother and family and a million-and-a-half Armenians!" I snapped, answering him in his own language.

The goateed officer Gnass jumped to his feet. "Ah, ha! So the prisoner speaks Turkish."

"As well as I," the interpreter said oozingly.

The Police Chief was quite pleased. "Excellent. We will continue the interrogation in Turkish." He waved an imperious finger at the interpreter. "You will translate the prisoner's statement into German."

The Turk responded with a deep bow. "Very well . . . Sir."

"Ask him why he committed this crime," Chief Gnass commanded.

"He's a Turk—he can go to hell!" I snapped in my poor German. I had spoken as much of the detested Turkish language as I intended. Now the translator might as well have been talking to the *Brandenburg Gate*. I remained silent now, my contempt for him and his native tongue making him flush scarlet. The Police Chief showed anger at first, but now surprised me by grinning understandingly. With a wave of his hand he dismissed the enraged Turk and ordered me back to my cell.

I have, on occasion, complained about the quality and taste of German coffee, but not even a German would drink the brew I was served on the following morning. However, the liquid was hot and I had just finished it when a guard escorted a visitor to my cell and then departed, leaving us alone.

My surprise turned to pleasure when I recognized him as Gevork Kalousdian whom I had met in Berlin and who brought me the good news that he was to be my interpreter. Our smiles linked us in bonds of renewed friendship.

Kalousdian spoke softly, his consoling words filling my eyes with tears. "I'm not one for making speeches, Soghomon, but I'll stand at your side until you and all our people are vindicated." His voice faltered. "I, too, lost my loved ones in the massacre. What more can I say?"

After a short interval—those precious moments in a man's life when two souls communicate without speaking—Kalousdian continued:

"You're quite famous now. The name Tehlirian is internationally known, especially among the Armenian people, no matter in what country they live. The newspapers are printing reams of copy about you."

"Fame doesn't appeal to me."

Kalousdian smiled. "Fame—publicity—call it what you will, it may not be appealing to you, but you can be sure it's going to be important to the prosecution. If they can make a political chess game out of the trial, they will. What you need most of all, Soghomon," he added thoughtfully, "is a good lawyer. No, not just a good lawyer, a genius."

"Lawyers like that don't come cheaply," I observed dryly, "and even if I had the money, where could I find one who would risk his reputation on a lost cause?" I faced Kalousdian squarely. "I neither intend to cringe, to beg forgiveness, nor to ask for leniency. I executed a criminal in the name of humanity and that is exactly what I shall tell the court."

We shook hands as Kalousdian prepared to leave. "I'm not promising anything, Soghomon," he said kindly, "but Armenians everywhere are rallying to your defense. Don't worry about legal counsel and expenses."

I wanted to thank him but the sudden lump in my throat prevented me from talking.

* * * * * * * * * *

Assistant Chief Inspector Schultzen was a cold, militant-looking officer who wasted little time on preliminaries. He turned to Gevork Kalousdian. "Ask him why he murdered Talaat Pasha."

Gevork interpreted and I answered crisply. "Because he was responsible for the extermination of a million-and-a-half of my people—and he was not murdered, he was executed."

Inspector Schultzen scribbled some notes on a pad. "Then you admit that you killed him?" he asked through Gevork.

"Of course I admit it!"

"Who were your accomplices?"

"I was alone," I told him.

True, I had had every possible assistance, from Yeranouhi to the far-flung offices of the Federation and their agents, but sometimes it is wiser to tell a small lie that hurts no one rather than utter an important truth that can only result in tragedy for everyone.

There was a note of curiosity in Inspector Schultzen's voice that was more personal than professional. "You must have hated him intensely. You say he killed a million-and-a-half of your people, but what did he ever do to you?"

Kalousdian interpreted slowly, his every syllable deliberate. I rose from my seat and leaned across the desk, my face within inches of the detective's. Unknowingly I was shouting.

Gevork Kalousdian eased me back into my chair. "*Yechbire, hampairootoun!*—Patience, brother! Compose yourself." The interpreter turned to Schultzen. "Would you be good enough to send for a glass of water, Sir? You can see Mr. Tehlirian is terribly upset."

"This is not the Grand Hotel," the inspector spat. "I asked a question and I expect an answer."

I regained control of my emotions although my throat felt as though it was lined with sandpaper. "What did Talaat do to me, you ask? He murdered my mother. It was he who caused the deaths of my brother and nearly every member of my family. He burned our home to the ground." I could have continued with a lengthy account of Talaat's injuries to my family but decided to wait.

Kalousdian interpreted Schultzen's self-satisfied observation. "Then your act was premeditated; a deliberately planned killing."

A hot retort rose to my lips when I caught Kalousdian's warning glance. "Silence!" he plainly cautioned.

I held my tongue.

The detective lit a cigarette. "Doesn't your conscience bother you?"

"No! Justice was done. My conscience is clear."

The police official asked something in guttural German. Kalousdian translated. "Your visa, what does it specify?"

"A student of mechanical engineering."

Schultzen smiled mirthlessly. "I'm afraid your student days are over, Tehlirian. You've incriminated yourself to such an extent that the law may go hard with you. One more thing: I have a reputation as a harsh man, especially when murder is involved. You may as well know that every word you said today will be used against you." Assistant Inspector Schultzen leaned back in his chair and exhaled a cloud of smoke. "Of course, you understand that I don't say this because of my personal feelings. As far as I'm concerned you are just a statistic on a police blotter." He dismissed me with a careless, "That will be all."

The first pale shaft of sunlight penetrated the tiny window of my cell. But the morning crackled with tension.

The time for the trial was approaching; the weeks of tortured uncertainty had hardened me for the days ahead.

I was ready.

* * * * * * * * *

The following day I faced a new interrogator, Chief Inspector Mandteufel, a man far more severe than Schultzen. Kalousdian warned me that the officer had a reputation for twisting statements in a manner that made Schultzen seem like a rank amateur. However, the interpreter bolstered my confidence by telling me that my countrymen had obtained three of Germany's legal giants to serve as my defense counsels.

To my later dismay I learned that the astute Mandteufel had trapped me into many self-incriminating "confessions." I had already made too many statements which could not be deleted from the records. Kalousdian, to his everlasting credit, conveniently forgot to sign the transcripts in an effort to bar the damaging testimony from being accepted in court.

Several days later I was transferred to the Berlin Central Prison where I remained throughout the trial. I was given a new prison uniform and the unexpected luxury of a bathtub. The rules were strict, the gong of a bell regulating our every activity. How I grew to despise the discordant gong that awakened us every morning! We would stand at attention, water pitcher in hand; a second gong informed us that the trustees were making the rounds, bringing fresh water; the third gong signified that we were to scrub our cells for inspection by the officer in charge. As for the meals, I wouldn't feed them to a Turk.

On the second day I was visited by the prison chaplain. He offered me a Bible, but when I asked for an Armenian Testament in exchange for the German one which I could not possibly read, the kindly chaplain referred my request to the Armenian Prelate in Berlin who presented me with one in our native language. He visited me regularly thereafter.

* * * * * * * * * *

The day of my legal ordeal was almost at hand when I first met the bearded, bespectacled Dr. Adolf von Gorton, the man who was to act as my chief defense counsel. Dr. von Gorton, after hearing my story, agreed that Gevork Kalousdian would be ideal as court interpreter and, undoubtedly acceptable to both prosecution and the defense. Courageous Hazor had volunteered to interpret but the world community of Armenians needed him much more than I. In any case the exposure would ruin his effectiveness as an undercover agent. I thanked him. Hazor had truly proven his friendship and loyalty.

Only yesterday Hazor described how he accompanied a group of enemy students to Talaat's funeral. As usual his Turkish features removed him from any suspicion. Many dignitaries were present at the burial, including Kemalist Turkey's Embassy officials, the diplomatic representatives of Germany and the Arab nations. Motion pictures were taken, but what interested me most were the threats made by Shekir, and by heads of the Arab League. Pledges were vowed by these Moslem Leagues to avenge the death of their hero. I shrugged. It was unimportant to me now that fate had caught up with the fiend, Talaat.

Several days later I met Dr. Johannes Wertenhauer, my second defense lawyer; bald, clean-shaven and dignified. His part in the plan of the defense was to obtain information about my personal life, periods of illnesses and reasons for executing Talaat. It was also at this time that Kalousdian informed me that virtually every German newspaper was against me. Indeed, they had openly offered their columns without charge to the Turks so that not only I, but all Armenians could be denounced. The reason, of course, was obvious: the Turks and the Germans had been military allies while the Armenian minority was now a convenient whipping boy who no longer had a nation to protect him. But my friends were by no means silent. They bought full-page advertisements to refute the trumped-up Turkish accusations.

It was toward the end of May when I finally met my third defense lawyer, Dr. Kurt Niemeyer, a handsome man in his late forties.

The bitter cold of winter was now making way for the spring and summer. I wondered if I would ever live to see the coming seasons.

One consolation warmed me. Even if I were to be found guilty and executed, the Turks would be exposed for their crimes against the Armenian people. I could only hope for one result: that the conscience of the world would be aroused so that the crime of genocide would be an act accountable to some kind of international court set up by a society of civilized nations, rather than punishable by an individual.

But I had little time for reflecting upon such weighty matters on that evening before the momentous trial. Visiting me was my chief defense attorney, Dr. Adolf von Gorton. He showed me a copy of the *Handles-Zeitung,* at that time one of the most widely circulated newspapers in all Germany. The editorial had already tried, convicted and sentenced me:

"Berlin: Tomorrow morning a vicious killer will appear before the bar of justice to explain, if he can, his reason for the cold-blooded murder of a Turkish statesman and humanitarian, Talaat Pasha, whose cooperation as an ally with Germany during the last war was proof of his friendship for our country.

"Soghomon Tehlirian, an Armenian fanatic, who has yet to express one word of gratitude to the Government of Turkey for the generous help it has given to the Armenians, deliberately and with malice aforethought, shot down the man who befriended his people.

"Germany enjoys a reputation as a government of law and order. Its judges must proclaim to the world that justice must and will be served. Tehlirian, whose fellow Armenians have been committing atrocities against the Turkish people for many years, has himself committed the greatest sin of all. He has taken the life of the man loved by Armenians and Turks alike.

"Justice demands that Soghomon Tehlirian pay the supreme penalty.

"He must hang by the neck until dead!"

The grandfatherly Dr. von Gorton put a comforting arm around my shoulder. "It isn't going to be easy, Son."

"Is there any chance at all?"

Dr. von Gorton put both hands on my shoulders. Our eyes met. "If you believe in God, you have a chance—a slight one."

I grasped his hand. "I have nothing to fear," I told him.

XIV. THE TRIAL OPENS

A hot wind, indicative of the sizzling day ahead, made the city of Berlin, even at that early hour of Thursday, June 2, 1921, uncomfortably warm. Every nerve and muscle in my body was a'tingle with anticipation, as the wall clock struck 9:15 a.m.

I was escorted by the bailiff into the courtroom and took my position in the prisoner's dock, to the right of the judge's bench. The sensationalism surrounding the trial and the reams of copy which filled the newspapers had attracted hundreds of people to the proceedings. The courtroom was crowded, every seat occupied by newspaper reporters and spectators. Outside, in the corridors and in the streets, disappointed crowds who had been unable to gain entry, milled about.

I scanned the sea of faces about me. Seated at my left and facing the bench were my lawyers, Chief Defense Counsel Adolf von Gorton, flanked by his assistants, Johannes Wertenhauer and Kurt Niemeyer. At his desk on my right side was Heinrich Kolnig, the brilliant, calculating Chief Prosecutor.

Dr. von Gorton had warned me of the expected hostility I would encounter but nevertheless I discovered a few friendly faces in the audience. Kalousdian, my interpreter, came over to wish me well and to instruct me in some minor details of court procedure. In the row of seats reserved for the defense witnesses I was delighted to see Eftian and his bride, Leona, my erstwhile German teacher. Both smiled at me reassuringly. Near them were the two landladies from whom I rented rooms after arriving in Berlin. There was also another couple in the witness section, a Mr. and Mrs. Terzibashian, both of whom I had heard about from Kalousdian. I was to thank the Almighty many times for the testimony Mrs. Terzibashian and her husband were to give later.

There was a scattering of other Armenian faces in the packed room. Among them I recognized Apelian, Ayvazian, Serkoyan, Sumpat, and to my utter astonishment, *"Bahbig"* —the fiery old Federation veteran I had met in Geneva and who had boasted that, had he been twenty years younger, he could have taken both

Mugurditchian and Talaat with one hand.

There were somber faces, too. Seated in the prosecutor's section was the woman in black—Mrs. Talaat, who now had good reason for the color of her clothing. But, other than the few friendly people whom I recognized, everyone else appeared to be openly hostile Germans or Turks whose hatred of me was a tangible, living thing.

At 9:17 a.m., Presiding Judge Erich Lemberg and his two associate justices, Karl Locke and Ernest Pathe, entered the courtroom. Everyone rose as they took their places on the bench.

Judge Lemberg cast a stern eye over the courtroom, silently announcing that this was *his* court and that he would brook no nonsense from anyone. He faced me squarely:

"Are you Soghomon Tehlirian, son of Khachador and Hnazant Tehlirian?"

"I am, your Honor."

"Are you represented in this trial by attorneys Adolf von Gorton, Johannes Wertenhauer and Kurt Niemeyer?"

"Yes, Sir."

"You were born in Erzinga, Turkey?"

"*No, Sir!*"

There was a moment of consternation in the courtroom as the presiding Judge sharply questioned the court recorder. Equally disturbed, the recorder could only refer to his notes.

Prosecutor Kolnig was about to make a statement when von Gorton leaped to his feet. "If it please the court, I believe I can explain my client's answer. As an Armenian he recognizes neither Soviet nor Turkish domination of his country. He was born in Erzinga, Armenia. The defense respectfully asks the court to recognize the defendant's birthplace as Erzinga, Armenia, rather than Turkey."

Judge Lemberg conferred briefly with his two associates and then addressed Dr. von Gorton: "While the court understands and sympathizes with the prisoner's feelings for his homeland we can only recognize political facts as they exist today. However, the recorder will note the birthplace of the accused as Erzinga, Armenia, a dominion of Turkey. Counsel for defense will instruct his client to answer 'yes' in accordance with this ruling."

Kalousdian interpreted every word into Armenian, loudly and distinctly.

It was at this point that the proceedings were interrupted and the courtroom thrown into a confused uproar. *Bahbig,* the irrepressible, ancient warrior, jumped from his seat and took a firm stance in the center aisle, in plain view of the five hundred people in the courtroom. "*Soud-eh! Soud-eh!* —Lies! Lies!" he shouted. "*Airzingah haiyoun guh bahdganee!* —Erzinga belongs to the Armenians! There is no need to mention the Turks!"

Judge Lemberg banged his gavel repeatedly in an effort to restore order. "The bailiffs will remove that man from the court at once!"

Bahbig, seeing several of the court police approach him, prepared for battle. "*Mehr haiyoutoun havedian beedi abree! Haigagan droshag vor hos eh poast!* —Our Armenia will live forever! Here is Armenia's flag to prove it!"

Amazed, and with my heart bursting with pride, I watched the fiery old soldier pull a bundle from inside his coat and unfurl the red, blue and orange flag of Armenia. Kicking and squirming, he was carried out of the room by a cordon of guards, still shouting his defiance, the flag held aloft.

It was several minutes before the order was restored. Judge Lemberg, his voice steely, warned: "If there is one more such outburst I will order this courtroom evacuated of all spectators. This is not an American political convention but a court of law—a German court of law—I intend to maintain the dignity of this court."

The Judge now addressed me: "You, Soghomon Tehlirian, are accused before this court on an indictment charging you with violating the law of Germany. I shall now read the indictment and it will be translated for you into Armenian:

**SOGHOMON TEHLIRIAN is
hereby charged as follows:**

NATURE OF OFFENSE:
　The accused, on March 15, 1921, violated the law of Germany by depriving another person of his life.

　PARTICULARS OF OFFENSE:
　(a) The accused committed an act of murder against the person of Talaat Pasha, a native of Turkey, and a resident of Berlin at the time of said crime.
　(b) The accused committed the act of murder in a manner charged as premeditated.
　(c) The motive for said crime was political.

(d) The accused was in full possession of his faculties at the time of said act and at the time of his deposition to the authorities.

A copy of this indictment was delivered to the counsel for the accused on the 18th day of May, 1921.

> *Heinrich Kolnig*
> Chief Prosecutor
> May 18, 1921."

When Kalousdian had finished the translation, the Presiding Judge asked: "Have you understood the indictment?"

"Yes, your Honor," I answered.

"You will now state yes or no, whether you are guilty or innocent of the charges of which you are accused."

Dr. von Gorton had clearly been waiting for this moment. Before I could answer, he stepped forward and addressed the tribunal: "May it please the court; I request permission to present an objection before my client answers the question of whether he is guilty or not."

"What is the nature of your objection?"

"My objections, your Honor, fall within three categories: One—the indictment charges the defendant with the crime of murder. But there are certain mitigating circumstances which have been recognized by every civilized nation on earth that excuse the act, thereby placing it beyond the realm of the crime called murder."

A look of surprise blossomed on Lemberg's face. "Is counsel for the defense claiming that the accused was justified in shooting the victim? Did he not confess to murder in his pre-trial deposition?"

"I submit that the defendant is not qualified to declare the nature of his act or to use any legal terminology. He stated that he had executed Talaat Pasha. It is this precise act which we intend to prove was justified."

"The court would be interested to hear how defense counsel justifies what his client calls execution."

"There are ample precedents, your Honor," Dr. von Gorton began. "I will offer these precedents to the court to prove that there have always been particular crimes such as piracy, illicit dealing in narcotics, mass murder, and more recently white slavery, which are recognized as criminal acts and punishable as *hostes generis humani* (enemies of the human race). Because there is no such body as an International Court to try these wrongdoers before the bar of justice, they are necessarily subject to punishment by anyone who can capture them. Surely, Talaat Pasha, as the organizer of a campaign of extermination which resulted in the deaths of almost all of the Armenian people can only be classified as an enemy of the human race. The indictment therefore should read, not 'murder' but, 'execution.'"

Dr. von Gorton studied his notes and then continued. "The indictment claims that the defendant's act was premeditated. But that is something which Dr. Kolnig, in his capacity as prosecutor, will have to prove. Was it premeditation or was it an act of compulsion? If the latter, then the law of Germany requires that my client be declared innocent of the act of which he is accused.

"There is a final point of objection which I respectfully submit to this court. Dr. Kolnig, the prosecutor, in the indictment which he signed, categorically assumed that the defendant was in full possession of his faculties at the time of the execution and at the time of his deposition to the police. That statement, your Honor, has not been substantiated in the medical reports I have studied. Further, that is a matter which the prosecutor is also obliged to prove during the course of this trial. Evidence alone can prove a man innocent or guilty; but this indictment is mere personal opinion.

"Because this indictment has been improperly drawn up and contains inaccuracies not consistent with law, I ask the Judges of this court to dismiss the case of Soghomon Tehlirian forthwith."

There was a stunned silence in the courtroom as Dr. von Gorton's superb impudence struck home. I must confess that even I gaped. I had shot a man to death. My lawyer, legal language notwithstanding, had brazenly asked that the case be thrown out of court on technical grounds. My confidence soared.

But I had yet to reckon with Dr. Kolnig, a prosecutor with an iron mind and a will to match.

Justice Lemberg permitted himself a faint smile. "I have no doubt," he commented dryly, "that the prosecution would be somewhat annoyed if this trial were to be terminated before it got started."

Kolnig was already on his feet, his face flushed with indignation. "Your Honor, counsel for the defense and I have met many times and at many trials. I respect him. But I respect the authority of this court to a far greater extent. It must be plain to the court that my learned opponent is indulging in nothing more than a display of courtroom histrionics. His flamboyant speech does not even merit an answer."

"You'd *better* answer if you hope to win your case," Judge Lemberg said grimly.

Kolnig sputtered and fumed for a few moments but quickly rose to the challenge, his remarkable ability asserting itself at the outset. "Counsel for the defense maintains that this ordinary act of political murder should be regarded as an execution. But I say an execution can only be made by a State and its authorized agencies. The accused represented no such State, and if he did, the crime was committed on German soil where no other country can claim jurisdiction.

"The defense counsel also declares that the victim was an enemy of the human race. I deny that. But whether he was or not is of no importance here. It is not the victim who is on trial but his killer: Soghomon Tehlirian.

"My opponent also refers to acts of piracy, white slavery and narcotics. I ask, your Honor, hasn't he gone far afield to prove a questionable point? What has that nonsense to do with this trial?"

Judge Lemberg stabbed the air with a bony finger. "Don't ask me, tell me!" he barked.

Kolnig was quite accustomed to the testy old judge. He continued as though he had not heard the caustic remark. "Dr. von Gorton objects to my use of the word premeditated and says that I will have to prove the point. He also asks that you reject the indictment because he claims it is inaccurately prepared. Now before the court even considers the preposterous demand that this case be dismissed, I should like to teach Herr von Gorton an elemental fact of law: there is no need to prove anything in an indictment. An indictment embodies the accusations which the prosecution is obliged to prove during the course of the trial. The State claims that the act was one of premeditated murder. Let the prisoner's lawyer convince the court otherwise.

"Finally, Dr. von Gorton argues that the medical reports which he studied are contrary to the description given in the indictment. All I can say is that I did not expect Herr von Gorton to jump for joy when he heard the indictment read in court. If he does not like it, he will be given every opportunity to correct the situation during these hearings. If it please the court, the indictment stands true and correct. I respectfully ask that the objection raised be disregarded so that we may get on with the trial."

Judge Lemberg and his two associate justices wasted no time in arriving at a decision. After a brief discussion among them, Lemberg announced their collective decision: "The court overrules all the objections raised by the counsel for the defense. The indictment was drawn up in full observance of the laws of the land and the court sees no reason why it should not be accepted."

Dr. von Gorton strode to the bench. "We respectfully ask that the judges give their reasons for their decision," he demanded impertinently, but well within his legal rights.

The trigger-tempered little judge, who might have been expected to give my lawyer a tongue-lashing, astonished us with his mild and reasonable reply: "This tribunal will enumerate the reasons for the decision in the second session of court, tomorrow. Court is adjourned."

We had been overruled! Whatever the reasons the judges might give, the fact remained that the opening skirmish was a devastating defeat for us. If this was a harbinger of what was to come, my future looked anything but bright.

XV. PARADE OF WITNESSES BEGINS

On this, the second day of the trial, the newspapers were in full cry for my conviction. The Press was especially incensed with Dr. von Gorton for what they called his unethical conduct. This editorial in the *Berliner Tageblatt* was typical of those carried in all German newspapers:

> "The trial of Soghomon Tehlirian presented a sorry spectacle in this, the first day of the proceedings. The prisoner is a self-confessed murderer. Even his own lawyer, Herr Adolf von Gorton, does not deny that his client shot down a man in the prime of his life. Yet von Gorton sought by every means to circumvent the law, attempting to evade justice through shadowy loopholes. Many lawyers would question the ethics of this once-respected attorney.
> "If the murderer, Tehlirian, is allowed to once again roam the streets of Berlin because of a mere legal technicality, no man, woman or child will be able to walk the streets of our fair city. We join in the plea of all decent people that Soghomon Tehlirian be found guilty of the crime he so freely admits and that von Gorton be reprimanded for his questionable defense."

Kalousdian was at my side in the prisoner's dock when Judge Lemberg rendered the court's decision:
"After the reading of the indictment, Defense Counsel von Gorton raised three preliminary objections. We will deal with them in the order in which they were presented:
"**(a)** The accused executed one Talaat Pasha for acts which are purported to be international crimes such as piracy, slavery and the like.
"**(b)** The accused's crime was not premeditated, but that he acted under compulsion and therefore in a state of mind over which he could not control his will.

"(c) The accused was not in full possession of his mental faculties, neither at the time of the commission of the crime nor during his confession to the police.

"We have studied these and your other objections carefully," Presiding Judge Lemberg went on. "This is the court's decision:

"Regarding those crimes which are recognized as international in character, punishable as *hostes generis humani,* none of these have been proven in this court. We can only recognize the act as stated in the indictment as a national act, committed on German soil and therefore within the jurisdiction of German law. Because the accused committed the act in Germany and the indictment correctly states the circumstances, the court rejects the objection made by the counsel for the defense.

"Regarding the second objection, the accused, in his deposition to the police, stated that he had long considered the act of which he is charged and to carry out this act he deliberately sought out the victim and slew him. But whether this act was premeditated or one of compulsion is a matter that must be proven in the course of this trial. We therefore find that the indictment was correctly presented on this point and the objection of the counsel for the defense is overruled.

"Regarding the third objection, the prosecutor has had the accused examined by medical doctors and it was on the findings of those examinations that he based his charge that the defendant was, in fact, in full possession of his reasoning powers when the crime was committed and when he made his deposition to the police. To Defense Counsel's argument we reply that the Prosecution had logical reasons for the charge while Defense produced no evidence to the contrary. We therefore overrule this third objection."

Judge Lemberg nodded to Dr. von Gorton pleasantly (and somewhat maliciously, I thought). "It is the unanimous ruling of this court that the indictment, *en toto,* is drawn up in full accordance with the law of Germany."

Prosecutor Kolnig then addressed the bench: "Your Honor, the indictment, having been presented to and accepted by the court, I demand that the prisoner be ordered to answer guilty or not guilty to the charges."

Dr. von Gorton's challenge had been defeated on every count.

* * * * * * * * *

Judge Lemberg peered at me over the rims of his glasses. "Soghomon Tehlirian, you heard and understood the indictment on the first day of this trial?"

"Yes, your Honor."

"Are you guilty or not guilty?"

"Not guilty! I executed Talaat Pasha but I am not guilty of murder. Talaat is the murderer. I only punished him for his crimes."

My denial created pandemonium in the courtroom. The prosecutor and my lawyer were both on their feet and shouting as Judge Lemberg furiously banged his gavel to restore order. When he succeeded in quieting the outraged Turks and the indignant Germans among the spectators, Prosecutor Kolnig, his voice strident, shouted to the Tribunal: "I object, your Honor! The prisoner did not answer the question; he made a self-serving statement. I insist that he be ordered to answer your question, yes or no, without flag-waving speeches."

Judge Lemberg not only sustained the objection but nailed me to the wall with a razor-sharp rebuke. He then repeated his question, but this time it was more in the nature of a demand. "You will answer guilty or not guilty to the murder of Talaat Pasha."

"Your Honor," von Gorton interrupted, "my client..."

Judge Lemberg sharply cut him off. "I must warn Counsel for Defense that you and your client observe court procedure or stand in contempt of court."

My interpreter, Kalousdian, looked me in the eyes. "*Soagamoan, badaskhaneh, aiyoe gam voch. Ait eh haidararootoun chopah* —Soghomon, you must answer either yes or no. That is the limit of your answer."

"How do you plead?" Judge Lemberg said impatiently.

"Innocent of the charge as worded in the indictment."

Thus the issue was joined. I was not a murderer, nor did I feel like one. It now devolved upon Dr. von Gorton to prove that I had done nothing more than bring down my heel on an enemy of mankind. Kolnig, for his part, would have to prove me guilty of murder.

What were my sensations? I only know that in my own humble way I had struck back at a beast whose talons had ripped and clawed eighty percent of my blood-brothers into extinction and robbed us of our 4,000-year-old homeland. I may have been satisfied, but I cannot say I was proud of what I had to do. As Dr. von Gorton put it, if an international court had existed, Talaat

Pasha would have met his fate just as decisively as he had at my hands. But, at least, I gave him an honorable exit. He was shot dead instantly. An international court would have sentenced him to the gallows after months of tortured waiting. A court would have dealt with him cruelly. I gave him mercy with a single bullet—a mercy he never showed in the ocean of blood he spilled on the soil of my beloved Armenia. Yet, he continued to conspire against the Christians, to work long hours in a vain effort in returning to power in Turkey and massacring the surviving Armenians. He died with the very sword he used to kill with.

* * * * * * * * * *

Kolnig, his manner supremely confident, began his opening address: "O Judges of Berlin, I stand before you accusing not one wretched man named Soghomon Tehlirian but thousands of ruthless Armenians, members and supporters of the Armenian Revolutionary Federation who have dedicated their lives to the wanton murder of innocent Turkish men, women and children. The accused, here in the prisoner's dock, is a member of that organization whose sole function is one of revenge against the legally constituted Government of Turkey. This man represents but one of the thousands of assassins who belong to or support an organization founded on the principles of anarchy.

"The accused has yet to repent, to utter one word of remorse for his heartless, premeditated murder of Talaat Pasha, a man respected and admired throughout the world. The acts of violence by the Armenian people against legal Turkish authority have been so well documented that they constitute a shame and disgrace to decent people everywhere.

"The murder of Talaat Pasha is more than an isolated killing. It is a planned atrocity in the continuing campaign of scheduled murders by Armenians against innocent statesmen who brought justice for all nationalities within the Turkish commonwealth of friends and neighbors.

"Most of the Armenian people, although they were helped in every conceivable way, became disloyal to their benefactors. Why? I shall tell you why: Firstly, the Armenian people are a weak people. They have no character, no culture, no mind of their own. Without the guidance of the Turkish people, they have nothing. Secondly, an international group of fanatics who arrogantly call themselves the Armenian Revolutionary Federation, aroused their weak-minded kinsmen to such a pitch that here, in this very courtroom, you have heard them term cold-blooded murder as justifiable.

"Judges of Berlin, I ask that you see this man, Soghomon Tehlirian, in his true light—a member of a worldwide band of killers who destroyed a soul without a qualm of conscience. I shall prove to this court and to the jury that the prisoner is a vicious murderer who took another man's life because, like countless thousands of others, his home happened to be damaged in an unintentional act of war. This was *political* murder, pure and simple. Soghomon Tehlirian stands indicted as a fiend who shot to death an eminently respected official of our traditional ally, Turkey, and an invited guest of this Government. I shall prove these contentions, syllable by syllable. And I shall rely on the wisdom of the jury and the judges to preserve the honor of German law in its decision against the arrogant prisoner, Soghomon Tehlirian."

Judge Lemberg interrupted the prosecutor at this point and called for a pre-luncheon recess at 10:30 a.m. The interval gave me a moment to talk to my lawyer. I was understandably nervous. "There's not a friendly face on the jury," I said through interpreter Kalousdian. "And why did he keep bringing the Federation into the speech? This was strictly a private affair between Talaat and me. He would have died at my hands whether an organization existed or not."

I gained very little reassurance from Dr. von Gorton's enigmatic answer: "The jury isn't as hostile as it is impartial. True, they may have been conditioned by all the unfavorable publicity in the press, but you leave them to me, Soghomon; that's my job. As for the Federation, Prosecutor Kolnig brought them into his speech so that he could establish the motive of politics and premeditation—it's easier if he can incriminate an entire organization."

My ignorance of the law at that time was obvious. "I guess he's right," I said, not thinking.

Dr. von Gorton quickly looked around. Fortunately, I had spoken in low tones. "Don't say that again," he said sharply. "Premeditation and political murder calls for the death penalty."

I made no answer, but Gevork Kalousdian grinned: "I didn't hear anything."

* * * * * * * * * *

Prosecutor Kolnig, in what he hoped was the beginning of my march to the gallows, read to the Tribunal the written summary report by Chief of Police Heinz Gnass. Now he called his first witness to the stand, Assistant Police Inspector Schultzen. "Please give your name and profession to the court."

"My name is Max Schultzen, Assistant Police Inspector Schultzen."

"In the depositions made to you by the prisoner, did he or did he not confess to the murder of Talaat Pasha?"

"Yes, Sir, he confessed."

"Did he confess that the murder was premeditated?"

Schultzen looked briefly at his notes. "Yes he did. He said, 'I have been trailing him for three long years.'"

"Did the prisoner exhibit any remorse?"

"May I quote him, Dr. Kolnig?"

"Please do."

Schultzen raised his notes several inches. "He said, 'My conscience is clear.'"

Kolnig looked pleased as he continued with his questions. "Then, as an experienced police official, would you say this was premeditated murder?"

For a moment I thought Dr. von Gorton would object to what was obviously a leading question. But he and his assistant attorneys exchanged a few quick remarks and then scribbled furiously on their onion-skinned tablets. Whatever it was they had in mind, I assumed, would be used in the cross-examination.

"Based on the confessions made by the prisoner," Schultzen responded, "I do not hesitate to say that this was without a doubt a premeditated murder."

A satisfied smile on his face, Kolnig bowed slightly to the witness: "Unless Defense Counsel wishes to question you, you may step down from the stand, Inspector Schultzen."

Dr. von Gorton and his deputy attorney, Niemeyer, exchanged a few hurried words. The former, as he stood up, said, "The Defense will cross-examine the Prosecution's witness."

Von Gorton strode to the witness stand, his face hard as he made eye contact with Schultzen. "You have an excellent reputation in Berlin as a police officer and a man of honor."

"Thank you, Dr. von Gorton."

"As an attorney, I have worked with you in previous cases, in this very courtroom and also in others. I believe that you respect me as I do you."

"Of course, Dr. von Gorton. Thank you, Dr. von Gorton."

"Then tell me, please," von Gorton asked, "why did you testify that Tehlirian's act was premeditated when, according to your own transcripts, the defendant never said it was an act of premeditation?"

Defensively, Schultzen replied, "He trailed the victim for three years. He even brought a Mauser automatic with him from Constantinople. It must have been premeditated!"

"You must have reasons for your deductions. No doubt they are based on your training. Will you please give the court your educational background?"

"I would be glad to," Schultzen proudly announced. "I am a graduate of the Charlottenburg Police Academy. I was one of the top ten in my graduating class."

"What are the qualifications for graduating with such high honors, Inspector Schultzen?"

"Modern investigative methods; understanding of the latest scientific detection techniques—you know, the latest methods."

"Were there any other requirements necessary to place you in the top ten of the graduating class at the police academy?"

"Well, there were calisthenics. I don't mean to boast, *Herr Doktore*, but I boosted my work twenty percent by doing eleven more push-ups than anyone else in the class."

"All that is very impressive, Sir," Dr. von Gorton acknowledged. "I admire your intellectual talents. Now please be good enough to outline for the court your education in medicine, the medical degrees you have earned and your experience in psychiatric techniques."

"I—I, well, Sir," Schultzen sputtered, "I'm a police official, not a doctor."

"Inspector Schultzen, your testimony contradicts the written medical reports from a group of specialists."

Schultzen suddenly looked very nervous. "I don't know what you mean."

"You have testified that Soghomon Tehlirian committed a premeditated act of murder—that because he was carrying a gun it could not have been otherwise. Yet qualified psychiatrists will testify that this may not have been premeditation but an act of compulsion. I ask you, Inspector Schultzen, in all frankness, do you know the medically-accepted difference between premeditation and compulsion?"

"Not exactly. As a police officer I would say it was premeditation. As far as the doctors are concerned, I am not qualified to argue with them about the difference between premeditation and compulsion."

His expression one of total triumph, Dr. von Gorton immediately pressed his advantage. "Then you no longer contend that this was premeditated murder?"

"No, Sir. That is—not exactly. I'm a police officer, not a doctor. Regardless of my personal opinion, as long as you put it that way, from a medical standpoint I cannot honestly say that it was premeditated. But, neither can a doctor do my work as a police official. That must be understood!"

Dr. von Gorton faced the three judges. "Gentlemen, in dismissing the prosecution's witness, I call attention to this court that Assistant Chief Inspector Schultzen is not only unqualified to declare my client's act as premeditated but he is unwilling to argue against medical authority as to whether the execution was one of premeditation or compulsion. I suggest he be disqualified."

The judges straightened in their chairs. "This court heard and is qualified to evaluate the testimony of the witness without any suggestions from Counsel for Defense," Judge Lemberg lectured sternly. "The Prosecution will continue with its case."

Dr. Kolnig called the Chief Inspector to the stand. "Be good enough to identity yourself, Sir."

"I am Ernest Mandteufel, Chief Police Inspector, city of Berlin."

"How long have you been Chief Inspector?"

"Eighteen years and five months."

Dr. von Gorton interrupted. "Your Honor, we are familiar with Chief Inspector Mandteufel and we accept him as a qualified police official."

Kolnig faced the witness. "We have in our records a series of confessions which the prisoner made during the course of your interrogations. I will read them to the court and at the conclusion I will ask you to corroborate that the statements made are true and correct."

"Objection!" Dr. von Gorton boomed. "The copy of the so-called confessions which the court furnished to me cannot be considered as admissible evidence because the accused understands only a smattering of German, while on the other hand, I believe Inspector Mandteufel understands not one word of Armenian."

Judge Lemberg broke in crossly. "The court understands that

a language barrier exists, but was not an interpreter present during the police interrogations?"

The police official and the prosecutor nodded in accord.

"Your Honor," von Gorton argued. "If the court will examine the transcript it will see that this document was not initialed or signed by an interpreter. It is up to the prosecution to prove that my client understood the questions being asked."

Judge Lemberg elevated a quizzical eyebrow. "Will the prosecutor kindly hand me that transcript?" he demanded of the dumbfounded Dr. Kolnig who had not noticed the absence of Kalousdian's signature.

The three judges examined the papers. Associate Justice Karl Locke directed a question to Inspector Mandteufel. "Inspector, was an interpreter present when you questioned the prisoner?"

"There was, your Honor."

"Is the same interpreter in this courtroom?"

Inspector Mandteufel pointed a shaking finger at Kalousdian. "This is the same man."

"It would seem proper," Judge Locke declared, "that the prosecutor would wish to question the interpreter to determine why he did not sign the transcript if he was there at all."

"I most certainly do," Dr. Kolnig said, his face flushed. "Inspector Mandteufel is excused and I call the interpreter to the witness stand."

Kalousdian took the stand and Kolnig started in. "What is your name?"

"Gevork Kalousdian."

"You have been serving as interpreter since shortly after the prisoner's arrest?"

"Yes."

"Now then, were you or were you not present in your capacity as an Armenian-German interpreter at the time Chief Inspector Mandteufel interrogated the accused?"

"Yes, I was present."

"In that case, tell the court why you did not sign the transcript of the questions and answers?"

"Because, Sir, Mr. Tehlirian did not understand the questions."

"What do you mean, he didn't understand? Aren't you a qualified interpreter?"

"Of course. But there is no way that Mr. Tehlirian could understand the questions because I did not understand them myself."

Anger shone in Kolnig's face. "Do you ask this court to believe that you, an officially recognized interpreter, did not understand a few simple questions?"

"They were not simple, Sir; they were so complicated I was unable to convey their meaning to Mr. Tehlirian."

Kolnig's face purpled and he was about to snap another question at Kalousdian when Dr. von Gorton again raised a quick objection. "Your Honor, the prosecution is baiting the witness. Mr. Kalousdian has stated that he didn't understand the Inspector's questions and therefore the defendant's answers cannot be accepted as relevant."

Judge Lemberg took over. "This whole thing sounds to me like a conspiracy of some kind. But I have no other alternative than to sustain the objection," he asserted. "Without the signature of an interpreter, this transcript cannot be considered as evidence and therefore cannot be read before the jury."

I stared at von Gorton and then Kalousdian. Had I heard it right? The self-incriminating statements I had been tricked into making by the wily police officer were damaging enough to hang me, yet the court had just refused to accept my "confession" as evidence. My respect for Dr. von Gorton climbed another rung.

But my ordeal was just beginning. Prosecutor Kolnig brought a procession of witnesses to the stand; some who testified that they had seen me shoot Talaat, and others who stated they had seen me stand over the fallen Turk, gun in hand. One woman testified that she had screamed hysterically. That was true enough; I can still hear that scream today, so many years later. The policeman to whom I had surrendered my Mauser automatic stated that I was in a dazed and battered condition at the time of my rescue from the angry crowd.

Each witness was asked one final question: "Did the prisoner appear to be ill at the time of the shooting or immediately after the crime?" Their answers were unvaryingly the same: "He seemed to be perfectly healthy and in full control of his mind. It was cold-blooded murder."

My spirits sank as the last of the witnesses returned to his seat. Certainly I had confessed to the execution of Talaat and I could not at first understand why Kolnig had gone to such lengths to prove that I had killed him. It was only when I studied the granite-hard, accusing faces of the members of the jury that I realized his purpose. Had a ballot been taken at that moment, I would have

PARADE OF WITNESSES BEGINS / 141

been found guilty on the first vote.

But once again the fast-thinking von Gorton gave me cause for reassurance. He demanded that every witness be recalled for cross-examination. To each he asked one question: "Will you kindly give the court your medical background to support your testimony that the defendant was in a normal state of mind at the time the victim was shot?"

"No medical background," they replied, in effect.

The witnesses were disposed of with mathematical precision and Judge Lemberg ordered that their testimony concerning my mental condition be stricken from the records. It was almost 1 p.m. when luncheon recess was called. The prosecution had gained little for its pains, except to substantiate what everyone knew—that I had executed a Turk. But the penalty—death by hanging—remained the same.

* * * * * * * * * *

The afternoon session again saw the Berlin courtroom swarming with people. Of my three lawyers, only Assistant Defense Counsel Johannes Wertenhauer was present. Dr. von Gorton and his other assistant, Niemeyer, were elsewhere with an Armenian student named Vahan Zakarian, assembling the evidence they intended to present, busily scheduling witnesses in my behalf. Zakarian served as official assistant interpreter to Kalousdian during the trial.

Wertenhauer, his bald pate glistening, nodded reassuringly to me. His initial approach, I quickly perceived, was to establish my standing in the community. First he called *Frau* Mildred Stelbaum and *Frau* Mae Lena Tiedman, my former landladies, both of whom stated that I was a respectable young student.

Now the prosecutor questioned the two women. "Would you say that the accused is a 'respectable' student and prompt with his rent?" Kolnig asked the ladies.

They answered affirmatively and Kolnig, grinning, dismissed them without another word.

The third witness, however, furnished the key that opened the door to the crucial issue in my case.

Wertenhauer, his voice that of a cultured gentleman, called: "Will *Fraulein* Leona Bailunzon please take the witness stand."

She did so and Wertenhauer began his questions. "Tell the court your occupation, *Fraulein*."

"I am a private tutor. I teach the German language."
"Your students are mostly foreigners, are they not?"
"That is so."
"It was in your capacity as a teacher that you met the defendant?"
"Yes, about six months ago."
"In your deposition you stated that the defendant became ill in your presence. Please describe the circumstances to the court."
"I asked him if there was anyone in his family who could help with his German lessons. For a moment he looked blank. Then he began to sway dizzily. He fell back onto a chair. He was moaning, but before he fainted I could hear the words, 'My family! All killed except one little girl. My people—gone!' Luckily my fiance arrived and managed to revive Mr. Tehlirian and take him home."
"According to your statements, *Fraulein* Bailunzon, there was nothing on the surface to indicate that the accused was ill? It was only when you mentioned his family that he lost consciousness?"
"Yes, that is true."
Wertenhauer stepped back. "Thank you. Unless the prosecutor wishes to ask questions, you may be excused."
"We will cross-examine the witness," Kolnig announced promptly. He waved a pencil within inches of Miss Bailunzon's face. "Young lady, do you realize that you are under oath and that any untrue statements you may make will constitute perjury?"
My lawyer momentarily lost his polished manner, his usually modulated voice now hoarse. "Your Honors," he protested, "there is no need to inform the witness that she is under oath nor to threaten her. May I remind the court that it is Soghomon Tehlirian who is the defendant in this case."
Judge Lemberg thrust his lower jaw out aggressively. "Young man, this court does not need to be reminded who is or is not on trial here. Please confine yourself to formal objections. And should we wish to be reminded of anything, we will ask." He now wagged a forefinger at Dr. Kolnig. "Unless you have good reason to believe that the witness is being untruthfull, you will cease that line of questioning."
"The question is withdrawn," Kolnig said hastily. He turned toward the witness. "You identified yourself as *Fraulein* Leona Bailunzon. Is it not a fact that this is no longer your name—that you recently married?"

"Yes, I was married on March 26. My name is now Leona Eftian."

Sarcasm leaped into Kolnig's voice. "Perhaps you can tell us why you have not advised the court as to your identity?"

"Because my identity has not changed," she responded coolly. "While I am called *Frau* Eftian in my private life, I have retained my maiden name for professional and legal purposes. My school still bears the name of 'Bailunzon' and I continue to sign all papers as I have always done in the past."

"Eftian: isn't that an Armenian name?"

"It is. My husband, Levon Eftian, was born in Erzeroum, a city in Armenia."

"Ah yes, Levon Eftian! Is your husband not a personal friend of the prisoner?"

"Yes, he is."

"Do you concede, *Frau* Eftian—you don't mind if I use your married name?—that you are sympathetic to the Armenian Cause?"

Her face quickly coloring, she replied, "I am under oath. My personal bias has nothing to do with my answers. I have been and shall continue to be truthful."

"You seem to place great value on your oath. I take it that you are a Christian woman. Tell the court, madame, in what church you were christened."

"I was baptized a Lutheran and have been a member of the Charlottenburg church for almost fifteen years."

"That is very interesting," Kolnig said triumphantly, "and I thank you for your candor. Tell us now, *Frau* Eftian, in what church were you married?"

"The Armenian Apostolic Church."

Kolnig dismissed Leona with a contemptuous gesture. "This witness," he said, "has virtually declared herself as an Armenian, married to an Armenian and inclined toward the Armenian religion with all of its cultures and traditions. Surely this court cannot accept the testimony of a woman whose obvious devotion to the Armenian people is so strong that she has practically become one of them. Can there be any doubt that she is favorably disposed towards the prisoner? I say no! Why did the defense go to such desperate lengths to introduce a witness under a concealed name? I'll tell you why—because her testimony about the alleged fainting spell would bolster their claim of inner compulsion. Your Honors, I ask that the court strike from the records her testimony regarding the prisoner's emotional condition. She surrendered her neutrality and became, despite her German birthright, an Armenian in every sense of the word."

Justice Lemberg removed his glasses and tapped them reflectively on his desk. He consulted briefly with his two associate judges. His decision was enunciated carefully. "The witness has declared under oath that she observed the defendant during an emotional crisis. The court has no reason to believe, nor was any evidence shown which would raise the suspicion that she was untruthful. The fact that she married an Armenian does not evince favoritism toward a third party; the defendant. All it shows is that she preferred one Christian church to another for the wedding ceremony. The court understands that the witness may be considered friendly toward the problems of her husband's people, but there is no valid reason to disqualify any part of the witness' testimony. As to the defendant's mental condition," Judge Lemberg concluded, "this court expects to hear the testimony of qualified medical men whom the defense and the prosecution have appointed, in addition to one appointed by the court. Our decisions will be based, in part, on their testimony and not necessarily on those of other witnesses."

It was not until later that I learned why the defense and the prosecution attached such importance to her statements. Judge Lemberg had made a momentous decision. Leona had planted the first seed in the minds of the jury that my mission stemmed from an inner compulsion.

Dr. Kolnig, in his future essays wrote: "While the eyewitness accounts of the Turkish atrocities certainly added strength to the arguments for the defense, this unassuming young lady may have tipped the balance on the side of Soghomon Tehlirian." ("The Tehlirian Case." Volume II, by Dr. Heinrich Kolnig. Published by the *Deutchland Barrister,* April, 1924, Germany.)

* * * * * * * * * *

That evening, von Gorton and interpreter Kalousdian visited me in my cell for our usual conference. I expressed my appreciation to Kalousdian for his statements on the witness stand and then directed my attention to von Gorton. "The way you handled the prosecution witnesses was remarkable. And this afternoon's performance by Dr. Wertenhauer was no less remarkable."

Dr. von Gorton nodded. However, he was not as pleased as I. "Keep this in mind, my boy; the judge only *demanded* their testimony be stricken from the records but no power on earth can order that spoken words be stricken from the *minds* of the jury. They'll remember, even though the judge ordered that they disregard every word."

My discouragement must have shown in my face. Kalousdian, grinning, turned to Dr. von Gorton. "Whose side are you on anyway?" His humor was infectious and we all smiled.

But as I lay on my wall-bunk that night my thoughts were anything but pleasant. Attorney von Gorton's parting words were that I do my best to relax over the weekend. "Your life," he had said, "may very well depend on the diagnoses of five doctors."

They were scheduled to testify next. Even now, after so many years, I cannot say whether I was proud or humiliated. The diagnoses were devastating.

XVI. ATROCITIES INTRODUCED

Deputy Judge Ernest Pathe conducted the hearings of the medical specialists on Monday, June 6, the fifth day after my trial began. Each of the doctors was closely questioned, and the prosecutor and my defense counsel acknowledged all five as qualified. With this, prosecution witness Dr. Wilhelm Stoemer was called to the stand.

Dr. Stoemer, his manner belligerent, told the court that he had examined me and was familiar with my typhus infection during the fight against the Turks, my history of dizzy spells, fainting and nausea. "It is my opinion," he concluded, "that these symptoms are those of organic rather than inorganic causes."

For the first time since the start of the trial, von Gorton glowered, but my knowledge of the subject was far too limited to understand the reason for his reaction.

Kolnig smiled and faced the bench. "We are in perfect accord with the doctor's conclusion," he told the judge.

"Does the defense have any questions?" Associate Justice Pathe asked.

Von Gorton nodded vigorously. "Yes, your Honor. In view of the medical reports that will be given by the defense witnesses, I would like to question the doctor."

"Then proceed."

Von Gorton got quickly to business with the witness, Dr. Stoemer. "Are you a psychiatrist, Sir?"

"I am not!" the doctor stormed indignantly. "I am a physician."

"It is your opinion that the defendant's tensions, dizzy spells and recurring illnesses are of a physical rather than a psychological source?"

"Not exactly, *Herr* von Gorton, but generally speaking, my diagnosis would be that the defendant is physically rather than emotionally disturbed."

"*Generally* speaking, Doctor? Are you not certain?"

"What I meant was that there are other factors which must be considered."

"Psychological factors, perhaps?"

Dr. Stoemer was now on the defensive. "To a degree. Aside from the purely organic factors, the accused could have committed the crime because of a sudden explosion of vital impulses after a long period of repression. I do not mean to imply that the defendant had no control over his will. I do say it is possible that his reaction to what he claims were Turkish atrocities might have affected his mental and physical condition."

Now it was Kolnig's turn to glower. He had not expected his own medical expert to be led astray so easily by the adroit von Gorton into an admission that psychological factors could be involved. He listened closely as my lawyer continued.

"These vital impulses which you mention," Dr. Stoemer, "are they not what you call compulsions?"

"They could be so regarded."

"Then what you are saying is that psychological factors cannot be discounted? That whether or not the defendant suffered from a physical illness is really of no consequence in the matter?"

"I did not *say* that!"

"But you did say that the defendant could have committed the act because of psychological reasons arising from a compulsion."

"Well he could have, but . . . "

"Thank you, Doctor, that will be all." Von Gorton was grinning.

Kolnig, clearly disappointed with his first medical witness, now called his next expert, Dr. Bruno Hagen. Dr. Hagen's statement was terse. "Whether or not the accused was able to control his will cannot fully be determined in the short time I have had to examine him. That is a matter which would take many, many months to determine. I can only say that he has been under great emotional stress for several years—if what he says about the alleged Turkish massacres is true. But, in my opinion, this was nevertheless an act of premeditation, and not compulsion."

Von Gorton elected to cross-examine. "Dr. Hagen," he began, "how do you reconcile your statement that the defendant acted under premeditation with your contradictory testimony that his condition could not be determined in the short time allotted to you by the court?"

The prosecution doctor was not as easily confused as his predecessor. "What I said, *Herr* von Gorton, was that it would take many months to *fully* determine his condition."

Von Gorton pounced on the answer. "Then, as a man of science, will you agree that if the defendant had been examined over a period of many months, your diagnosis might result in an opinion of compulsion rather than premeditation?"

"These things are too nebulous," Dr. Hagen answered obstinately. "Although new findings might conceivably change my opinion, the uncertainty, the vagueness . . . "

Von Gorton turned to Judge Pathe. "Your Honor," he protested, "the witness was asked a simple question; one that need be answered only yes or no. Neither the jury nor I can understand these evasive answers."

Judge Pathe nodded to the witness. "Counsel for Defense asked you a relevant question concerning a statement which you yourself volunteered. He wants to know, and so do we, if your opinion might have changed had you examined the defendant over a long period of time. Please give a direct answer to the question."

Slowly, painfully, Dr. Hagen replied. "If further examination could shed any new light on the defendant's mental processes, I would, of course, alter my opinion."

Judge Lemberg, who had not uttered a word since court convened that morning, banged a tiny fist on his table. "Even I don't understand you!" he roared. "Answer yes or no!"

"Yes," Dr. Hagen answered meekly.

"Yes, you would change your opinion?" von Gorton asked pleasantly.

"Yes, I would change my opinion. But . . . "

"That will be all, Dr. Hagen. Thank you."

"But, Sir...!"

Judge Lemberg snapped an interruption. "Counsel for the Defense said, '*That* will be all!'"

At this time, Judge Lemberg called the court's witness, Dr. Edmund Foerster, to the stand.

"Doctor, can you tell us, in plain language," Judge Lemberg asked, "whether the accused is ill and, if so, did this illness compel him to commit the crime for which he is indicted?"

"It is possible, your Honor, that Dr. Stoemer's diagnosis is correct and that the defendant suffers from a physical ailment which results in the fainting spells. However, I cannot rule out emotional trauma that could have arisen when he witnessed his home in ruins and his family murdered."

"We are not doctors, Sir. Clarify your interpretation of

trauma."

"Let me make it clearer . . . "

"Please do!" Judge Lemberg impatiently interrupted.

"It seems that the defendant was unable to deviate from what he called his 'mission'—an unconscious need to right what he believed to be a terrible wrong. In that one area he could be said to be emotionally disturbed. I realize that this is not a completely qualified answer but my personal belief is that the defendant, emotionally disturbed or not, acted with premeditation. However, I must add, that the science of psychology has not yet advanced to such a degree that anyone can say positively whether or not the accused killed through compulsion or premeditation—my conclusion, you understand, is only an opinion."

"Are you telling the court that you doubt the validity of psychological examinations?"

"Where there is a man's life at stake, your Honor, and in this particular case, yes."

"Well, a man's life *is* at stake. Do you still say it was premeditated?"

In a voice betraying uncertainty, Dr. Foerster replied, "I—uh—yes, it was premeditated."

Judge Lemberg leaned back with a sigh. "The court is not entirely satisfied with Dr. Foerster's testimony. Unless his answers are clarified by the attorneys representing the defense and prosecution, we will resume our questioning later. *Herr* Kolnig, question if you wish."

"You agree with Dr. Stoemer that the prisoner's condition is physical rather than emotional?"

"Well, I agree that the physical symptoms cannot be ignored. However, he was suffering an inner need to right a wrong."

"So he stalked the unfortunate victim, Talaat Pasha, and killed him because he thought he had been wronged?"

"You might put it that way. Everything points to premeditated murder."

"Tell us, Doctor," Kolnig pressed, "why do you rule out compulsion?"

"I can only repeat what I just said to the court—psychology has not attained that point where anyone can draw a fine line between premeditation and compulsion; particularly in a case like this. Again, I say, everything points towards premeditation."

Kolnig, satisfied, was willing to accept the qualified answer. "No further questions," he said.

"Well, I have some questions," Judge Lemberg interjected. "Dr. Foerster, if it is not possible to draw a fine line between compulsion and premeditation, it would be interesting to know how you arrived at your own conclusion."

"Your Honor, all signs . . . "

"We heard all about the signs, Doctor. Just tell the court your reasons. Now I am not refuting your conclusion; you may very well be right. All I want to know is *why* —w-h-y!"

Dr. Foerster's face turned pink and he controlled his resentment with difficulty. In all truth, it was very difficult to like the fiery little judge.

"As a doctor, and based on my examinations, it is my opinion that this was premeditated murder, fine line or not. This was no compulsive act."

"That's better. Why didn't you say so in the first place instead of wasting the court's time?" Judge Lemberg grumbled. He glanced at my lawyer. "Counsel for Defense may question the witness."

Von Gorton, a consummate actor, now posed as a genial comrade to the doctor on the witness stand. His opening questions were couched in a friendly manner. "I must say, Dr. Foerster, that your testimony was quite impressive. As you say, psychology has not been so perfected that the difference between compulsion and premeditation can always be determined. Your frankness, Doctor, is refreshing."

"Thank you, *Herr* von Gorton. But I was not speaking generally. This particular case is unique."

"I agree. No doubt you refer to the fine line which you mentioned?"

Prosecutor Kolnig, sensing the drift of the questioning, offered an objection. "Your Honor, the good doctor has already answered that point fully to your own satisfaction. I see no reason to continue."

"Well, I see plenty of reason," Judge Lemberg retorted, "and I do not recall saying I was satisfied. In any event, the witness volunteered the information and it is certainly relevant to the case. It also follows, then, that questions are admissible. Objection overruled."

Von Gorton continued. "Doctor, in your testimony you said that the defendant was unable to deviate from his mission—that he suffered from an unconscious need to right a terrible wrong. Is that not compulsion?"

"Well, if you want to quote me out of context..." he hesitated and looked at Judge Lemberg as though expecting him to reprove the lawyer.

Judge Lemberg took an opposite view. "Yes, he wants to quote you out of context. It seems that is the only way to get an understandable reply today. Now please answer; was the defendant's urge an act of compulsion or not?"

Thoroughly cowed by the aggressive, junior-sized judge, Dr. Foerster mumbled, "I would say that such a long-standing urge *might* be considered compulsive, but again this is a fine line..."

"Dr. Foerster," Judge Lemberg interrupted, "it appears to me that you are deliberately evading your responsibilities as a witness for the court. Nobody asked you about fine lines. Answer the question!"

"It *could* be compulsion."

Smiling benignly, von Gorton asked, "Is that your conclusion now?"

"It is not!" Dr. Foerster replied in anger. "I only said it *could* be. It is still my belief that the act was premeditated."

"Dr. Foerster, if you doubt the validity of modern science, whether this case is unique or not, then there must be others who also share your doubts. Surely you are not the only doctor in the world who believes as you do."

"Of course not; many doctors agree with me."

"Oh? About how many?"

"I can't answer that definitely, *Herr* von Gorton. I would say half."

"I'll accept that, Doctor. Now then, if half the doctors agree with you, then it is reasonable to say that the other half do not. Is that correct?"

"Well, I really ... uh ... yes."

Von Gorton was grinning as he continued. "Then fifty percent of all doctors in the world say that the defendant's act was compulsive and not, as you said, premeditated?"

"I...I...I..."

"Never mind, Doctor. I have no further questions."

Judge Lemberg was not quite finished with the witness. "This fine line you spoke of—by your own admission, half of the doctors would be on one side of the line and the other half on the opposite side?"

"Yes, your Honor," Dr. Foerster said unhappily.

"Well, all I can say is that when this court requested a neutral doctor it certainly got what it asked for. You are excused, Sir." Judge Lemberg now addressed von Gorton. "The court will hear the doctors presented by Counsel for the Defense. I might also add that this trial is moving at a snail's pace. I hope the evidence to be given will proceed more rapidly than in the past," he said, wiping his brow and rearranging his glasses. He now frowned at the three doctors who had just finished their testimony.

Dr. Hugo Liebmann was the first medical witness in my behalf. Judge Lemberg sank down in his chair, the top of his head barely visible above his desk. Once again Associate Justice Pathe presided. "Be good enough, Doctor, to present your opinion, and as briefly as possible."

"As a psychiatrist and also as one who has practiced internal medicine," Dr. Liebmann began mildly, "I cannot agree with the opinions expressed by my colleagues. My examinations have produced no evidence of physical malfunction. The accused appears to be a serious-minded young man whose act was the result of emotional injury. He sincerely believes that he sustained tremendous personal and national losses. These could well have created a powerful need for retribution in his unconscious mind. Whether or not the atrocities actually happened is not of prime importance. Simply put, he was compelled to commit the act. One might say he had very little mastery over his will, if indeed he had any control over it at all. It is my contention that the defendant suffered from a psychological, rather than an organic disturbance. His was beyond a doubt a compulsive act."

The courtroom was silent and it was obvious that von Gorton was quite pleased with Dr. Liebmann's testimony. Not so the prosecutor. Kolnig had been taking notes as the witness spoke. His voice was sharp and incisive: "You claim to be a psychiatrist?"

"I *am* a psychiatrist. My degree . . ."

Judge Pathe interrupted with a show of impatience. "*Herr* Kolnig, both the defense and the prosecution have already agreed that the medical men appearing here are qualified. It is therefore not necessary to examine them in that respect."

"Your Honor," Kolnig protested, "I only wish to show that, as a psychiatrist, Dr. Liebmann is prejudiced toward the science of physical medicine. His testimony should be ruled out because of bias. I demand that this court dismiss him as an unqualified witness."

"Objection, your Honor!" von Gorton shouted. "The prosecutor has his facts twisted. It is Dr. Stoemer's testimony which should be stricken because he is unqualified in psychiatric matters."

Justice Pathe rapped his gavel repeatedly. "Silence!" he demanded. "This is not a debating forum on the values of one branch of medicine as against another. We will permit no further discussion of the matter. Mr. Prosecutor, please continue your questioning. But keep in mind that you *will* refrain from instructing this court to act according to your personal wishes."

Kolnig hesitated and then tore into Dr. Liebmann's statements as though he would rip them to tatters. But he was unable to dent the psychiatrist's testimony. His basic difference with the preceding doctors remained on the record.

The second doctor to appear in my defense, and the last of the medical experts, was Dr. Richard Kassirer—the same physician who treated me during my illness soon after I had arrived in Berlin. His testimony touched upon my recurring dizzy spells, complications of the typhus infection and my general condition. His summation was equally as brief: "In conclusion, the defendant was motivated by compulsion. This was not and could not be premeditated."

"No further questions of the witness," von Gorton said contentedly.

Kolnig approached the witness slowly, like a lion stalking a lamb. "*Herr Doktore,* are you a psychiatrist?"

"No, I am a general practitioner."

"Then can you tell me why you contradicted Dr. Stoemer, who is also a general practitioner?"

Dr. Kassirer shook his head. "I would not go so far as to say I contradicted my learned colleague. It is quite possible that Dr. Stoemer could be right. Extended examinations might very well show a combination of emotional and physical causes that resulted in the commission of the crime."

"But you do agree with Dr. Stoemer's contention that the accused was physically ill—that his condition had little, if anything, to do with his emotional state—that it was premeditated, political murder?"

"No, I cannot agree to that. Such a diagnosis could only be made after extended examinations. May I say, Sir, that my examinations date back several months before the commission of the crime."

The prosecution was clearly taken by surprise. "I was not

informed of your friendship with the prisoner."

"Not friendship, *Herr* Kolnig; a doctor-patient relationship," Dr. Kassirer answered evenly.

Kolnig apparently had no wish to pursue the issue. He addressed the bench. "If the court please, I see no point in the further questioning of the witness. Nor does it seem quite ethical for the defense to produce a witness whose testimony is based on examinations not shared by the other four doctors. I maintain, your Honor, that Dr. Kassirer should be disqualified."

"Objection, your Honor!" von Gorton called. "The prosecution contends that the defense has somehow acted unethically. This witness was brought into court because he alone has had the opportunity of the extended examinations discussed by the other doctors. For that very reason, and in the interests of justice, his testimony should be welcomed by the court."

Judge Pathe queried my old physician. "Dr. Kassirer, how well acquainted are you with the accused?"

"He was my patient, your Honor; nothing else."

"You were not friends?"

"We were friendly, of course, but not within the meaning as you phrased it."

Judge Pathe exchanged a few words with his two fellow judges and then asked one final question. "What was your diagnosis of his illness at that time?"

"Nervous exhaustion."

"Thank you, Doctor," said the judge.

Von Gorton was all smiles. "The defense rests."

"No further questions," muttered prosecutor Kolnig.

Judge Lemberg came to life. "Speak up, young man. We're not in someone's parlor."

"I said no FURTHER QUESTIONS!" Kolnig shouted hoarsely.

Von Gorton made the mistake of grinning and the irascible old judge turned on him. "Just what is it you find so humorous, Sir?" he snarled. My lawyer's grin disappeared instantly.

But whatever humor I might have felt was quickly dispelled by the jury, all of whom wore puzzled masks. It was evident that the medical men had confused them as well as the spectators. We were soon to learn why the prosecution and the defense attached so much significance to the findings of the doctors. I can only remember that I felt a momentary desire to explode—to shout that even they, with all their medical learning, could not know the true meaning of my need to execute Talaat. Motive? How could they, or anyone else, seek motives in the face of the destruction of a whole nation and nearly all of its peaceful Christian population?

Judge Pathe's gavel brought the morning session to an end.

* * * * * * * * * *

Court reconvened after the luncheon recess and Dr. von Gorton, one hand fingering the lapel of his coat, gestured to the jury with the other. At his desk, Kolnig scribbled furiously as his opponent spoke. The issue revolved around one focal point: Was my act premeditated or not? My lawyer began by dissecting Article 51 of the German legal code.

"Your Honors, members of the jury; Article 51 is surrounded by many legal complications. It was based on an old Prussian code establishing a premeditated crime as one which was conceived fourteen days or more before the enactment of the actual crime.

"But, Gentlemen, we are now dealing with modern law and a new legal code. In the new interpretation the crucial question is: Was there premeditation at the very moment the crime was committed—what was the defendant's mental and emotional condition at the precise moment he committed the crime? The law also states that the will must be free from inner compulsion or external pressure if there can possibly be premeditation.

"Mr. Tehlirian's life is in your hands. I ask you, was he free from anger, sorrow, the tragic memories of the past, inner turmoil, at the exact moment he committed his act? Obviously he was not. Therefore, under the law, he cannot be held responsible for committing the act."

Von Gorton paced before the jury. "As for the inner tensions and psychological factors, let us consider the statements made by the court's witnesses. Dr. William Stoemer, a physician, but untrained in the science of psychiatry, stated boldly that the accused suffered from some kind of organic disturbance, but that his free will was not affected. Dr. Hugo Liebmann, on the other hand, found no basis for that diagnosis and stated that in his opinion Tehlirian's inner tensions and compulsions, arising from the past, made him an ill man. Dr. Richard Kassirer was neutral and virtually agreed with both views. Dr. Bruno Hagen's testimony supported Dr. Stoemer. As to Dr. Edmund Foerster, he said that psychological tests point towards the accused as being an emotionally ill man. The net result of this testimony shows two doctors agreeing on premeditation, two others contending that it was compulsion and one neutral. Simplified, they just could not agree that it was premeditated murder."

Dr. von Gorton stepped nearer the jury box. "The Supreme Court has ruled that where there is no free will, there is no responsibility. Was *Herr* Tehlirian able to make logical decisions, of his free will, when he grabbed the Mauser automatic and pursued Talaat Pasha? Opinion among the doctors is evenly divided. But, mark this well, the division of thought is not whether the defendant was extremely disturbed but whether it arose from organic or psychological reasons. I say to you, Gentlemen, that the defendant was compelled to commit his act. His action was sparked by the indescribable horrors of the Turkish massacres. The fact still remains that the end result was compulsion."

Von Gorton bowed formally to the tribunal. "In view of the medical testimony, which I believe establishes compulsion, not premeditation as the reason for the crime, I ask that Article 51 be invoked and my client set free."

I stared in amazement at my bold attorney. The details of my confession-so-called were still wet on the front pages of every metropolitan newspaper in the world, but here was this distinguished-looking, elderly lawyer, demanding for the second time that I be set free. The complications of the law may have frustrated me but my admiration for Dr. von Gorton's ability knew no bounds.

Prosecutor Kolnig's voice rang loud and clear. "Your Honor," he said, facing Judge Lemberg, "the defense has given a distorted and false picture of the circumstances surrounding this trial. In fact, every word that Dr. von Gorton uttered concerning the Turkish problem should be stricken from the records—in fact, I *demand* that it be stricken from the records."

Justice Lemberg had not enjoyed his lunch or perhaps he was suffering from indigestion. He snapped, "Then why didn't you object?"

"But...but..." Dr. Kolnig stammered, "this is my first opportunity. No proof has been offered that such atrocities are anything more than outrageous lies. I submit that they are nothing more than falsehoods, concocted by the prisoner in an effort to cloak the murder of an innocent man in the name of the flag of Armenia— a nation which does not even exist."

For the first time I breathed a sigh of relief that the old warrior, *Bahbig,* was not present, or a new revolution might have started.

Von Gorton sprang from his chair. "We have documentary

evidence and eyewitnesses . . . "

Whatever my lawyer was about to say will forever be lost to posterity. Judge Lemberg interrupted and fixed von Gorton with a glare. "*Herr* von Gorton," he said icily, "you were permitted to speak during your address to the court and you will allow the same opportunity to the prosecution. Any objections should be made formally and in accordance with accepted procedure. I will permit no further interruptions such as this; bear that in mind."

Von Gorton, his face flushed with anger and embarrassment, remained silent. The crusty old judge ordered the prosecutor to continue.

Kolnig, who may have felt sympathy for his opponent, but pleased with anything that might hurt the defense, took quick advantage of the opportunity.

"I cannot say that I blame Defense Counsel for taking any desperate measures he can invent to confound the court's presentation of this case, and Judge Lemberg is to be commended for putting a stop to it."

"Don't commend me; go ahead with your case," Judge Lemberg demanded irritably.

Kolnig sighed. He should have known better. Fussy and irritable though he might be, there would be no boot-licking in Lemberg's court. Kolnig again focused his attention on the jury.

"I address you now, not as a prosecutor, but as a fellow citizen," Kolnig began. "You have been bombarded by the defense with technicalities surrounding Article 51. But I say to you, brother Berliners, that Article 51 does not condone cold-blooded murder! And it was cold-blooded because, despite the eloquent speech made by *Herr* von Gorton, the prisoner did, in fact, seek out and kill a man without cause or reason. That selfsame Article 51 stipulates that a premeditated killing falls within the confines of the law.

"I agree with only one conclusion by the Counsel for the Defense, and that is, the medical experts who testified this morning were not in agreement. However, we can all agree on three points: Firstly, the Turkish and Armenian people experienced political differences which have now been settled. Secondly, we can produce evidence to show that the prisoner was either a member of the Armenian Revolutionary Federation—a gang of killers—or else was closely associated with that group of political assassins. Thirdly, the prisoner, together with his fellow conspirators, hunted Talaat Pasha across the face of two continents as though the Turkish statesman was a wild beast. It was here on a peaceful street in the city of Berlin where the accused, encouraged by the Armenian Revolutionary Federation, committed political assassination. Premeditated? Can anything be so premeditated as this unprovoked act which took three years to complete?"

Von Gorton rose slowly, like a spiral of cigarette smoke.

"You have an objection?" Judge Lemberg snapped.

"Yes, your Honor, in a manner of speaking. The prosecution asked a question. With the court's permission, we'd like to answer."

Judge Lemberg jerked his silver-thatched head. "The prosecutor has clearly not finished his summation as you were allowed to do. You may answer, but in view of your past performance in this trial, *Herr* von Gorton, it is only fair to tell you that if your answer is found irrelevant and immaterial, you could be held in contempt of court."

Once again my lawyer presented his formal bow. "What I have to say, your Honor, is quite relevant. The prosecution asked what could be relevant behind what he called an unprovoked act. The defense has documentary evidence that the Turkish atrocities against the Armenian people were even more revolting than Soghomon Tehlirian has stated. What is more, we are prepared to bring eyewitnesses whose oral testimony will corroborate the documents."

Kolnig was on his feet. "Objection! Your Honor, I object on the grounds that such testimony would be irrelevant to the case. It would serve no purpose. Obviously it is a deliberate move to discredit the reputation of the victim, the Turkish people and their nation."

"Your point is well taken, Dr. Kolnig. But the court would like to know what Dr. von Gorton has in mind." He now addressed von Gorton. "On what legal grounds does Defense wish to enter such evidence?"

"To prove our contention of compulsion rather than premeditation, your Honor," von Gorton said forcefully. "The pith and marrow of our defense is that Soghomon Tehlirian was compelled to complete his mission. If we are not allowed to prove a reason for that compulsion then we have no case and German law is a myth."

Judge Lemberg compressed his thin lips into a tight line. He shook an arthritic finger at von Gorton. "This court needs no flowery speeches about the myth or actuality of German law. And I'll thank you to leave the lectures to me." After a brief conference with his associate justices, Judge Lemberg straightened in his chair. "The court overrules the Prosecutor's objection. We wish to listen to Defense Counsel's evidence."

I saw a dream come true. The Turkish holocaust that destroyed my family and scattered the few survivors of my people around the world was now about to be brought into the open. Whether or not I climbed those last few steps to the gallows was of secondary importance. Talaat and the Turkish hierarchy were to be exposed in this Berlin court, to say nothing of the world's newspapers. The first act of genocide since Biblical days—the first in the 20th century—would now be revealed and the living soul of the Armenian people vindicated. I breathed a prayer for all of my countrymen who were slain at the foot of the Cross by the Turks. My words were silent but heartfelt:

"Thank you, God."

XVII. TURKISH HORRORS PROVEN

The weather report for that Tuesday, June 7, 1921, read "Hot and Humid." But it was not long before a chill descended upon the courtroom as witness after witness testified to such bestial crimes that spectators wept and even case-hardened journalists were stricken dumb. An aura, like a collective heartache, settled about the listeners as the tales of anguish unfolded. One could easily visualize a keen-edged, upraised crescent being brandished like a sword, slashing at a bleeding Armenian cross.

The spine-chilling accounts began with testimony given by Mrs. Christine Terzibashian of Erzeroum, Armenia. Under the gentle urgings of Dr. Adolf von Gorton, Mrs. Terzibashian began to speak, steadily at first and then falteringly as the poignant memories of the grim past became vividly real:

"In the early morning of June 3, 1915, just six years ago, the Turks ordered our entire population—maybe ten thousand or more—to leave the city. They said we were being moved for 'strategic reasons.' But they *lied!* There were no Turks or Kurds among us—only Armenians. My husband, Ardash, and I, along with countless others, were sent in walking caravans out of the city to an undisclosed destination; where, we didn't know. In eight days, five hundred families were driven from Erzeroum, each averaging about twenty persons; parents, children, uncles, cousins and other relatives. The Turks said we were being sent to Erzinga but we soon neared another city, Papert. As we approached the outskirts we began to see piles of corpses—Armenian dead. Many of the older people had fallen during the death march because of starvation, thirst and torture; or they were just killed. We were beaten, forced on at bayonet-point, without food, water or rest. When we arrived at Papert, Turkish mobs attacked us and stole what little belongings were left to us. Almost a third of our caravan were axed to death."

A horrified, incredulous hush descended upon the courtroom as Mrs. Terzibashian covered her face with her hands. Judge Lemberg, his stern features now softened with compassion, waited patiently for her to regain her composure. Now she looked up again, her eyes reddened.

"There were twenty people in my family and only three of us, including my husband, Ardash, survived. They butchered us with axes, swords and bayonets and"—her voice broke and she wrung her handkerchief—*"badchar cheegar* —for no reason."

Judge Lemberg, his face ashen, tried to calm the witness. "I know it is quite difficult for you to relive those hours, Mrs. Terzibashian, but it is important that we learn all the facts."

Mrs. Terzibashian finally managed to continue. "The few of us who survived were goaded on without food or water. A few miles along the road we were halted. About five hundred of our men were pulled from their families and slaughtered right before our eyes; their bodies thrown into a river. Many who knelt in prayer died under a rain of gunfire. The Turks shouted: 'Move on, your Christ can't help you now!' Our neighbor's eight-year-old daughter, Sayran, knelt beside her mother in prayer. A Turkish soldier drew his knife and went for the child. Those who tried to stop him, including Sayran's mother, were axed to death. The child kept on with her prayer; I don't know why! Pretty little Sayran..." Mrs. Terzibashian sobbed quietly. "She was so afraid, she could not stop; she did not until the Turk..."—her words crept over quivering lips—"... cut her tongue out."

There was silence.

Courageously she continued: "They prodded us onward, stabbing, kicking, beating the fallen to their feet. Somehow we reached Malatia, only to find that we were not allowed to enter the city. Instead, we were driven into the mountains. There, again, they separated the male survivors—including my husband, Ardash—and marched them some fifty yards away and axed them to death while their wives and daughters screamed. Somehow, thank God, a few escaped into the mountains; later to be rescued by some friendly Kurds."

Her eyes were now focused on a young man, who looked years older than his actual age, seated in the first row of the section reserved for witnesses. Kalousdian, at her side, comforted her. He now glanced towards the tribunal and irrationally explained, "Please, be patient, she wishes to continue. Yes . . . he is—the gentleman is her husband. She wants to continue, I'm sure . . ." His words were drowned. Mrs. Terzibashian broke into heavy sobs that carried throughout the horrified courtroom.

Justice Lemberg, whose heart we had thought was made of

granite, leaned forward and asked the bailiff to bring the distraught woman a glass of water. The peppery little judge surprised us by saying, "Mrs. Terzibashian, this court is anxious to arrive at the truth, but we have no wish to cause you such distress. If you wish, Madame, we would be glad to postpone your testimony until tomorrow?"

She shook her head. "*Nereghootoun guh khntrehm, shunoragal yehm dser medsahbadmootoum* —My apologies, and thank you so very much, your Honor, I'm all right now. May I continue?"

Lemberg hesitated and then bowed graciously—a tribute to a valiant woman.

Mrs. Terzibashian went on. "The Turks violated all the women and girls; children and the elderly alike. Some of us tried to resist but the Turks, howling with lust, assaulted us anyway and then cleaved skulls of our females with swords and axes. It was terrible—just terrible! The arms of pregnant women were hacked off; they were stabbed in their bellies with bayonets, their unborn babies spewing to the ground. But the Turks laughed. Yes, they just *laughed!*"

Many spectators in the courtroom, their emotions unleashed, were stamping their feet, denouncing the Turks. Others, who could not bring themselves to believe the accusations, yelled their indignant questions. Judge Lemberg banged his gavel and shouted repeatedly for order. Seemingly, minutes passed before order was restored. "Any repetition of this disturbance and I will clear the courtroom of all spectators," the diminutive judge barked. He turned toward the witness stand. "Please continue, Mrs. Terzibashian."

"The soldiers made us fall on our knees and pray for Talaat Pasha's long life and health," the witness went on. "We were forced to thank him for his generosity in allowing us to stay alive so long."

As far as I was concerned, I was vindicated right there and then. Mrs. Terzibashian had driven the last nail in Talaat's coffin. I listened attentively, my heart dripping tears, as she continued.

"I was one of the fortunate ones. I escaped near the city of Samsek. The others? They died in the deserts, or were shot and then thrown into the river. I was free, but without a home, a family or country."

The courtroom buzzed with conversation. Dr. von Gorton arose and faced the jurists. "It is quite understandable that some of you find it difficult to believe Mrs. Terzibashian's testimony. It is always difficult for decent people to understand that there are anomalies such as Talaat and his fellow Turks who committed such inhuman acts against a helpless minority." He stepped back to the table and picked up a folder of papers. "May it please the court, these documents are affidavits of several hundred eyewitnesses that will support the experiences Mrs. Terzibashian just related."

Prosecutor Kolnig sprang to the alert. "Your Honors," he declared stentorianly, "I object to the introduction of any affidavits contrived to support the testimony of the witness."

"What is the reason for your objection, Mr. Prosecutor?" Judge Lemberg asked.

"If the court will permit an observation, war is a disgraceful but recurring phenomena of modern civilization," asserted Kolnig. "An ethnic group of people who seem to enjoy calling themselves Armenians, took it upon themselves to defy the legally constituted Turkish regime and in so doing, precipitated armed conflict. Now, I ask the court and the gentlemen of the jury, shall we give credence to the laments of a victim of war when the real issue is simply a question of whether or not the prisoner shot down a man on the streets of Berlin? Down through the ages, innocent people have lost their lives and their property because of policies of State—policies over which they had no control. Just a few minutes ago a witness for the defense came before you, whining that she had been subjected to fantastic brutalities. But what was her objective? Was it an idealistic motive that would resolve the differences between the Armenian rebels and the lawful Turkish government? No! She appeared here only to vent her spite. Through the consequences of war, which all nations accept, she suffered a loss of property and the lives of those who were dear to her. For this I express my deep sympathy."

What was he getting at, I wondered. No *war* existed between Turkey and Armenia—we were citizens of the Empire—yet he dared call the murder of one-million-and-a-half unarmed civilians ... war. Yet, except for his last statements, some of the things he had said were true. At times Kolnig sounded more like a witness for the defense than a prosecuting attorney. His next sentence jolted me back to grim reality.

"However," Kolnig went on, every word a battering ram, "the individual tragedies suffered by the civilian population are handmaidens to the wars between nations. While there are undoubtedly many others who suffered similar personal losses, we again maintain that the seeking out of one individual, years after the illegal Armenian revolt had been halted, and murdering him on foreign soil cannot be described as anything but an act of vengeful, political assassination. Your Honor, we have all suffered personal agonies through acts of war. I ask you, as a human being endowed with a God-given soul, is there anyone here who can condone *murder!* —especially because of the aggressive actions of the victim's country? *No!* No, indeed. For in that case, all of us who bear resentment against our transient enemies—given the opportunity—would be held accountable.

"This court has heard the testimony of a hysterical Armenian woman in support of the murderer who stands before you so defiantly at this moment. She has contributed nothing to the evidence. Her appeal has been purely emotional, as has the defendant's. Not one shred of fact, mind you, not one!—has been introduced to corroborate her fantastic testimony. If objectivity is to be our goal, I must demand that this court consider only that which is factual. Mrs. Terzibashian has presented an emotional diatribe with no substantiating evidence to confirm her highly-colored accusations. Therefore I ask this court to exclude her testimony from the record. She is, and quite understandably, a prejudiced person; not an acceptable witness. The dignity of German law is at stake. *Our* law. And, *our* law demands fact, not mere opinions based on bias."

Dr. von Gorton's objections were being voiced even as Judge Lemberg raised a questioning eyebrow. "Your Honor," my attorney declared, "the defense is prepared to place on the witness stand persons of high repute and acknowledged authority who will substantiate the testimony of Mrs. Terzibashian. In addition, we are ready to introduce documentary evidence to bolster the attestations of our experts concerning the Turkish Crime."

Judge Lemberg discussed the issue with his two associate judges. "The court will consider the testimony of experts and the documents which the defense deems necessary to this case," he ruled after a few minutes deliberation.

So it was that the official documentation of the tragedy of the Armenian people was aired in court—sons and daughters of the first Christians on earth, who had for centuries died defending the Faith and had sustained their greatest mortal loss during the Massacre of 1915 at the hands of frenzied Islamic Turks. The next witness, Dr. Lepsius, was to rip away the Turkish veil of secrecy that had for so long shrouded the Armenian blood-bath.

* * * * * * * * * *

"Your Honors, Gentlemen of the Jury," Dr. von Gorton began, a sheaf of documents in his hand. "It will be quickly apparent that the testimony to be given by our next witness forms the bedrock of our case. Because he is indeed our key witness. I ask the court's indulgence so that I may properly introduce him as an authority."

"In what field does he qualify?" Judge Lemberg asked.

"He is qualified as an internationally known authority on Armenian affairs, your Honor. His field is theology but he has long since proven his capabilities in sociology and in the political and military sciences. As a distinguished author, his books and articles have been well received throughout the world. A long-time resident of Armenia and other areas of the Ottoman Empire, he has for years championed closer social, religious and economic ties between the Armenian and German peoples."

Judge Lemberg hesitated a short moment. "The court would like to see some of these literary works before passing on his qualifications as an expert."

Von Gorton nodded, pleased. "I have here several of his books, including a copy of 'The Secret Reports of Reverend Johannes Lepsius: The Massacres of the Armenian People.' It is this very same Rev. Lepsius whom the defense would call as its next witness." The lawyer handed the publications to the judge. Other books were included such as *Bericht Uber Lage Des Armenisehen Volkes In der Turkei, Deutchland Und Armenien.*

Kolnig sprang to his feet. "Objection, your Honor!" the prosecutor called forcefully. "The so-called 'Secret Reports' which the defense would have you consider has no substance in validity or authority. It was not only banned by our German Government but was even confiscated by the police because of its traitorous accusations and distortions of the truth. In fact, your Honor, our own authorities have described the reports as prefabricated lies and nonsense. I would be glad to furnish to this court the names of the officials and the various departments who have gone on record in opposition to this fanciful account of trumped-up fairy tales—which only sought to destroy the Turkish and German military alliance. As one who had read these 'Secret Reports' I join with my colleagues in branding the document as devoid of all truth."

Judge Lemberg polished his spectacles and glared at von Gorton. "The prosecution's charges are serious ones," he said fiercely. "Does Counsel for Defense still wish to introduce the next witness as an expert?"

"We certainly do, your Honor. I believe that we can explain the reasons behind the banning of Rev. Lepsius' reports on the Armenian Question. But, if the court will allow, I should like to preface my explanation with some background data so that the entire issue will be crystal clear."

Kolnig again objected. "Your Honor, I protest this unseemly use of the court's time to vindicate a man who is not even on trial here. I have offered to bring evidence which will show that the proposed witness and his reports have been condemned by the leading authorities of Germany. His previous writings have shown him to be totally unfamiliar with German and Turkish relationships and he cannot, indeed *should not* be accepted as a qualified expert in this trial."

Judge Lemberg leaned back and reflectively tapped his teeth with a pencil. For a moment he and his associates conferred. Finally, Judge Lemberg spoke. "It is this court's decision that the prosecutor's arguments will be taken into consideration at the time of its judgment. Meanwhile, in order that the ends of justice may be served, Counsel for Defense should also be allowed to conclude his argument in behalf of his witness. He is also granted permission to preface his remarks as requested. Please proceed, Counsel."

"Thank you, your Honor," von Gorton said. "First, may I say that, too often, we Germans tend to think collectively. Particularly are we gullible to official propaganda. Sometimes it would appear that right and wrong is measured by prevailing German needs and interests. But right, like truth, is universal, without beginning or end. It was a policy of the military leaders of this nation during its alliance with the Turkish Empire to mislead the masses—a fact which we all acknowledge."

"I acknowledge nothing of a sort!" Lemberg snapped. "But, please continue."

"We were told that it was the French who mistreated the Armenians and that the Armenians in turn were massacring the Turks. But in this moral desert, parched of truth and covered with the dry sands of bombast and propaganda, a few isolated voices could be heard. Yes, these brave voices were raised despite the ever-present danger of arrest and imprisonment because they dared tell the truth. Perhaps the most vehement of these outraged Christians was the Rev. Johannes Lepsius. In April, 1915, Rev. Lepsius, as president of the German-Armenian Ecclesiastic Mission, journeyed to Turkey to investigate the stories he had heard of the Turkish butcheries being inflicted upon Christians: Armenians, many Greeks and some Jews.

"The unspeakable crimes which Rev. Lepsius witnessed and documented represent the core of this case. We understand the reason for Prosecutor Kolnig's bitter fight to keep this witness from testifying. The result will show that the accused, Soghomon Tehlirian, not only suffered a nightmarish compulsion but it is small wonder he did not go completely berserk.

"It is interesting to note that even our Emperor, Kaiser Wilhelm II, was also appalled at the reports of the Turkish barbarisms. But, unfortunately, our German High Command, anxious to avoid an open rift with their ally in the war against the Western Powers, dissuaded him from making an official appeal to the 'Young Turks'. Instead, Rev. Lepsius carried His Majesty's personal appeal to the Turkish leaders in Constantinople to halt the massacres. However, when Talaat Pasha, Enver and Djemal learned of Rev. Lepsius' investigations he was forthwith summoned to explain the reason for his activities. Our Emperor's appeal was deliberately ignored. Rev. Lepsius was ordered to leave Turkey immediately with the warning that every member of the German-Armenian Ecclesiastic Mission was now considered to be *persona non grata*. Moreover, they declared that any delegate of this Christian body would be executed should they again set foot on Turkish soil."

Judge Lemberg looked up sharply at the sound of a collective hiss from the spectators. He rapped his gavel. In the prisoner's dock, carried away by the revelations that aroused the spectators, I had momentarily forgotten that it was I who was on trial. The spontaneous expression of disapproval that swept the courtroom was the first sign of public sympathy in my behalf since the time of my arrest. The section reserved for the press was as busy as an anthill in a field of wheat at harvest time. Reporters scribbled furiously as though not to miss a single word. I quickly returned my attention to von Gorton.

"Soon after his return to Germany, Rev. Lepsius published his report," my lawyer explained. "The truths inherent in his analysis were also authenticated by documents in the archives of the German Ministry of Foreign Affairs. But our Army officers had no intention of allowing the public to learn that they had been apathetic and in some cases even condoned the massacres. The reports were plainly detrimental to our concepts of morality, so the Military High command ordered that the book be banned. All printed copies were confiscated and burned. However, Rev. Lepsius fled to Holland with the original manuscript where it was re-published. Later it appeared in the French and many other languages. The reason it is called a 'secret report' is that it was not only smuggled out of Turkey, but later, a few copies were covertly brought into Germany in spite of the ban."

Judge Lemberg meditated long and earnestly. "Are you prepared to substantiate your arguments in defense of this book?"

"I am, your Honor."

"Then you are ordered to bring this proof into court so that the judges may examine it. Meanwhile the court is impressed with the presentation made in behalf of the witness. Counsel for Defense may proceed."

Kolnig started to protest. "Your Honor . . . "

"I distinctly said Counsel for Defense may proceed," Judge Lemberg said levelly. "Perhaps the prosecutor did not hear."

"Pardon, Sir," Kolnig muttered.

Judge Lemberg glanced at the huge wall clock and placed both palms on his desk. "The hour is late," he announced. "It is just as well we adjourn for the day. Court will reconvene tomorrow morning at nine o'clock."

We all rose as the judges filed out of the courtroom.

* * * * * * * * *

"I hope that Rev. Lepsius lives up to your expectations," I said to von Gorton that evening when he visited me in my cell.

The lawyer smiled as Kalousdian translated. "My expectations are, Soghomon, that the good Reverend will demolish the prosecutor's case against you."

"You *actually* believe that?" I asked eagerly.

"I didn't say that. I said those are my *expectations*."

There was a moment of void. His cautious smile, however, was reassuring. I could scarcely sleep that night for the excitement that bubbled and boiled within me. This key witness, a minister of the Gospel, would open a door for me. Whether that door led to freedom or to the hangman rested in the will of God and in the testimony of one of His disciples.

XVIII. KEY WITNESSES DISCLOSE ATROCITIES

"I call the Rev. Johannes Lepsius to the witness stand," von Gorton announced.

Every eye in the courtroom was trained on the slim, sixtyish minister as he ascended the stand. He was a commanding figure, about five-feet-nine inches in height and weighing some 150 pounds. He had a carved face, somber and exact in expression, distinguished by a short, iron-gray beard. Silvered, wavy hair swooped back from his temples to his crown like the wings of an albino raven. Though somewhat frail in his well-tailored, vested suit, he exuded a dynamic personality that caught and held rapt attention; however, there was about him an aesthetic quality that softened what might have otherwise been a forbidding manner. More than any other man I have ever known he had a faculty for being able to speak of soul-shattering crimes in one breath and, in the next, rise to lyrical heights of sheer poetry. I remember thinking what a privilege it must have been for his congregation to listen to him.

Rev. Lepsius was sworn in, identified and questioned briefly about his background, a pure formality since Judge Lemberg had already qualified him as an expert witness. His manner was scholarly, almost pedantic, as though addressing a class of students, but his words fell softly like dewdrops from a flower warmed by the sun. "If I am to discuss the recent holocaust which decimated the Armenian people," he began, in answer to von Gorton's opening questions, "it might be best to give a brief resume of the Crown Jewel that was Armenia before she was ravaged by the Turks."

Von Gorton lifted an inquiring eyebrow toward Judge Lemberg who nodded assent. The lawyer, in turn, responded affirmatively. "Please do, Reverend."

Lepsius inclined his head politely in a gesture of appreciation. "When one speaks of Armenia, he must speak with reverence. For here was located the Garden of Eden, the cradle of the human race—the cradle of civilization. Armenia is landmarked by its towering 17,000-foot Mount Ararat where Noah, sheltered in the Ark, viewed the flooded plains, valleys and plateaus below. Here, Cain, the tiller of the soil, killed his brother, Abel, the keeper of the sheep. Noah's great-great grandson, Haik, was the first king of Armenia. (COMMENT: Armenia was named after King Haik. In the Armenian language, Haiastan is Armenia.) Here flowed the four Biblical rivers: Pison, Gihon, Hiddekel and Phrath, today known as Cyrus, Araxes, Tigris and Euphrates. If you were to travel the route from Persia, through Armenia, to the Black Sea, you would traverse the site of the Garden of Eden which today touches upon the cities of Van, Bitlis, Moush, Erzeroum, Sassoun and Erzinga.

"At the height of its power the ancient Kingdom of Armenia, with a population of 33,000,000, consisted of 500,000 square miles—larger than our Germany and France combined—of fertile tableland extending from the Black Sea and the Caucasus Mountains to Persia and Syria. The land is rich, fertile, rugged and beautiful. Armenia had five dynasties: Haiguzun or Yervantian, Artaxiad, Arsacid, Bahgradian and Reubenian. Tigranes the Great and the Mamikonians are but a few of the many great Armenian leaders. It was King Tigranes who married the daughter of Mithridates, King of Pontus. Tigranes defeated the Cappadocians, Parthians, Assyrians and crossed swords with Pompey and his Roman legions and Alexander the Great and his forces.

"Armenia is the Motherland and all other lands are her daughters; but she is fairer than any other. Even her mountain tops of perpetual snow are a crown of her glory, supplying the beautiful rivers below and then penetrating every corner of the land, through hundreds of miles giving life to fields, vineyards, orchards and turning mills, to finally rest in the Caspian Sea, the Black Sea and the Gulf of Persia. She feeds her own noble lakes such as Sevan, Urumiah and Van. Her fields are fertile to the extent that it is said that two melons is a camel's load.

"May I quote from a statement made by the honorable Englishman, James Bryce: 'Armenia is blessed with every gift of nature God has bestowed. Deep-rooted, her history coincides with the recorded history of the first man. It does not go back to the Mayflower or Norman the Conqueror, but begins with the Garden of Eden. The Armenians' first recorded ancestors are found in the Book of Genesis.'

"The Armenian Church—Gregorian Apostolic—was founded by St. Gregory the Illuminator in the 4th Century A.D. (COMMENT: Not to be confused with the Catholic ecclesiastical popes of later dates—540 to 1585 A.D.) Armenians have defended Christianity against fire-worshippers, Persians, Romans and a host of others. Spiritual wealth is at the core of the Armenian character. If the Armenians had not defended Christianity, there would be no Christianity today. (COMMENT: Armenia's neighbor, Persia (Iran) practiced Zoroastrianism. Intending to force the Armenians to accept their faith, the Persians attacked Armenia, but the Armenians refused to give up their faith. The Christian Armenians, with only 66,000 defenders, confronted the numerically superior Persian force of 220,000. Field Commander Vartan Mamigonian was killed immediately. Although the Armenians were defeated, they held on to their faith. Thirty years later, the martyred field commander's nephew, General Vahan Mamigonian, carrying a Banner of the Cross, confronted the hordes of Persians and dealt heavy losses on the Persians. The General's victory assured the survival of Christianity.) Thaddeus, Bartholomew and John the Baptist preached in Armenia and, it was under the reign of the first Christian king—King Durtad (Tiridates)—that Armenia became the first Christian nation on earth in the year 301 A.D.

(COMMENT: The Armenian Apostolic Church was established directly by Jesus Christ through his apostles, Thaddeus and Bartholomew. At the Feast of Pentecost, described in the Holy Bible in The Book of Acts, a mighty wind filled the room and tongues of fire descended upon the heads of the apostles, and they were filled with the Holy Ghost and began to speak in different tongues. God spoke to Thaddeus and Bartholomew and directed them to travel to Armenia and convert the Armenian nation. The apostles carried the Shroud of Jesus which was placed on the King's face. He was immediately healed of leprosy. Thaddeus and Bartholomew held an active ministry of healing there from 35 A.D. to 45 A.D., both in different areas of the nation. Thaddeus was executed in the city of Magou, in what is now Iran, but at that time still a part of Greater Armenia. The apostle Bartholomew was beheaded at Aghbag in 60 A.D. The martyred apostle is buried near the city of Bashkaleh. The Armenians built two churches in their honor, one at Artaza, and the other at Albac. The Christian movement spread quickly, and among the many other apostles who travelled the mountains and valleys of Armenia, had been St. John the Baptist and St. Paul, who was born in Tarsus in Lesser Armenia and said in ancient Armenian manuscripts to have had an Armenian mother. In 301 A.D., inspired by Jesus' directive to Christianize Armenia through his apostles and the work of St. Gregory the Illuminator, the Armenian spiritual leader, the king ordered Armenia to accept Christianity as a national religion — thus Armenia became the first nation to embrace Christianity.)

"The Armenian is Aryan, of the white race, Indo-European; his homeland forty centuries old. The Armenian Church was established twenty years before the Greek and thirty-two years before the Catholic Church. In the 7th Century there arose a power in the East, destined to become one of the greatest threats to Christianity—to the Armenians: Islamism. Like a plague, Mohammed's militant religion spread from Mecca to the Gibraltar. When it reached Armenia it could not penetrate; although their kingdom could be burned to ashes and their people enslaved, the Armenians refused to surrender their faith in Jesus Christ.

"In the 5th Century—the Golden Age—St. Mesrop and St. Sahag, both born in the Armenian cultural center of Moush, revolutionized Armenian religion, literature, art and music. St. Mesrop wrote the Armenian Bible and together with St. Sahag created the thirty-six letter Armenian alphabet. (COMMENT: The Armenian translation of the Holy Bible became known as the "Queen of Translations." The Prophet Isaiah wrote, "The entire land of Armenia was filled with the knowledge of the Lord, as the water covers the sea.") Countless masterpieces were produced by Armenian artists during this period. Greek classics, including the writings of Eusebitus, were translated. The originals were lost and the Armenian translations were the only source available to our modern world.

"Six centuries ago, appeared the Turks. Sporadic persecutions took place over the centuries. In 1876 the notorious Sultan Hamid II became the ruler of Ottoman Turkey. Barbarisms against the Sultan's Armenian subjects became prevalent because they would not surrender their Christian faith for Mohammedanism. England's Sir Gladstone denounced the Turks: 'The Turks are the blind destroyers; they have created nothing—they are a human cancer crawling across the face of the earth.' When I asked an Armenian whether he would prefer Russian rule instead of the Turks—for the Russians had claimed to be their new protectors—he answered: 'The Turk lops off our heads; the Russian digs us up by our roots.'

"At the turn of the 20th Century, this mountainous region was appropriately termed the Switzerland of Asia Minor, almost reaching the Caucasus on the North, the Black Sea on the West, Mesopotamia on the South and the Caspian Sea on the East.

"It was a peaceful, verdant land—the 4,000-year-old homeland of the Armenians—which the Islamic hordes invaded, turning it into a living hell. Three thousand years before the primitive Turks were ever recorded in history, the Armenians, a civilized people, were already tilling the soil of that ancient and hallowed center of the then known world.

"How was it possible, six centuries ago, for the Turkish barbarians, only a step removed from their Neanderthal fathers, to conquer the progressive Armenian people? The answer is obvious: a militant, armed minority has always been able to conquer a peaceful, unarmed majority—culture and refinement notwithstanding."

Kolnig was on his feet, his objection raucous in the hushed courtroom. "Objection! If it please the court, this is an obvious attempt to sway the jury though emotion rather than documented or eyewitness evidence. We cannot tolerate this in a German court of law."

"It seems to me," Judge Lemberg observed dryly, "that much of what the witness stated is very well documented in the Holy Bible and in countless numbers of textbooks in our institutions of learning."

"But this is an appeal to sheer emotion!"

Lemberg explained, "Not at all. We must take into consideration that the witness is a minister of the Gospel and is comfortable in the use of expressive oratory. He is not accustomed, as you are, Dr. Kolnig, to the prescribed confines of legal language which must be nakedly formal. While this is not the pulpit, we recognize Rev. Lepsius' leanings and accept his descriptions. Frankly, I'm rather enlightened by them." There was no question that he, too, like everyone else in the room, was mesmerized by the articulate and eloquent minister. (COMMENT: In his essays, the late Prosecutor Heinrich Kolnig wrote: "I confess that I, too, was entranced with Rev. Johannes Lepsius' eloquent story." *The Tehlirian Case* —Vol. III, Chapter XVII)

"The witness may continue," Lemberg said.

Rev. Lepsius smiled faintly. "While the origin of the first organized Turkish massacres are lost in antiquity," he said, "it is definitely established that wholesale murders occurred in the second decade of the 19th Century."

Kolnig again bellowed his disapproval. "Objection, your Honor! There can be no conceivable relevancy in any happenings of a hundred years ago. If Counsel for the Defense seeks to use ancient history to substantiate his plea of compulsion, then surely this tribunal will sustain me."

"May it please the court," von Gorton interjected. "It is important that we establish a definite time in which the Turkish massacres started; at least within the past century. Prosecutor Kolnig himself has argued that the prisoner had no cause for committing his act. It is our intention to prove otherwise. But before we do, we must also prove that not only Talaat and his 'Young Turks' massacred Tehlirian's people but so did most of their predecessors."

Judge Lemberg wore a questioning look. "To be quite candid, Dr. von Gorton, the only way to legally *prove* murder is to present evidence of the *corpus delicti*."

In my prisoner's box I wondered what Dr. von Gorton's answer would be. Like many others who are not familiar with law, I had always thought that *corpus delicti* simply is a Latin phrase meaning the "body of the crime." To criminal lawyers it signifies the basic elements of a criminal offence. There were two fundamental charges which von Gorton hoped to prove: Mass-murder (genocide), and the looting of Armenian property. Mass-murder, in this case, meant not only the murder of a million-and-a-half of my people but also their crimes against humanity, which included continued persecutions and the attempted destruction of the Armenian culture and religion. Further, it also meant the deportation of nearly a half-million people, condemned to live in exile for the rest of their lives. Although I knew nothing of the legal terminology at the time, Judge Lemberg was clearly as knowledgeable about the legal complications surrounding mass-murder (genocide) as was von Gorton; perhaps more so. Not quite comprehending, I listened engrossed as von Gorton answered the judge.

"Your Honor, it is a matter of record that before the most recent Turkish persecutions, which began in 1915, there were 1,850,000 Armenians alive in their homeland. At the end of 1918, only forty-two months later, there were less than 350,000 survivors—all living outside their ancient homeland. Thus, with documents to support the evidence that more than 1,500,000 people disappeared at the hands of Talaat and his 'Young Turks,' we hope to establish at least *prima facie* proof of the *corpus delicti*.

"If the court will permit, I shall introduce evidence to show that these last massacres were an integral part of the Turkish plan to exterminate the entire Armenian people—a plan which dates back at least to 1822.

"I shall also bring evidence to show that 350,000 survivors were forcibly deported from their native land and that land confiscated. Some fled to comparative safety in the Caucasus. But, today, these survivors are scattered throughout the world. The result, your Honor, was that an entire nation—an entire culture disappeared—wiped out, if I may, through murder, deportation and plunder.

"It is our intention to furnish documentary proof of these atrocities. We shall also bring historians, minsters of the Gospel, military officials and others, to corroborate the written evidence. No doubt this is the first case on record that such people, none of them lawyers, have been called to establish the *corpus delicti*. I ask the court's indulgence because this is the only way that we can show the vast extermination of life and property, all of which constituted such a tremendous loss to the Armenian people. It will also show why my client, Soghomon Tehlirian, was compelled to act as he did."

To my surprise, Kolnig nodded approval even as Judge Lemberg gave his assent. "The court agrees that the defense is justified in establishing the *prima facie* evidence of the *corpus delicti*. You may continue with your case, Dr. von Gorton."

My lawyer gave a quick, appreciative nod to Kolnig for his agreement with the legal interpretation. "Rev. Lepsius stated that the massacres could be traced to the year 1822," von Gorton said. "Although the persecutions go back six centuries, we will, for the purpose of this trial, accept his statement and herewith offer the documentation. It reads as follows:

UNIVERSITY OF LEIPZIG
Department of Middle-East History
**Chronological Listing of Eight Authenticated
Massacres of Christians Committed by
The Turkish Government.**

YEAR   NO. SLAIN   BY ORDER OF:

Year	Victims	Ruler
1822	50,000 Greeks and Armenians	Sultan Mahmoud, (Grandfather of Abdul Hamid II)
1850	10,000 Armenians and Nestorians	Sultan Mejit, (Father of Abdul Hamid II)
1860	11,000 Maronites and Syrians	Sultan Mejit
1876	15,000 Bulgarians	Sultan Ariz * (Uncle of Abdul Hamid II)
1894	10,000 Armenians	Sultan Abdul Hamid II
1895-1908	325,000 Armenians	Sultan Abdul Hamid II
1909	30,000 Armenians	Talaat Pasha, Enver, Djemal and others in the Young Turk Party
1915-1918	1,500,000 Armenians	Talaat Pasha, Enver, Djemal and others in the Young Turk Party

* (COMMENT: When Sultan Aziz visited Europe in July of 1875, his shoes were filled with "Moslem soil." This was done so that he could continue to walk on undefiled earth while in the land of the "infidel" Christians, and thus avoid "disgracing" Allah.)

"We will mark this as an exhibit for the defense," Judge Lemberg said, accepting the proffered document.

Rev. Lepsius continued his testimony. "Since the court has a partial list of the massacres, reaching back to 1822, I will confine my remarks to those which occurred in 1908 and thereafter, under the regime of the 'Young Turk Party,' also known as the *Ittihad-*

Tehlirian's mother, Hnazant, and his brother, Misak, are seated next to Soghomon, 14. Standing behind them is his brother, Avedis, medical student at the American College who died with his mother when the Turks razed Erzinga to ashes. (Photo: Archives of Avak Z. Avakian)

Tehlirian's father, Khachador, who survived because he was in Serbia at the time of the massacres. The young girl is Tehlirian's niece, Armenoohi, Misak's daughter, a survivor.
(Photo: Archives of Avak Z. Avakian)

Soghomon Tehlirian's schoolteacher, Armenag Melik, with his lovely 22-year-old bride at Erzinga. Turkish cavalrymen raided the city and abducted her. He never saw her again.
(Photo: Archives of Avak Z. Avakian)

Armenian corpses strewn across the desert of Der el Zor, farther than the eye can see. (Photo: Archives of Avak Z. Avakian)

Liberated by Armenian Volunteer Army soldiers, these youngsters are now in safe hands. In the background a member of the Armenian Red Cross can be seen standing just behind victim on the left in the front row.
(Photo: Archives of Avak Z. Avakian)

A Bible in his pocket, rifle in his hand, and cloaked in the vestments of his office, a bishop of the Armenian Apostolic Church leads a group of fellow clergymen to protect the women and children who found sanctuary in the *Sourp Garabed* (St. Charles) Monastery near the city of Moush. This episode followed the desecration of their churches and the disembowelment of Gregorian priests. 1,500 Turk soldiers killed this small band to the last man and then set fire to the monastery, burning alive every woman and child inside.
(Photo: Archives of Avak Z. Avakian)

General Gevork Chavoush, *Fedeii* leader, Armenian Fighting Elite. These were guerrillas who fought the oppressors from the hills. Chavoush, from the city of Moush, was one of Armenia's greatest heroes.
(Photo: Archives of Avak Z. Avakian)

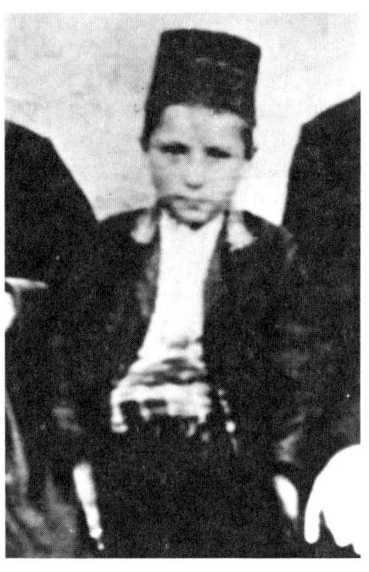 

Six-year-old Zakar Avakian, the author's first cousin, brother of tiny Shooshig. He was typical of the "future enemies of the Turkish Empire" Talaat ordered to death by sword, axe, or fire. (Photo: Archives of Avak Z. Avakian)

Three-year-old Shooshig Avakian, the author's first cousin, met death in 1915 at Moush, Armenia, when the Turks set fire to their home and at gun point kept the Avakian family of five inside the structure to burn to death. (Photo: Archives of Avak Z. Avakian)

Christians! "Tiny Golgotha" was the name given to this mountain of skulls of the Armenian victims of the desert Der el Zor in Northern Syria, where nearly a million died in 1915. (Photo: Archives of Avak Z. Avakian)

Armenian priests pose before a collection of bones and skeletons, grim reminders of the first Genocide in the 20th Century. A collection of bones from Der el Zor, shown, was shipped to Cilicia and placed below the altar of the Martyr's Church. (Photo: Archives of Avak Z. Avakian)

Altar of martyrdom. A memorial shrine to the victims of the 1915 Genocide. Armenians of Beirut, Lebanon pay homage to the Christian martyrs who died at the hands of the Moslem Turks, during the period of April 11-24, annually. This shrine is in the garden of the Catholicos. (Azbarez Publishing Company)

New York American, Sunday, January 19, 1919, published this special section titled: "To Restore Ravished Armenia: after centuries of persecution of the oldest of the Christian peoples." Top left: Mt. Ararat where Noah built his Ark. Center top: ARMENIA IN THE SCRIPTURES: unhappy land whose people trace their descent from the family of Noah. Right top: Cain driven from Armenia. The Garden of Eden is situated near the city of Erzeroum. Cain, after killing his brother, Abel, was driven from Armenia. Bottom left: St. Ripsime, nun who fled Rome and returned to Armenia. Center: Mt. Ararat in Armenia. Noah's Ark, bearing the vestige of the human race and specimens of all animals, were saved from the flood. They rested in the Ark on Mt. Ararat. Bottom right: Widowed mother of three when Turks murdered her husband in the Massacres. (New York American)

Mount Ararat, the most famous of mountains. Here, Noah rested his Ark on the Mount. Armenia's sacred mountain is the heart of the "cradle of civilization."
(Photo: National Geographic Society)

King Haik, great-great grandson of Noah, was Armenia's first king. Armenia was named after him: Haiastan: Armenia.
(Painting: Hovannes Babessian. Atlas of Historic Armenia)

"Ruins of the church of St. Gregory at Ani, the ancient capital of Armenia. 800 years ago this church was built by Christian Armenians and dedicated to their patron saint, St. Gregory. Top left: Stone carving of 10th century Armenian church wall engraved with Adam and Eve and tree of life and serpent story. Bottom left: Ruined walls and arches of church at Ani." (New York American)

First Christian king and queen: King Tiridates and Queen Ashken of Armenia; 4th century A.D.
(Painting: Hovannes Babessian. Atlas of Historical Armenia)

Number 4 Hardenburgstrasse, Talaat's lair. Here, marked by the X, the notorious Turkish mass-murderer, Talaat Pasha, was executed on March 15, 1921, in Berlin, Germany.
(Photo: Memoirs of Soghomon Tehlirian)

Charlotenburg courtroom where a High German Court tried Soghomon Tehlirian for his execution of Talaat Pasha. The trial began on June 2, 1921.
(Photo: Archives of Avak Z. Avakian)

Adolf von Gorton, Chief Defense Counsel, who represented Soghomon Tehlirian at his trial in Berlin, Germany. (Photo: Archives of Avak Z. Avakian)

LEFT: Assistant defense attorney, Johannes Wertenhauer. RIGHT: Assistant defense attorney, Kurt Niemeyer. (Photo: Archives of Avak Z. Avakian)

Dr. Johannes Lepsius, German theologian, key witness for the defense, at the trial of Soghomon Tehlirian. An outstanding authority on Armenia, he wrote the "Secret Reports" of the Turkish Genocide against the Armenians.
(Photo: Archives of Avak Z. Avakian)

The author's parents, Mrs. Surpoohi (Antoyan) Avakian, 18, and Avak Zakar Avakian, 28, at their wedding, February 18, 1907 in Fresno, California. Both were survivors of the 1894-96 Massacre by the Red Sultan, Abdul Hamid II. Their combined testimony was submitted in writing to Tehlirian's attorneys. (Author's collection)

Father Yegishe Mekhitarian, in his office at the Holy Trinity Armenian Apostolic Church in Fresno, California. Born in Moush, Armenia, he was to become one of the victims of the 1915 massacres. He escaped the Turks and dedicated his life to the priesthood. He became an important figure in the Armenian Church throughout the world. He served as Prelate of North Africa and Southern Europe and held many important posts in America. His written testimony was submitted to Tehlirian's attorneys; he and Tehlirian later became close friends. (Photo: Armenian Apostolic Church Archives)

Simon Vratzian, premier of the Free Independent Republic of Armenia. The free republic lasted from 1918 to 1920, when it succumbed under a combined Turko-Soviet attack and became the first captive nation of 20th century Communism. It is now the Soviet Republic of Armenia: one of 15 Soviet republics. (Photo: Archives of Avak Z. Avakian)

Henry Morgenthau, American Ambassador to Turkey from 1913 to 1916. He wrote his bitter report on the Turkish Genocide of the Armenians in September, 1915, in which he said, in part, "After 450 years, the evil Turk has come to the end of her misrule of her Christian subjects. Her dominion over the Christians and Jews has been one of savagery. They stand convicted of wholesale murder in the first degree, of committing the most atrocious crimes and beastly tortures of the ages."
(Photo: Archives of Avak Z. Avakian)

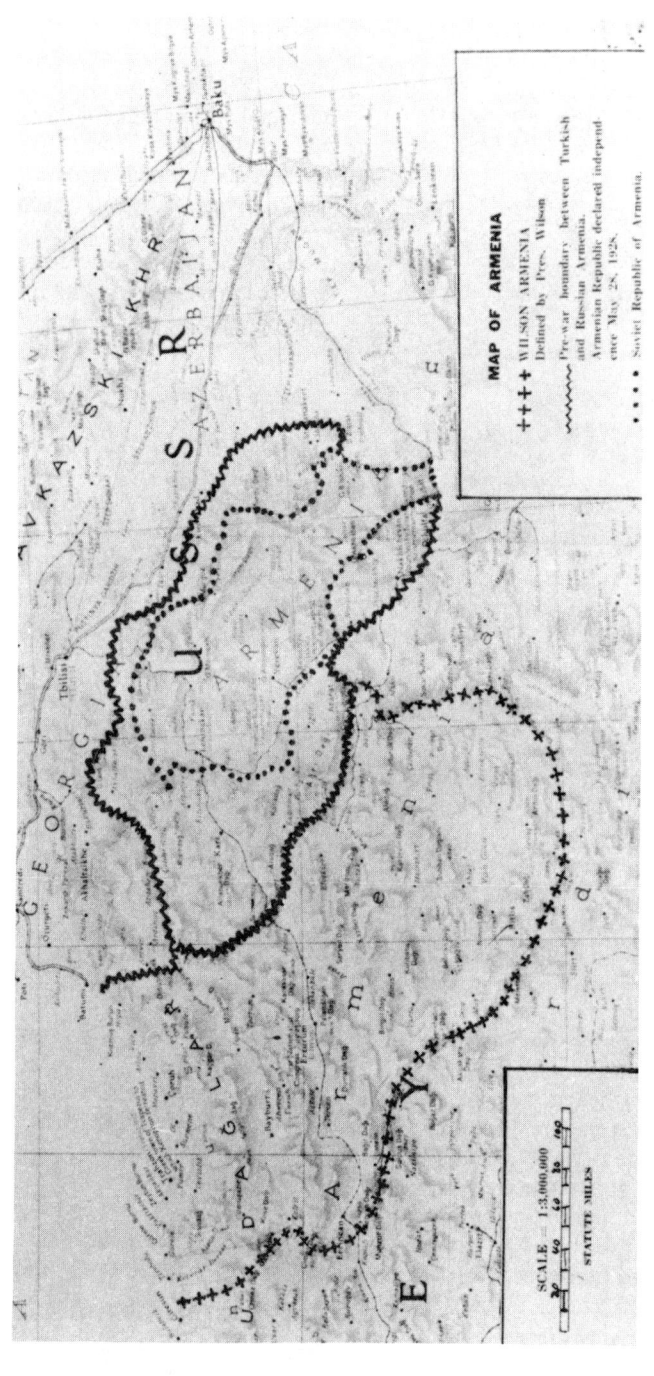

The boundaries proposed by President Woodrow Wilson for what he envisioned as an independent Armenia. (Map: Hairenik Publishing Company. Official organ of the A.R.F.)

President Woodrow Wilson. His constant fight for justice to the Armenians and other small nations is history. He proposed a definite territory for the Armenians; however, the United States Congress denied his proposal for an American mandate over Armenia. Probably, President Herbert Hoover is the only American who comes close to the affection held by Armenians for President Wilson. Wilson's dream for an independent Armenia was crushed in 1920 when Kemal of Turkey and Lenin of the Soviet Union attacked and captured the infant republic. All promises previously made at the treaty table to Wilson were nullified. (Photo: The Fresno Bee Newspaper)

Some of the cabinet members of the Independent Republic of Armenia, murdered on the very steps of the Armenian Parliament Building at Yerevan, in December, 1920 by invading Communists. The Armenian Republic, just over two years old, became the first country to fall victim to Communist aggression by the Soviet Union. (Photo: Archives of Avak Z. Avakian)

Ismet Pasha, top military advisor to Kemal Pasha, leader of Turkey after World War I and fellow Young Turk. In 1919 and 1922, Ismet was responsible for the massacre of 250,000 Armenians, Greeks and many Jews. So elated was Kemal's "Man With The Gun," Ismet Pasha, at his success in the wholesale slaughter of 30,000 Greek Christians of the city of Inonu that he fiendishly added the name of that Greek city to his: thus his name became Ismet Inonu! The very same Ismet Inonu who later was Premier of Turkey and a candidate for the 1965 Nobel Peace Prize: despite his criminal history. (Photo: Associated Press News)

Terraki Party or Committee of Union and Progress. It is interesting to note that when the 'Young Turks' assumed power, they restored their constitution which supposedly guaranteed freedom, equality and fraternity to all Turkish subjects. Thus the Armenian minority was lulled into a false sense of security. But six months after Talaat and his associates seized the reigns of government, and with the plaudits of Europe ringing in their ears because of their vaunted 'love of democracy,' they annihilated more than 30,000 of the Armenian population of Adana. Why? There were two reasons, neither of which coincide with the Turkish explanation. Let me explain:

"The Turks, at first, replied to a horrified Europe that the slaughter was the work of the deposed Sultan and his followers. When that story was received with skepticism they then claimed that the extermination was necessary because the Armenians of that city were plotting a revolution. The hidden truth behind the bloodshed was; **(a)** the wealth to be gained by the looting of Armenian property and, **(b)** the assurance of Paradise for killing Christians, as promised in the Koran. The Armenian people were desperate to believe that the 'Young Turks' would adhere to the new constitution. They accepted the official explanation. It wasn't long, however, before they learned that it was not an isolated massacre by the Sultan and his followers but just another episode in the systematic campaign of wholesale murder which was now the official policy of the Turkish government."

Judge Lemberg interrupted. "Do you have any evidence, Rev. Lepsius?"

Von Gorton anticipated Lepsius' answer. "We do, your Honor. The witness has turned over to us several documents in addition to many others which we were able to secure. With the court's permission I shall now read a report written by the prominent historian and author, Herbert Adams Gibbons, Ph.D., as recorded in the United States Congressional Record: (COMMENT: Dr. Gibbons was the author of "The Decline and Fall of the Ottoman Empire," "Turkey's World Panturanism," and other texts.)

"'I was in Adana in April, 1909. From the very beginning I was in position to become intimately acquainted with the Armenians in Turkey and to find out their true sentiments towards the 'Young Turks' and the new regime. They were fervently loyal to the new administration. The Turks rewarded this loyalty by massacring 30,000 of them in Adana, Cilicia and Northern Syria. Their blood was spilled before my very eyes in Adana. I was with the few survivors in different places after the fury of the massacre had abated.

"'The self-serving explanations given by the Turkish Government were false. They themselves finally admitted that Sultan Hamid had nothing to do with the massacre. The accusation that all the Armenians were plotting a revolution is another falsehood. (COMMENT: At the World Congress of the Federation held on May 20, 1914, in the city of Erzeroum, Armenia, Armenian leaders issued a proclamation to the *Ittahad-Terraki* Regime: "<u>In the event of open conflict with Russia, we shall continue to support our Ottoman Government as we have for six centuries</u>." Some 200,000 Armenian young men joined the Turkish armed forces to serve. Before year's end, all 200,000 were systematically murdered by official order of Talaat.) It has been demonstrated, to the satisfaction of every competent neutral source, that there was no foundation for this charge.

"'In retrospect it sounds incredible but I witnessed the Armenians' pathetically eager acceptance of the original explanation when it was first delivered. The announcement was made by a Turkish officer in behalf of Talaat Pasha, the Minister of Interior. He brazenly told the Armenian remnant that their kinsmen had fallen in the struggle against the Sultan's counter-revolutionists and that many 'Young Turks' had also died alongside their Armenian brothers. The few Armenians who were left cheered hoarsely as they were again promised 'liberty, equality and fraternity' under the new 'constitution.' Exactly six years later these few survivors were rounded up and also killed, by the order of Talaat Pasha.'"

Von Gorton placed the document and several others on Judge Lemberg's desk. "We are prepared, Sir," he said, "to introduce further evidence and shall do so as the witnesses testify."

Lepsius, on the stand, consulted his notes and resumed his testimony. "On June 28, 1914, Archduke Franz Ferdinand's death by assassination precipitated the World War, with Turkey on German's side, against the Allies. (COMMENT: Thirty-five days after Ferdinand's assassination, on August 2, 1914, Talaat, in a secret meeting with high German officials, signed the Turko-German War Pact.) Shortly thereafter and continuing almost until the close of the war with the Western Powers, the Turks drenched their Armenian subjects in a blood-bath unprecedented in history.

"Our German High Command had already sent such key

officers as General Limon von Sanders to Turkey, in 1913, to reorganize their army and transportation facilities and it was on the advice of these military figures that a national conscription system was inaugurated. This draft of manpower fitted in perfectly with the Turkish master plan of extermination. All able-bodied Armenian men were called to military service—some 200,000. The Turkish government then pressed a great many other Armenians, above military age, into forced labor where they were told they would be assigned to work projects in distant cities. They were never to be seen again. All of them—fathers, brothers, uncles and other relatives—were murdered in cold blood. With the Armenian communities cleared of most of its men, the Turks next ordered all weapons to be surrendered. The population was now defenseless and the Turks, although at war with such formidable powers as Britain, France and Russia, found the time and means to prepare for another persecution of this innocent minority. The Christian martyrs were about to be sacrificed on the flaming altars of Islamic hatred."

Somewhere in the courtroom I heard a muffled sob. I, too, found it difficult to subdue my emotions. Every word that Rev. Lepsius uttered was a dagger that opened long-closed wounds. A group of Armenians among the spectators leaned forward, their faces revealing the tragedy in their souls. I could hear my own heart pounding as the witness relived for us that twilight of horror.

"The procedure for annihilation was as efficient as it was devilish," the scholarly witness continued. "First, under the guise of conciliation, the Turks called for meetings with the most prominent members of Armenian communities throughout the nation. The meetings were always held on the outskirts of each city. There they were murdered. The systematic killings soon resulted in the desired effect—the Armenians were left virtually leaderless. Resistance was now almost impossible.

"The next move Talaat Pasha made was to order the relocation of all people in one city in Armenia after another. 'For strategic reasons due to the war,' they were told. But when the evacuations started, often with but twenty-four hours notice or none at all, only the Armenians were moved, while the Moslem population remained. The subterfuge, 'strategic reasons,' was successfully employed almost to the end.

"That is how the deportations began. The deportees were forced to write letters to their relatives back home and in other cities stating that they were happy and prosperous. In this manner the later groups of Armenian evacuees were led to believe that they were actually being transferred to new colonies where they would be 'safe from the danger of war' and where their temporary living and working conditions would be pleasant. These letters were written before the unfortunate victims ever reached their destinations. Each caravan embarked on what was literally a death march. For example, from the Anatolian area alone, ninety percent died en route.

"Males were assembled into groups and, within sight of their loved ones, were shot. Women and girls were ravished by the Moslem guards and then slain. Many of the ill and starving were left to die in the desert. Others, their wrists bound behind their backs, were thrown into rivers, their skulls first shattered. Even so, the small terminal camps became overcrowded with each successive arrival of Armenians. To make room for the half-dead newcomers the Turks would divert thousands of them to the deserts and rivers where they were killed. The grisly display of Turkish ferocity has no parallel in the history of mankind. Neither Ivan the Terrible nor Ghengis Khan ever conceived such an unholy plot against humanity."

Rev. Lepsius faced the bench. "I have given pertinent documents, including many eyewitness statements to *Herr* von Gorton. There is little more I can add, your Honor," Lepsius whispered, sorrowfully.

Said Judge Lemberg with difficulty, "Unless the prosecution has any questions, you may be excused, Pastor Lepsius, and I may commend you for your informative testimony."

"No questions," Kolnig said.

Was I mistaken or did I detect a glimmer of sympathy in the prosecutor's ordinarily harsh voice? I watched von Gorton as he rose ponderously to address the bench. "If it please the court, I will read one of the eyewitness' statements given to me by Rev. Lepsius."

"Please identify the author," Lemberg said.

"This is the sworn testimony submitted by Miss Aroos Haloian of the city of Erzeroum. Miss Haloian's statement was made under oath to the Joint Allied Investigation Committee, appointed by The Honorable Woodrow Wilson, President of the United States."

Judge Lemberg displayed one of his rare smiles. "That's quite an impressive introduction. The court will be pleased to hear the eyewitness' testimony."

KEY WITNESSES DISCLOSE ATROCITIES / 181

Von Gorton cleared his throat and then read:

"'I am using my maiden name, Aroos Haloian, because I was unmarried at the time of the massacres. I am now employed as an archivist in Armenian history. On June 14, 1915, I and five hundred other Armenians in the city of Erzeroum were ordered to accompany a squad of about a dozen Turkish militia. We had been told to prepare for a long journey but that we would be given good homes and jobs at our destination. I remember thinking it peculiar that despite our many questions, we were never told our destination. Our fears, though, were allayed by the Turkish mayor who made a speech about the fine future ahead of us. He even smiled, shook hands and bid us adieu, telling us 'please don't forget to write.' He pointed out that we need have no fear of the British, French or Russians who were then fighting Turkey and Germany.

"'That was how he explained the presence of our armed Turkish escort. We Armenians smiled to ourselves. We knew the Allied Powers would never harm us. We often silently prayed for their victory—not because we may have had political differences with Turkey (we were always loyal to the Government) but because we wanted to become one with the other Christian nations of the world. True, Germany was a Christian nation and an ally of Turkey but we feared the Prussian militarists just as other Christian nations did.

"'We marched out of Erzeroum with a gay tune on our lips, *Erk Asadooteeyahn* (Song of Freedom). But our caravan had no sooner reached the outskirts when our militia was reinforced by a phalanx of Turkish cavalrymen, each horseman armed with a rifle, saber and razor-sharp axe which was standard equipment until the end of the war. Immediately the glad song we were singing froze on our lips as the awful truth burst upon us in one blinding, horrifying flash. From gaiety we went to black despair. This was just another of the death marches that our parents and grandparents had told us about. I looked at the strained, white faces about me. Yes, my fellow Armenians had also recognized the fate that awaited us. We were being led to our doom!

"'All around me my relatives and neighbors were now being beaten and robbed of their possessions. A group of cavalrymen seized Agavne, my twelve-year-old niece. Her clothes were ripped from her bleeding body as she was dragged away, screaming in terror, to a clump of bushes. We were forbidden to bury her ravished little body.

"'I looked about for a place to hide but suddenly I was grabbed by the hair and thrown to the ground. The few possessions that I had were taken from me. I could see the terrible lust in their faces. Shrieking, squirming, biting and clawing, I tried to escape. My terror only seemed to madden them. One of the Turks, perspiration standing out on his forehead like globules of oil, raised his axe. I closed my eyes in prayer as the hatchet descended. Although nearly unconscious I realized that my scalp was being torn from my head. Later I learned that I was not the only girl who had been scalped. This was a common procedure used by the Turks in their search for jewelry and gold which might be hidden in our hair. I do not know why I was not left to die with the rest. I made bandages with my petticoat, wrapped them around my mutilated head and stumbled on with the rest of my people.

"'On the eighth day of our march, with almost half of us dead of starvation, thirst, exhaustion and torture, we were halted just before noon. A Turkish officer ordered the few surviving males among us to step aside. Before we quite realized what was happening, the Turkish guards leaped upon them. Within twenty minutes every male over fifteen years of age was slaughtered—hacked to death. Sick at heart, numb in mind and body, we finally reached the banks of a broad river. Heaps of corpses were piled up on either side of the road. The carnage was indescribable. There was the traditional mark of the Moslem: hundreds of corpses mutilated—hands hacked off at the wrists; a foot missing; an arm or a leg chopped off; decapitated bodies by the dozen. Dully resigned, we awaited our imminent death. As the Turks closed in we sank to our knees and asked the Lord to bring us to Heaven with our menfolk.

"'Unarmed, utterly helpless, cowering in fright, we watched the Turks as they assembled our male children, from infants feeding at the breast, to boys of fifteen. Several women who struggled with the Turks were axed to the ground; they didn't have a chance. The children had their wrists bound behind them; a bullet was fired through their temples and then they were thrown into the Euphrates River. The little boys who had not yet died of their bullet wounds made great sport for the Turks. They shot at the bobbing heads until they disappeared. Some of the mothers among us went mad and were also murdered.

"'The death march fulfilled its intended function. Of the five hundred of us who started on the march, I am the only known survivor. Just before we reached our destination I managed to crawl, undetected, into the underbrush. Unlike the rest of our caravan who were slain down to the last man, woman and child, I was rescued by a band of kindly nomads and nursed back to health. When the Western armies invaded the Palestine area I was questioned by the intelligence staff of the Joint Allied Investigation Committee, and this statement is part of the sworn testimony given before that body.

>
> *Aroos Haloian*
> Paris, France
> December 5, 1918

(Acknowledged) *The Honorable Woodrow Wilson*
President of the United States
Washington, D.C.
February 15, 1919.'"

A stunned silence surrounded us as Dr. von Gorton sat down. Except for the Turks among the spectators, every face was a portrait in shock. Judge Lemberg's voice was strained as he broke the stillness. "The court wishes to examine the testimony and documents presented by the defense. We will therefore adjourn until Monday morning." He was pale as he gathered his robe about him and left the bench. I remember feeling a pang of sympathy for the jurist. The horror reflected in his manner was obviously intense. Yet it was but a glimmer as compared to the agony that had gripped my soul for so many years.

XIX. INTERMEZZO

The change of attitude, as mirrored in the press, was very heartwarming. I even noticed a new measure of respect among my jailers. Extra butter and coffee were brought to me, and the guards, who had once been cold and forbidding, now smiled and occasionally chatted with me when Kalousdian was present to translate. Even Chief Inspector Mandteufel visited me in my cell that weekend, bringing with him a supply of newspapers. He was still gruff but as he left he put a hand on my shoulder. "If I had known what you went through, Mr. Tehlirian," he said, half apologetically, "I would have acted differently when we first met. Good luck!"

Letters and cablegrams were arriving from all over the world; from close friends, from members of the Federation, and even from total strangers. As I read the many encouraging communications my heart brimmed with gratitude for their loyalty and concern. My darling Anahid's letter brought a mist to my eyes. Her faith in me had not wavered for an instant. She wrote cheerfully of the life we would have together and entreated me to face my ordeal unafraid. Every syllable sang of her love. I pressed the pages to my cheek, my loneliness overwhelming. She had enclosed in her letter a small gold medallion of St. Gregory the Illuminator, the founder of the Armenian Church.

Some of the letters contained personal accounts of suffering endured under the Turks—obviously written to bolster my case. These I turned over to Dr. von Gorton who, in turn, presented them to the court. Among the writers was Armenag Melik, who had been my schoolteacher in Erzinga. Writing from the United States, he told me of the 1915 massacre in which 20,000 unarmed, peaceful Armenians were wiped out in our city. As a captain in the Armenian Volunteer Forces, belatedly organized to fight off the rampaging Turks, Melik, who had lost his bride to the Turks, also verified the murder of my family in Erzinga and the gutting of our homes. His lovely wife, only twenty-two years old, was swept up into the arms of Turkish cavalrymen and abducted—he never saw her again. He ended his letter with a testimonial in my behalf.

It has been said that I did not receive the support of the Federation during my trial. Officially, the Federation could not very well figure in the case. Unofficially, however, many individual members supported me, as had Armenians throughout the world, by submitting documentary proof of the Turkish atrocities and contributing to a mutual fund used to retain my lawyers. One letter which figured importantly in my trial came from a faraway, but familiar city: Fresno, California. It was written by one of the pioneers of the Federation in America, Avak Zakar Avakian (the author's father), a man highly regarded by Armenians everywhere. It was this same Avakian who first informed Dr. Nazariantz of my mission.

Brother Avakian, who came from the city of Moush, touched on the massacres which began in 1894 and extended to 1896, under the direction of the beastly Sultan Hamid II. That slaughter, Avakian pointed out, had left the Armenians with 325,000 dead and an additional half-million exiled to all corners of the globe. Wrote Avakian in part:

"My earliest recollection of the Turkish abuse of the Armenians goes back to the year 1895 when I was thirteen years old. My father, Zakar, a cabinet maker, was returning home from his day's work when he and scores of other Armenians were seized by squads of Turkish soldiers. Desperately my father fought for his life. During the melee he received a severe knife wound in his left temple and he was left in the street for dead—but not before he had disarmed and killed one of them. I saw the entire incident. Together with neighbors we managed to bring my father home.

"The following months saw the burning of our homes and the wanton killing of our people. Before it was over the seventeen members of our immediate family had been reduced to a pitiful three. My mother, Shooshig, was gone; my aunts, uncles, nieces and cousins also murdered. We found refuge in *Sourp Garabed* —St. Charles Monastery—which we used as a fort. Alongside my father and the other adults, my younger brother, Dickran, and I also fought in defense of our lives. At the time of escape, except for small pockets of resistance such as ours, there were very few survivors in the city of Moush. It was a dark, starless night when my father led us to safety. We joined a caravan of refugees, many of them wounded and bleeding, and made our way to Jerusalem.

From there we journeyed to Egypt where we sailed to France and then on to our new home in America.

"My wife Surpoohi's family suffered as did mine. There were twenty-five in her family when the Turks attacked their home city of Bitlis. Although my wife was but a child, the terror of that night when the Turks swooped down on the households of her town remains a searing nightmare. The men fought valiantly to save their women and children from certain death. In the struggle many of the men lost their lives. Surpoohi's two older sisters, Lucy and Sophia, were set upon by the Turkish cavalrymen, savagely beaten, and then, abducted. Like many of the other girls in Bitlis, my wife's sisters were never to return.

"Surpoohi's family was in the textile business. Once the Turks had completed their first round of terror—and after confiscating all material goods—they burned the entire city. The devastation was nearly complete. This was repeated all over Bitlis and the surrounding villages: confiscation, pillage, rape and murder—and for no reason except that we were Christians.

"I write of these massacres, Soghomon, my brave brother-Armenian, in the event that you might need an eyewitness account. *Azvadtz coor haid ulah* —May God be with you.

Avak Zakar Avakian"

Next was a letter from a nineteen-year-old youth named Yeghishe Mekhitarian, later to represent the Armenian Apostolic Church as Prelate of North Africa and Southern Europe and then in America, where he lived in Fresno, California. His description, while typical of the many other atrocities I had seen or heard of, was signally poignant. He wrote:

"You do not know me, but my name is Yeghishe Mekhitarian, of Khanous, *villayet* of Moush. (Soghomon Tehlirian and Reverend-Father Mekhitarian were later to become intimate friends.) I am a student of theology at the Armenian Theological University at Jerusalem. I pray God, with all my heart, that this account of my experiences—added to the grace of our Saviour—will be of some help to you.

"I can attest to the villainy of Talaat during his ungodly reign of terror which began in 1915. At the time, I was a twelve-year-old choir boy under the ministry of Bishop Krikorees Balakian, who, according to the newspapers, is one of your witnesses.

(Father Mekhitarian later was ordained by Bishop Balakian, who was the lone survivor of the infamous massacre of three hundred civic leaders in Constantinople.) The Turks descended on our placid community on the night of June 15, 1915, after we had finished choir practice, and encircled our village. One by one they captured our leaders and hacked them to death, cutting the brains from their bodies. In two days, forty-three of my family were brutally murdered before my very eyes. It seems cold and indifferent to say 'my family was exterminated'—a family can be any size. But my loved ones who were slain included my father, my precious mother, my adored and adoring grandmother and grandfather, my uncles and aunts—all of my blood who were dear to me.

"Those who were not immediately killed were driven to Erzeroum, although some were taken elsewhere to their doom. The Turks were determined that we would not perpetuate our kind. Our babies were thrown into the Araxes River. The Turks ate like gluttons; we were forced to eat grass and wild berries. They allowed us no water and we suffered indescribable agonies. We stumbled along, our feet sore and bleeding, for about fifty miles when, thank our Lord, I escaped. Originally there were several thousand of us but nearly all died on the way. The few who reached their destination were herded into a church where they were burned alive, according to the native villagers who swore under oath that this massacre occurred.

"I was recaptured in Kharpert, where I was sold into slavery for three years. I witnessed three young Armenian girls being sold into slavery for seventy-five cents. (COMMENT: As late as 1963, slavery was practiced among the Moslems, particularly in Saudi Arabia.)

"Again I escaped, worked my way to Jerusalem where I am now studying for the priesthood.

"While the agonies which I experienced, the loss of my flesh and blood, the death marches and endless torture, may be typical of what many of our people have endured, I feel that it is important that you should know that wherever I went, the one name that always arose—the one individual considered responsible for the slaughter, was Talaat.

"As a man of God I cannot condone your taking a life, but as a human being I can understand the urge that prompted you to stop an evil man before he carried through his plans to commit further atrocities against our people and their neighbors. I saw with my own eyes the persecutions, the killings, burnings; it was an act against God. We pray that merciful justice will be done.

> In the Saviour's Name,
> *Yeghishe Mekhitarian*
> Armenian Theological Seminary
> Jerusalem."

There was another letter, authenticated by the Joint Allied Investigation Committee, which I knew would be valuable to Dr. von Gorton. Related by Arto DeMirjian, it gave evidence of the 1915 massacre. Said DeMirjian:

"I was a young man in the year 1915 when 10,000 Armenians were deported from our city of Kharpert. Men, women and children were marched in the blazing sun, surrounded by Turks armed to the teeth. For forty-five days we were herded across the scorched plains until we reached the Yeprod River. More than half of us, including my father and mother, died on the march because of the intense heat, starvation, thirst and the cruel beatings. Thousands of us were shot without reason or pity. I managed to escape with the help of a compassionate tribesman. Later I learned that nearly all of the captured Armenians who had reached the Yeprod River perished at the hands of the Turks.

"I hope, Mr. Tehlirian, that this painful recital will be of use to you in your trial. Somehow, I know that you will be freed soon.

> *Arto DeMirjian*
> New York, New York."

Carefully I folded the letters and replaced them in their envelopes, my heart heavy, although I was thankful for their statements. There were so many—and, I knew that there were thousands of my countrymen who had similar experiences to tell. I breathed a prayer and leaned back, too overwhelmed to read another letter that evening—when suddenly my eyes caught a letter addressed from a Father Alex Speropoulos, of the Greek Orthodox Church, of Smyrna. I opened the envelope. He wrote that he had eyewitnessed the murder of several Armenian priests and that he had seen the Turks destroy and burn to the ground two Armenian churches. He detailed the slaughter of nearly a hundred Greek women and children and two Jews. One Greek priest had been decapitated when he tried to help save an Armenian priest whom the Turks had set afire. The massacre had taken place in a village on the outskirts of Smyrna in 1916. Father Speropoulos explained briefly that he had been wounded in the melee but had miraculously escaped death. He concluded with a prayer for all of the victims of the massacre—Greeks, Armenians and Jews—and said that he would pray for my acquittal. His last words brought tears to my eyes: "Son, you are not only a hero to the Armenians but to the Greek people as well. Every Christian and civilized nation in the world will soon know you as their international hero. My blessings."

Again I was reliving those fearsome days when, as a soldier in the Armenian Volunteer Army, I, too, witnessed many of the Turkish depredations and killings. I was lost in morbid recollections when footsteps sounded in the corridor. In a moment, Gevork Kalousdian and Dr. von Gorton appeared at my cell door and were admitted by the jailer. When we had exchanged greetings, I indicated the mass of letters and telegrams on the table. "You'll find some of those quite interesting," I said to my lawyer, wearily.

Von Gorton's eyes widened. "You've read them all?"

I shook my head. "I don't think I can stand any more," I said. "I'll go through the rest this weekend."

Kalousdian extended a letter to me. "I have one more for you to read, Soghomon."

I waved it away. "Gevork, please, I'm too tired and depressed to read another word."

"Not for this you aren't," he smiled. "Go ahead and look at it." He thrust the letter into my hands.

On the back of the envelope was the sender's name and address. Suddenly my hands began to tremble as the name, inscribed in fine Armenian characters, leaped out at me:

Yeranouhi—*Yeranouhi Danielian!*

"Well aren't you going to open it?" Kalousdian asked while von Gorton studied the other correspondence.

My voice seemed to have gone hoarse. "If—if you don't mind, I'd prefer to read this alone."

Kalousdian laughed aloud. "We know when we're not wanted," said my Armenian friend. Von Gorton smiled and nodded agreement. "We'll be by tomorrow for further discussions. Meanwhile, Soghomon, good night to you."

I sank on my cot and slowly withdrew Yeranouhi's letter:

"My Dear Soghomon,

"Even though we have not seen each other for nearly two years, you are still very close to me. I have often regretted leaving you in Constantinople so abruptly. True, my life was in danger, but so was yours. I, too, had a mission—to work and fight for the cause that is so dear to us both—the liberation of our poor, captive Armenia.

"As you may know I am working as a teacher and also a free-lance writer. Additionally, I am associate editor of an Armenian weekly here on the West Coast. In this way I help carry out our militant program—through the printed and spoken word.

"I am sorry we did not meet when you were in Boston during your visit to Federation headquarters. Armen Garo wrote me a very sweet letter in which he explained that you wanted to come to California but that Federation plans made that impossible.

"The news of Talaat's punishment is in all the papers here and has made the front page of every Armenian newspaper, as well as many English language papers, in America. There is great rejoicing among us as this marks the first time that one of our persecuted people has struck back at anyone in such high authority as the vile Talaat. Naturally we understand that Talaat's death could not pay for the one-and-a-half million he murdered and those he planned to murder if he had lived. But, as you yourself once said, at least he can kill no more. Had you not punished this madman, God alone knows how many more of us would have met death at his hands.

"Federation agents have definite proof that he was planning another coup in Turkey. But even if he was successful we wonder if things could be worse than they are under the wicked and pitiless Kemal Pasha. The Federation is now in possession of undeniable evidence that Kemal has embarked on a massacre of the Greek people, remnant Armenians and other non-Islamic minorities. Oh, how long will the world allow these Moslems to continue killing their subjects and neighbors!!

"We are all praying that you will be acquitted. Already you have become a symbol not only of physical but of spiritual courage. You will forgive me, I know, for an editorial I wrote last week titled 'Soghomon Tehlirian—a Living Legend.'

"Have you heard from Anahid lately? You always used to talk of how lovely she was. Perhaps I should not mention my deep feelings at such a critical time in your life. My only excuse is that, while I may be a patriot, I am also a woman.

"Oh dear, I almost forgot. Enclosed is a check to help pay for your defense, a gift from the Armenian people of this area. (COMMENT: Yeranouhi's sister, Araxie, told this author that Yeranouhi had taken up no such collection. The check represented her entire personal savings.)

"You will not be able to see me but I will be standing beside you, soul and spirit, when the verdict is announced. Continue to trust in the love and mercy of Jesus, and know that you are under Divine protection.

"Someday soon, if it be the will of God, we shall meet again.

> Always,
> *Yeranouhi*"

The letter affected me deeply. She called me "courageous." But I did not feel heroic as I finished Yeranouhi's letter. I turned to my side and cried into my folded arms. I wept for Yeranouhi—yes, for all the Yeranouhis. She was like a hurt dove whose wings fluttered and beat against life's locked doors. But, why?—why did I cry? I do not know. Tiny, radiantly beautiful, determined, valiant little Yeranouhi—she possessed the pure heart of a child and the spirit of a heroine. Nervously I fumbled in my pockets for a cigarette, when instead, my fingers found the medallion. My thoughts swept over the miles. "Anahid—my sweet Anahid, where are you?" I was whispering, feeling an unyielding longing for her.

My sleep was enriched with visions of the two women who had made my life a song of loveliness. It started as a rapturous dream, focused on an altar where Anahid and I knelt before the smiling Archbishop Zaven whom I had known in Constantinople and Paris. I slipped the wedding ring on Anahid's finger, my heart bursting with happiness. I lifted her veil for the wedding kiss and bent over her.

I gasped. Yeranouhi's tear-stained face was turned up to me. With the swiftness that it had appeared, her face was gone and I stood alone—only the clouds above me.

("..........??")

I awoke in a cold sweat, feeling as though I had been asleep for a hundred years.

XX. TALAAT EXPOSED AS AUTHOR OF GENOCIDE

One cloudburst after another, punctuated by ear-splitting claps of thunder and zigzagging flashes of lightening, filled the usually balmy night. The appearance of the sudden storm upon Berlin was as unpredictable as my fate in the days ahead.

Now, on the morning of Monday, June 13, the driving sheets of rain finally slackened into a somewhat lighter but steady downpour. Inside the courtroom, rubbered and newspapered spectators fumbled with their umbrellas and raincoats, looking uncomfortable in their damp clothing. Judge Lemberg had just finished explaining his reason for accepting, as admissible evidence, the documents and letters which had been presented on the previous Friday.

In the witness box was Bishop Krikorees Balakian, whose diocese was centered in Constantinople. Beside him was my solicitous, ever-present interpreter, Kalousdian. I do not pretend to know how the astute Dr. von Gorton and his staff managed to find this Armenian Prelate. I remembered the Bishop well. Yeranouhi had once told me that he was the lone survivor of the top three hundred Armenian leaders of Constantinople who had been betrayed to Talaat by the renegade, Mugurditchian. I had settled accounts with that rogue. I was as eager and curious to hear the testimony of the next witness as anyone in the courtroom. Von Gorton, his manner respectful and his voice gentle, questioned the aging religious leader, *Yebiscopos* (Bishop) Krikorees Balakian, who was now on the witness stand. "Your Eminence, from the documents in my possession and which I shall introduce for the record, I understand that you were the only survivor of the infamous 'Constantinople Massacre'?"

"That is correct."

"Tell the court, your Reverence, of the circumstances of that incident."

"It was no mere incident, Dr. von Gorton, but a tragic loss to the Armenians, Christianity, Mankind; a blasphemy against our

Heavenly Father. There were three hundred of us in Constantinople who were striving to keep the Armenian culture, tradition and Christian heritage alive. Not only for our children and their children, but for all men throughout the world. But we were betrayed with the kiss of Judas."

"What do you mean?"

"We were betrayed by one of our own—a man named Mugurditchian, marked forever as a symbol of treachery—and for a few pieces of silver. It was he who played on the trust and affection of his own people. Zealously, this traitor and his Turkish associates compiled a list of three hundred of us; educators, teachers, doctors, engineers, poets, writers, clergymen—all leaders. May his soul be forgiven—he turned this list over to Talaat."

". . . And when Talaat got the list?"

"They were ... all killed." The response came slowly, sorrowfully.

"Bishop Balakian, you and all the other leaders were imprisoned together?"

"Yes—that is so."

"The three hundred—none of the others are alive today?"

"They were . . . murdered," the Bishop replied, his voice choking. "May their souls rest peacefully. I am the only one who survived the stabbings, shootings, axe killings; some of the writers and poets—they cut off their fingers; the priests—their tongues cut out so they—the Turks—said, 'You won't talk of Christ and Mary in the land of Allah' ... The victims are only dead physically; the spirit is very much alive. Today I am an old man. There will be a day when the grass will not be green, all over this world, and all the sheep will return to the green slopes of Ararat where the Armenian shepherd awaits the flock given to him from above. You'll see, more will die before the grass will no longer be green. Constantinople was only the beginning. There is—"

"—This massacre of the leaders, Bishop—you ascribe this to Mugurditchian?" von Gorton asked, interrupting the Bishop.

"No—no! The poor soul was a deluded tool."

"Who then! *Who!?*" my attorney stressed, trying to elicit a precise answer.

The Bishop nearly shouted his response. "There was only *one* man possessed with the evil genius necessary to manipulate these misguided souls—and for whatever purpose his ungodly mind conceived. The Devil incarnate—Talaat—*Talaat Pasha!*"

(COMMENT: Bishop Balakian's supplementary report, in

writing, revealed that the Moslem Turks branded many Armenians with the "Mark of the Cross," so that Christians could easily be identified. The "mark"—a cross about three-quarters of an inch—was inscribed on the mocked person's forehead, cheek, temple, arm, wrist or hand, often at the base of the thumb. Usually, three methods were used to mark Christians: One, blue tattoo; Two, burned into the skin surface; Three, carved into the skin surface. Even decades later, many of the Genocide survivors bear proof of Talaat's Islamic hatred of Christianity. Bishop Balakian listed methods used by the Turks when plundering churches. For example: gold was scraped from Bibles, parchments, crosses and many other such valuable possessions of the Church.)

* * * * * * * * *

I was breathing again: neither Bishop Balakian or von Gorton had involved me with the traitor, Mugurditchian. Later, Kalousdian assured me that it would have made no difference because it would not have been admissible.

Quickly my attention went to General Liman von Sanders, who was the next witness to take the stand. A forceful-looking man in his early sixties, he was well over six feet tall, with piercing blue eyes, a waxed mustache and a healthy head of silvering hair, which was parted in the middle. His posture was ramrod stiff, a stereotype of the Prussian military elite, and, as testimony revealed, he could well boast of an action-filled background.

I first learned about the German general from Dr. von Gorton when he and Kalousdian visited me Sunday in my cell. It was General von Sanders whom the Kaiser had appointed as chief of Germany's military delegation to Constantinople in 1913, with strict orders to reorganize the Turkish Army. It was clear, even then, that prior to hostilities, Germany and Turkey had decided upon war against the Allies. General von Sanders, I had been warned, although one of my witnesses, was blindly loyal to Germany's military system and he might be expected to deny Germany's involvement in the massacres; even to the extent of defending the "Young Turk" leaders who were his confederates during the war. This information caused me a few hours of anxiety. But Dr. von Gorton, smiling thinly, assured me that he would extract from the General whatever information we needed.

"You can't get blood out of a turnip," I muttered. My lawyer grinned at my use of the English proverb, then replied, "Some turnips are oranges but don't know it."

I had cause to remember Dr. von Gorton's words as he approached the witness box, confronting the erect General von Sanders. My lawyer's voice was low and even: "I assume, General, that because of your tenure in Turkey you have knowledge of the massacres of the Armenian people. Is my assumption correct?"

"Your assumption, *Herr* von Gorton, is, let us say, partially correct. The massacres are an established fact. But there is some question that the leaders of the Turkish hierarchy—the Government, if you prefer—can be implicated in those atrocities."

"That is a surprising statement, General. Will you be kind enough to explain?"

"Yes, of course. Before the war, Turkey possessed an excellent police force—85,000 well-trained and well-disciplined men. But, eventually they were absorbed into the regular army. The auxiliary police force that replaced the regulars was comprised mostly of Turkish misfits, opportunists and criminals. Obviously, disciplining these men was an almost impossible task. Therefore, it is my belief that the illegal acts were committed by those of the substitute police and not the regular Turkish soldiers. It is also my belief that these atrocities were probably not intended by the Turkish Government but were committed by the irresponsible underlings in the auxiliary police force—on their own initiative."

"Now, General, as one of Germany's finest military men, among the best ever to graduate from the Prussian Military College, your sense of observation must be extremely keen. Did it not occur to you that many of the atrocious acts were committed, not by the police alone, but by soldiers of the regular army?"

"Yes—possibly."

"That remains to be determined. Now then, did you also not take into consideration that there were others equally as guilty?"

"I do not quite follow you, *Herr* von Gorton."

"I will be explicit. The facts are these: the army and the police committed wholesale, unprovoked murder upon this Christian minority, but!—it was the Turkish people—let me repeat, Sir, the average Turkish people—*citizens*—who joined the massacres with the overt and often active approval of the authorities. You yourself have stated that Turkey's militia was well-disciplined, proving even further that rigid authority did, in fact, exist. Surely you will agree that under such strict authority, neither the citizenry, the armed forces, nor the police could have engaged in the bloody killings unless the Government itself was involved. You are a military man, General von Sanders. If your troops were to murder innocent, defenseless people with whom you were not even at war—and in this case civil war—you would either have them court-martialed or else admit that the acts were perpetrated with your direct connivance or your tacit approval—if not by your direct order."

"That is true, *Herr* von Gorton. As a Commander I am responsible for the actions of my subordinates."

"Thank you, General. I only sought to draw a parallel. The *precise* situation existed in Turkey. As the supreme authority, the Turkish Government must be held accountable for the crimes?"

"Stated that way, Sir, the chain of command is clear. Subordinates cannot and do not make policy." General von Sanders paused briefly, then resumed speaking. "I—I wish to revise my earlier estimation. Militarily speaking, it was the Turkish Government that, as an official policy of State, sought to exterminate the Christians of Armenian extraction."

"Precisely, General von Sanders," said von Gorton, bowing slightly. "May I compliment you on your candor. It is not everyone who would reverse himself with such sincerity. However, you brought up a point that interests me and which I am sure will interest the court. I refer to your mention of the Christian minority. Will you elaborate, please?"

"Certainly. It must be understood that the Turks were partially imbued with the idea of a *Jehad* —a holy war. The Armenians, among the earliest and most devout Christians on earth, were a prime target for the Turkish people who were conditioned to believe that treating them harshly was religiously sanctioned according to the Islamic faith."

"Agreed. I notice, however, that you say the Turks were only partially affected by religious fanaticism. Were there other reasons?"

"Yes, there were. First, let me explain the official Turkish view which their propagandists circulated throughout the world: that the Armenian minority was planning a revolt against the Government in order to set up a homeland for themselves. The administration cautiously explained to the outside world that, as a consequence, it was forced to use stern, repressive measures to quell what they termed an incipient revolt. However, this was but an excuse, a subterfuge to camouflage the real reasons for the massacres. I have mentioned religious fanaticism but there was another reason—a purely materialistic one."

". . . And that was?"

"Wherever and whenever the mass murders occurred there was invariably, without exception, the companion motive of greed. Killings were always followed by, or in conjunction with, the looting, the plunder, the robbery of all earthly possessions of their victims. To attribute any overriding idealistic motive for the massacres is impossible in the face of what really happened to the persecuted Armenians."

"Exactly!" von Gorton agreed. "Now, tell us, General, how long a period did you spend in Turkey?"

"I was stationed in Turkey for five years, from 1913 to 1918."

"Then you were there long enough to determine the extent of the massacres?"

"Yes."

"In your pre-trial deposition, General, you stated that you were assigned to reorganize the Turkish Army at the request of the Kaiser. Actually you were a liaison officer for the German Government and your primary function was to prepare the Turks for eventual warfare as your ally. Is that not correct?"

"Well—I would say so. Yes."

"Tell me, Sir, did you ever accept a position in the Turkish Army?"

"I did. It was Enver Pasha, the Minister of War, who appointed me to the position of Inspector-General of the Turkish Army. My appointment was made at the direct request of Enver's political superior, Talaat Pasha, who, it was quite obvious, was seeking the future support of Germany for his own ambitions."

"Very well, General. I have asked these questions for a definite purpose. What I want to know is whether, in your high position as Inspector-General, you were aware of the atrocities committed by members of Turkey's armed forces and others?"

"Of course, I was aware. It was my business to know what was happening in my command."

"I am sure you did not approve," von Gorton asserted.

"Certainly not! At first, Ambassador Baron von Waggenheim would not intercede for the Armenians. After his death in October, 1915, Ambassador Wolf-Metternich and I protested strongly on several occasions but we were curtly informed that we, as Germans, had no business interfering in Turkish internal affairs. I might add, *Herr* von Gorton, I did not feel then, nor do I now, that the mass-murder of a race is an internal affair. The offending party should be punished by organized society. Turkey claimed that it was engaged in an unofficial war against the Armenians. I use the word 'unofficial' because the Armenain people were subjects of the Turkish Government and a State cannot make war on its own citizens. Officially, however, the Islamic political forces within Turkey had declared a war to the death against this Christian minority. Some of the Turks, at any rate, cannot be excused from punishment under international law."

"Some of them, General? Are not the assassins all equally guilty?"

"Morally, yes. But as an officer of the military I can only say that under international military code—I refer to the Hague Conference of 1899 and 1907—most civilians and noncommissioned officers may be guilty of crimes under their own domestic laws, but not according to international law. They committed crimes against the Armenian people but we must assume that they were ignorant of the fact that they were breaking the law established by the nations of the world at the Hague and at Geneva. However, we do know that commissioned officers, especially those of higher rank, realize that they are breaking the established international laws of humanity; that by participating in the massacres they are self-branded war criminals and subject to punishment by whoever obtains jurisdiction over their persons. There were many such criminals—war criminals, if you please."

"In your capacity as Inspector-General of the Turkish Army," von Gorton said deliberately, "tell the court please—what man would be considered the chief war criminal according to international law—the one man who issued orders for the mass murders?"

"Talaat!"

Von Gorton executed his formal bow, bending stiffly at the waist. "You are excused, General, and thank you."

"He is *not* excused!" Judge Lemberg barked. "This court will excuse the witness and all other witnesses whenever necessary. I am sure, *Herr* von Gorton, that when you attended law school you were taught about a procedure called cross-examination. I'm reasonably certain you have a passing knowledge of the term. Is that not true?"

Von Gorton, his face livid with humiliation, mumbled something and sat down.

"*Herr* von Gorton," the tyrannical little judge cried, "I asked you a question. Please be good enough to answer so that all of us will be enlightened by your answer. You will also stand up when you address the court. Now then, have you or have you not heard of the technique, cross-examination?"

"I have, your Honor," von Gorton said, his voice strangled.

Judge Lemberg nodded to Kolnig. "Does the prosecution wish to cross-examine?"

"Yes, your Honor," Kolnig answered, grinning at von Gorton's discomfiture. He rose to face the bench.

"Very well, *Herr* Kolnig, but before you proceed, I suggest you erase that silly smirk from your face or I will have something to say to you in my chambers."

Kolnig sobered immediately. (COMMENT: Once, during their student days at Berlin Law School, he and von Gorton had hanged Lemberg in effigy. In his memoirs, Kolnig wrote: "Now, in the courtroom, I experienced a fleeting wish that von Gorton and I had done away with the irascible old curmudgeon in actuality.")

"General von Sanders," Kolnig began, "you started your testimony by saying that you did not believe that the Turkish Government was responsible for the atrocities, did you not?"

"Yes, but . . ."

"Well, Talaat Pasha was a leader of that government. So, by your own admission, he was not responsible for the alleged crimes against the Armenians."

"If my memory serves me correctly, Sir, I reversed my original opinion. I testified at first that it was the underlings who committed the unsanctioned acts, but in light of the testimony given during the trial, I am convinced now that soldiers and petty officers cannot continue such crimes without the knowledge and approval of their commanding officers."

"It is very strange that a man of your perception and recognized ability could command an army for so long and rest content in the knowledge that they were well disciplined—and then, within a few minutes, suddenly reverse all those years of thinking. Come, General, is that what you want us to believe?"

"What we are discussing here is political, moral and legal. My business concerns only the military. As a career officer I have no apologies to make for strengthening Turkey, our wartime ally. As to other considerations, I believe *Herr* von Gorton is correct."

"Oh, so you *believe* he is correct? I ask you, General, have you ever witnessed a massacre of Armenian people?"

"Well—no, I have not."

"Tell the court, please, have you ever seen one single Armenian citizen persecuted, let alone killed?"

"No, but I knew what was happening. It was my duty as Inspector-General of the Turkish Army to know what was on—"

"—Just a moment, Sir!" Kolnig interrupted. "I do not imply, and I most certainly don't want you to infer that your truthfulness is being questioned, but you can't expect the jury to believe anything other than that you are grossly mistaken, or, at the very least, confused in your beliefs. Let me sum up your testimony, General: **One,** you said that you held long-standing convictions that it was Turkish underlings who committed the atrocities. But with just a few select words from *Herr* von Gorton, you conveniently changed your mind and accused Talaat. *Two,* you claimed that as a commanding officer it was your job to know what was going on within the lesser military ranks, yet all you are able to verify are rumors—hearsay evidence, which is not acceptable in any court. **Third,** you have never personally seen an Armenian injured, yet you apparently expect this court to believe that the Armenian people were oppressed—persecuted. I can only say, Sir, you seem unusually unaware of the activities of those under your command."

"I am a military administrator, *Herr* Kolnig," the General replied indignantly, "an officer of the General Staff, a graduate of the most reputable military college in the world; I have been honored many times for service to my country—I am not a petty snoop! Every military establishment has its Intelligence Service and their reports are usually accepted. The Intelligence reports confirm that Minister of Interior Talaat was the chief director of the massacres. It was he—"

"—I must again interrupt you, General. You do not know these things of your own experience. Intelligence Corps or *not!* —your testimony is merely hearsay and not acceptable."

Prosecutor Kolnig turned to the bench. "I ask that the Tribunal disqualify this witness."

"The Defense," von Gorton interjected, before Judge Lemberg could speak, "maintains that the General is not only qualified but is one of our expert witnesses. General von Sanders depends upon the reliability of this court. Our national administration may not have first-hand knowledge of what we say and do here, but it accepts the decisions made by this court because of the authority vested in it. By the same token we must accept the statements made by General von Sanders' Intelligence staff."

Judge Lemberg glared. "All right. Nobody asked for a lesson in civics. The court recognizes the General as a qualified witness and accepts the reports given to him by his Intelligence officers."

Von Gorton thanked him and then said, "Your Honor, I have a dozen documents which I now introduce to support the General's statements that Talaat was the master-mind who deliberately set out to annihilate a nation of people."

"What kind of documents?"

"They are telegrams, Sir, sent by Talaat to various officials, ordering wholesale murders. If it please the court, I would like to read six of them into the record. Five of these were dispatched to all commanding officers of the Turkish Army and regional authorities through the office of the Governor of Aleppo, and the sixth directly to those authorities."

"You may read them."

Von Gorton's voice was clipped, clear and concise as he identified and read the decoded, cabled messages:

ORDER #630
June 20, 1915

It was communicated to you, on April 15 of this year, that the Government, by order of the Committee of Union and Progress, commands you to destroy completely, all Armenians living in Turkey.

I further order that all who oppose this decision must be instantly removed from the official staff of the Empire. An immediate end must be put to the existence of the Armenians, however severe the measures taken may be, and no regard must be paid to their age or sex.

Talaat Pasha
Minister of Interior
Constantinople

ORDER #637
August 6, 1915

Collect and keep only those Armenian orphans who are too young to remember the circumstances surrounding the deaths of their parents. Abandon the older children in the desert or send them to the Euphrates River with the caravans of adults.

> *Talaat Pasha*
> Minister of Interior
> Constantinople

ORDER #642
September 21, 1915

My order # 637 is rescinded. This is not the time to give way to sentiment. Send all children, whether or not they remember their parents, to the deserts and rivers and inform me when these future enemies of our Empire have been liquidated.

> *Talaat Pasha*
> Minister of Interior
> Constantinople

ORDER #691
November 23, 1915

Destroy by secret means all escaping Armenians of the Eastern Provinces who attempt to pass through your territory.

> *Talaat Pasha*
> Minister of Interior
> Constantinople

ORDER #748
December 1, 1915

Despite the known necessity to dispose of the known Armenian clergy, I am informed that some have been permitted to emigrate to Syria and Jerusalem. Such permission is unpardonable. The only place of exile for such seditious Christians is the grave. I order you to act accordingly.

> *Talaat Pasha*
> Minister of Interior
> Constantinople

ORDER #867
February 15, 1916
General Field Headquarters

To All Commanding Officers:

In order to eliminate the dissident Armenian minority, the Imperial Government hereby orders the extermination of all those remaining within the Turkish Empire. The following directives are to be strictly observed:

1—All Armenians, regardless of age or sex, are to be escorted to secluded areas and disposed of immediately.

2—All Armenians remaining in the Imperial Armies are to be separated from their divisions without creating disturbances. They are to be taken away from the public eye and shot as traitors in our ranks.

Enver Pasha
Minister of War

By order of:
Talaat Pasha
Minister of Interior
Constantinople

Von Gorton packaged the six telegrams he had just finished reading and handed them up to Judge Lemberg, along with another sheaf of incriminating documents.
"Has the prosecution studied these telegrams and other papers?" Judge Lemberg inquired.
"We have, your Honor," Kolnig announced.
"In that case, I direct the clerk to mark them with their respective exhibit numbers." He glanced at the big clock. "This Tribunal has a great deal of evidence to study. We will therefore adjourn court until tomorrow morning."
As far as I was concerned, tomorrow, Tuesday, June 14, was the one day of the trial which held the most significance for me. It was clear that Adolf von Gorton was satisfied with the progress of the case. It was equally clear that Heinrich Kolnig was growing

more apprehensive. The telegrams and other documents that Talaat had signed with his own blood-stained hand were enough in themselves to convince even the most skeptical that he was the chief architect of the plan to annihilate my people down to the last nursing infant.

But as the trial progressed I grew increasingly uneasy. It seemed to me that von Gorton was beclouding what I considered an honorable act—my execution of Talaat—in the fogs and mists of legalistic subterfuges. In my cell I had insisted several times that my lawyer call me to the witness stand so that I might remind the world, a world that had apparently forgotten that the Armenian people—who had adopted Christianity sixteen hundred and twenty years ago—had been persecuted to the brink of extinction. There was also another, vital reason. If my act was to be respected as a symbol of retributive justice, it could not—it *must* not be hidden behind legal maneuverings. Compulsion? I know little of the language of psychology but I knew then, and I know now, that there was more to it than that.

During his evening visits von Gorton had flatly refused to allow me to appear as a witness in my own defense. At first I acceded, yielding each time he would promise to openly justify in court the real reason that led to Talaat's execution. He had not done so; at least to my satisfaction. There was only one more witness to be heard from: Shia Bey, Secretary of the Turkish Embassy in Berlin. I was determined that I would take the stand. Von Gorton would no longer deny me this one last opportunity.

Tonight, when he and Kalousdian came to my cell to discus the last day of testimony, we would have it out—once and for all!

XXI. I DEMAND TO TESTIFY

A beam of moonlight penetrated the small, barred window of my cell. It was seven in the evening and I had just finished what the prison guards jocularly called "dinner" when suddenly my old interrogator, Chief Inspector Mandteufel, together with my interpreter, appeared outside my cell. The door was unlocked by a guard and they entered. I nodded a hello to Kalousdian and looked up inquiringly at the inspector from where I was lying on the bunk. But this was not the police officer I had known; he was Mandteufel the man. He punched me playfully on the shoulders, his manner friendly, reminding me of an affectionate St. Bernard. I was not surprised; his attitude had grown increasingly cordial.

"Hello, Soghomon, remember me?" Mandteufel asked, grinning.

"I'm not likely to forget."

"*Ackh*, I'm not as bad as all that," he said, extending a huge palm.

We shook hands, smiling at each other like a couple of schoolboys. "You have a visitor," Mandteufel said.

"Who?"

"Your attorney, *Herr* von Gorton. He's waiting for you in my office."

My surprise was evident. "We've always conferred here in my cell. Why the change?" Kalousdian translated rapidly.

"Well . . . " he paused, embarrassed, "I thought you'd like to have a conference room rather than *this*." He indicated my cell with a disdainful sweep of his arm. Ignoring my pleased expression of appreciation, he escorted me to his office and, with a pleasant comment, left me at the door.

Von Gorton greeted me warmly as Kalousdian handed me a letter. It was from my angel, Anahid. (I read and re-read the letter later that night; her devotion shining between every line like a lustrous pearl. God, I loved her!)

My cigarette and von Gorton's cigar were glowing when he abruptly came to the point: "You knew, of course, that the Turkish

Secretary in the Berlin Embassy, Shia Bey, was scheduled to testify tomorrow." It was as much an assertion as a question. (COMMENT: Shia Bey was the official who had obtained Talaat's lair and suggested Talaat's alias, Ali Salieh Bey.)

"*Was?* He's going to be on the witness stand, isn't he?"

Von Gorton shook his head. "We don't know. He sent word to Dr. Kolnig just a few hours ago that he wasn't certain whether he would testify at all."

"Why not?"

"He claims illness."

"I don't believe it!" I blurted out.

"Neither do I," von Gorton agreed. "I don't think Kolnig does either. He's tried on several occasions to see Secretary Shia Bey, but each time he was told he is too ill to receive visitors. I think the Turks want as little as possible to do with this trial. They simply can't afford the notoriety. Kolnig and I talked it over at dinner and he confessed that he was doubtful of Shia Bey's appearance ever since he was first contacted. When you realize that Turkey's present leader, Kemal Pasha, was a former 'Young Turk,' there's little wonder that he refused to have Talaat's body returned to Turkey for burial. (COMMENT: Talaat's remains, in Berlin for nearly four decades, were returned to Istanbul in 1957 and re-interred in Ankara following an elaborate ceremony with full national honors.) They're anxious to avoid involvement in the case; unless it's completely to their advantage internationally. I believe, and this is just an educated guess, that Kemal will order Shia Bey not to testify, or else! And, if he hasn't already, he'll recall him to Turkey. The Turks are up to something, you can be sure of that."

I knew perfectly well what that "or else" meant and I could not honestly say that I would blame Shia Bey if he did obey Kemal's order; if von Gorton's assumptions were true. Von Gorton assured me of two things: either we would win a point, if Shia failed to appear, or, stand to lose one if he did. The prosecution, he said, was in dire need of a witness to support the Turkish viewpoint—at this point of the proceedings. Whatever would happen tomorrow, I had decided on the course of action I was determined to pursue.

"Dr. von Gorton," I began, plunging to the heart of my argument, "I insist that I testify in my own behalf. Tomorrow, Tuesday, is the last opportunity I'll have to defend myself in my own words. You yourself said that you and Kolnig expected to present your summations tomorrow. Thereafter everything will be in the hands of the jury."

"Are you still trying to vindicate your honor and integrity?" von Gorton asked testily.

"Hell no!" I snapped. "Not mine alone; the honor and integrity of the Armenian people—and, all people who have died for Christianity. The world has already forgotten that a million-and-a-half innocent human beings were slaughtered. To me, this trial is important only if it reminds people everywhere of what happened. It must teach some kind of lesson—that vigilance is the only kind of security they can rely on. If there is no lesson learned from this trial, then Talaat's execution was meaningless—and when? When in the days and years ahead will rise another Talaat? How many innocents will again be slaughtered?"

"Well now, Soghomon, that's a mighty pretty speech—and admirable. But I'm a lawyer, not a statesman. I was not retained to espouse Armenian patriotism or teach lessons to the world. Frankly, while I deplore the Turkish atrocities, right now I don't give a *damn* about the massacres of the Armenian people."

"Now look here . . . !"

"No, *you* look here, *Son!* You take your plan to try war criminals to Geneva—if you come out of this alive. I have one job to do—and that's to keep Soghomon Tehlirian's neck out of a noose. For your information, it's your neck I'm talking about. Don't think for a minute that the jury will acquit you only because the Turkish Government committed mass-murder. Sure they'll have compassion for the slain, but you can bet your life—and I don't intend to gamble on that bet—that Judge Lemberg will instruct the jury to stick to the facts in the case."

"But you can't separate the massacres from this case!" I protested hotly.

Von Gorton lifted a quizzical eyebrow. "I can't? Soghomon, I not only can but I will—*I must.* Now don't misunderstand me; I'll discuss the massacres in my summation. Not so much because I expect to arouse sympathy from the jury but because I want it to serve as a reminder that the atrocities are relevant to the plea of compulsion. If they understand more than that, all the better. Right now it's you I'm concerned about."

"All right, I don't care how you manage it, just so I have a chance to tell the story *myself,*" I persisted stubbornly.

"Your life is in jeopardy; this is no time to talk about the Turkish crimes. We aren't even sure that the plea of compulsion will be successful. There's one more thing I want to discuss with you." Von Gorton relit his cigar, puffed once or twice and then continued. "I haven't been ignoring your request to take the stand. In fact, I discussed that very question with my colleagues, Wertenhauer and Niemeyer. We all agreed it wouldn't be wise—you've already made your point. Don't underestimate Kolnig. He's a clever prosecutor and wily as a fox. He may seem vaguely sympathetic toward the Armenians at times, but don't think he'll lessen his attack. He's an ambitious man. It's common knowledge that he has his eye on a judgeship; some say he may even be our next mayor. Politically he can't afford to lose this case and he knows it."

"I've *got* to take the stand in my own defense."

"If you do," von Gorton warned, "it's quite likely you'll nullify our strategy. You'd be exposing yourself to Kolnig. Right now he's desperate and he'll try anything to convince that jury that it *was* politics, not compulsion, that led you to shoot Talaat. You can be sure that he'll demand the death penalty for political murder."

Kalousdian lit my cigarette. "He's right," Kalousdian said kindly. "I understand your reasons; the Turks murdered my family, too."

"There's no alternative," I protested doggedly.

Von Gorton flicked a cigar ash on Mandteufel's new carpet, ignoring the cuspidor at his feet. "There is. If the jury seems inclined to favor Kolnig's plea for political assassination, I might make a deal with him so that we can change our plea from compulsion to insanity."

For a few moments his words made no impression on me; he was simply explaining the boggling complexities of the case. Then, slowly, his meaning became clear and his words ran together like a drum roll of disaster, sounding and echoing in my brain.

Kalousdian placed his hand over my tightly clenched fist. "*Antardeh, Soagomoan* —Easy, Soghomon," he urged firmly.

Von Gorton spoke before I could compose myself to answer. "I can see that you're distressed, young man—I don't blame you. It's better than going to the gallows."

I pounded my fist on the table. "Insanity!?" I blurted, finally regaining my voice. "You want the world to think I'm insane? Do you realize what a plea like that would mean?"

"It could mean that your chances to escape conviction as a

political murderer would be considerably improved."

"I'm not insane! It *wasn't* a political murder—it was an execution!" I yelled. "How the hell can you sit there so calmly and suggest I spend the rest of my life in an asylum?"

"It wouldn't be for the rest of your life. In all probability you'd be committed to an institution for a few years and then released—a free man."

"How many are a *few years?*" I asked sarcastically. "Five? Ten? Twenty?"

"It could be any number. But we'd be working for your release all the time," he said soothingly.

My voice was cold. "No doubt you expect my fiance, Anahid, to wait twenty years for me; to marry an old man just released from an asylum—a man whose only defense was that he was criminally insane?"

"You don't understand . . . "

"I understand one thing: if I plead insanity, then my act will have no purpose. The judgment will defeat every principle that has meaning for me. I said this before and I say it again, Dr. von Gorton, and don't tell me I'm making a speech: for six hundred years the Turks have been murdering my people for no reason than they were Christians. Just six years ago they butchered eighty percent of us in cold blood, drove 350,000 survivors from our 4,000-year-old homeland, robbed us of our country. Out of the ashes of that Islamic-created hell, we fought back as they advanced on our place of refuge in the Caucasus. By the grace of God, we defeated them and founded our own Republic, the only true democracy in the Middle East. Seven months ago the Turks conspired with the Russian Bolsheviks and the slaughters began all over again. The Russian Bolsheviks conquered our two-year-old country and gave land to Turkey as a reward. But—we would have never lost our ancient homeland in the first place if it hadn't been for one man who conceived and was responsible for the 1915 Massacre—*Talaat!*"

I smashed my cigarette in the ash tray. "Yes, I executed him! I killed that evil bastard! I shot him as a warning to his followers and any future mass-murderers. I wanted to remind the world that they did nothing to arrest these criminals; to get them to remember the Turkish crimes. Then, someday they might even enact laws to deter others from imitating Talaat in the future—maybe. I shot him so that people everywhere would realize that there's a lesson to be learned: no man can murder an entire nation of people—the first Christians—and escape mortal judgment. Talaat fled Turkey three years ago—yet Armenians were still being killed. He planned to kill more. You think it was a pleasure to kill Talaat? Oh, no. That was a filthy job—like tangling with an octopus with leprosy. If what I had to do was political murder, then I'm guilty—but I'm not insane! An insane man cannot exact retribution; he *cannot* administer justice. They said only the State can execute a criminal—why didn't they execute Talaat? Talaat's death *must not*—for God's sake, *cannot* be dismissed as an assault by a madman. Sure, I want to live, but not by degrading my people; Christianity itself. I'm not insane; nor was I when I executed Talaat."

There were tears in Gevork Kalousdian's eyes; tears of pride, perhaps—and personal affection only an Armenian can sense—a feeling of kinship genuine Christians experience but find difficult to put into words. He put an arm about my shoulder; unable to speak. Von Gorton arose from his chair and walked to the window. The silence was acute. At length the lawyer squared his shoulders and turned to me.

"Soghomon," he said huskily, "I'm tired—tired of listening to what every man on earth should be hearing and doing something about. I guess I never really understood—never understood you or what happened to your people; right now—I just *think* I do. I respect you; more than any client I have ever represented." He faltered for a moment and then continued with a brusqueness I knew he did not feel. "All right, forget the insanity plea. I'll not forget the lesson you want to teach—it may never go beyond the courtroom. One thing: I insist you do not take the stand, Soghomon. In my summation I'll hold a lighted torch over the Turkish atrocities just as you yourself would if you were testifying. Not that you insist—but because I *want* to!"

I pressed his hand in mine. "*Azvadtz kez ortneh*—God bless you," I whispered fervently.

XXII. PROSECUTION AND DEFENSE REST

Tuesday, June 14, 1921.

Every seat in the Palace of Justice was occupied. Reporters from every major news media in the world were in the section reserved for journalists. Also represented were members of "Reuters," the British telegraphic news outlet; the Associated Press, and the United Press; the latter agency having just invaded the European market that year.

There were many familiar faces among the spectators. My friends dotted the audience as thickly as stars in an Armenian summer sky and were just as pleasant to behold. In the fifth row, much to my surprise, was my old friend, *Bahbig,* who I learned later, had been attending the proceedings unnoticed. I remember murmuring a quiet prayer that the tempestuous, fervently patriotic old man would not disrupt the hearings as he had done almost two weeks ago when he unfurled the Armenian flag in the courtroom. I was gratified to see the alert features of the dynamic statesman, Dr. Libarid Nazariantz, whose inspiring speech just a few months ago had galvanized me into the last spurt of energy I needed to satisfy my vow.

Suddenly my attention was drawn to Dr. Kolnig. Seated ramrod-stiff at his side was a Turkish Army officer with the crown of arrogance—a blazing red fez—carefully placed on one knee. "Shia Bey, the Embassy Secretary, of course," I assumed. He wore a winged mustache and he had that chalky expression that lacked human warmth—typical of the military of that nation of butchers. Von Gorton hurried a whisper, "He's not Shia Bey—but he'll be just as difficult to handle."

Judge Lemberg launched the court session with an ear-splitting crash from his gavel, and instructed Dr. Kolnig to begin.

"Your Honors," Kolnig said, "as I have informed you, Secretary Shia Bey of the Turkish Embassy here in Berlin is ill. I would like at this time to call his replacement to the stand, if I may."

"What are his qualifications?" Lemberg asked.

"He is the chief aide to Secretary Shia Bey—well qualified,

your Honor."

After a series of verbal exchanges between von Gorton and Kolnig, the Turkish officer was sworn in. Von Gorton worried me; he had not persevered.

Fez in hand, the Turkish officer marched to the bench, clicked heels and executed a bow, sweeping the *tarboosh* across his knees. Slightly concerned about the officer's over-courteous behavior, Judge Lemberg glared at him over the rim of his glasses. The officer executed an about-face, two heel clicks and two bows— once to the jury and then to the audience.

"Sir," Kolnig asked, "would you please give the court your name, rank and position of authority?"

"Major Djami, chief aide to Secretary Shia Bey of the Turkish Embassy in Berlin. The Secretary regrets that he is unable to appear; his illness has even become the concern of his excellency, Kemal Pasha. Secretary Shia Bey is now in Constantinople to be examined and treated by Turkish specialists—we have the world's finest, you know."

"I see. I will make my questions brief. Now then, Major, having served as a commanding officer in the Turkish Army in Asia Minor and throughout the Middle East, have you ever heard of Armenians being mistreated?"

"Sir, I know nothing of these rumors. I do know that Armenians have always received preferential treatment in our country. However, I do have a telegram from Secretary Shia Bey which I have been instructed to read."

"Your Honor," Kolnig requested, "may the witness read the telegram?"

"He may," Lemberg replied.

"As I have said, Secretary Shia has been quite ill—uh, even His Excellency, Kemal Pasha, is concerned." Now the Major stood up to read. "'Dr. Heinrich Kolnig: I regret that I am unable to be present at the trial of the assassin of our beloved former Prime Minister, Talaat Pasha; to observe German justice in action; to hear the verdict and watch the Armenian marched to the gallows. The entire world shares our grief and mourns the death of a great statesman and humanitarian—Talaat Pasha. I know that you will inform the court—the world—of the sufferings of the Turkish people at the hands of the seditious Armenians. Mankind was robbed of Talaat's genius; his compassion—his tolerance of all people and their religion.

"'He was born in Edirne, in 1874, to poor parents who

nurtured him to adulthood with deep love and affection, traditional of Turkish family life. His parents endured many sacrifices to send their son to the law school at Salonika. He served his country, his people and Islam with devotion and self-sacrifice. In 1908 he instituted a constitution which guaranteed rights to all subjects; especially the Christians. He represented Edirne as a Member of Parliament and soon became Deputy Speaker. In 1909 he was appointed Minister of Interior by the glorious *Ittihad-Terraki* Committee. In 1916 Talaat Pasha became Prime Minister of Turkey—a well-earned reward for his efforts during the struggle for national survival, when the Allied aggressors threatened to destroy Turkey and the precious land of our ally, Germany.

"'Even after assuming the highest office of the land, he remained humble. He lived in a modest home along the back streets of the old section in Constantinople; shunning public acclaim; though he deserved it the most.

"'It is ironic that Talaat Pasha, who loved the Armenians and respected their Christian beliefs, should be shot down in cold blood in peaceful Berlin, as though he were a beast. Concerned for the safety of Armenian men, women and children, he transferred them to new communities, away from the danger zones. He provided them with a police and military escort—issued food, finances and supplies. They traveled in comfort and, en route, Turkish villagers met them at the crossroads to assist them in any way possible.

"'But the Armenians deceived him; became traitorous to the nation who had helped them in earnest. They launched a program of shame: massacring Turkish men, women and children throughout the Eastern provinces; simply because they were Moslems. They are a disgrace to the Christian religion. Our Government files are filled with cases against these Armenian criminals who fled Turkey by the thousands to escape justice. Greedy Armenian leaders incited the masses into a holy war. Rebellious mobs murdered their Moslem neighbors, destroyed dozens of Mosques and murdered our Islamic priests. Talaat knew the fanatics belonged to secret societies and thus, he did not blame all Armenians. He telegrammed the decent leaders, begging them to intercede and halt the massacres. He recalled General Kazim Karabekir from the Front, where he was sorely needed, and sent him to the area of disturbance to assist Armenian leaders in the restoration of peace and brotherhood. Rather than anger, he responded to the Armenians with love and understanding. He built new churches, new schools and improved their communities. Yet the ungrateful Armenians pierced a sword in his back.

"'For six centuries we have shared the wealth of Turkish culture with these primitives. We have allowed them as guests in our ancient land. Oh, why? Why? We shall ask tomorrow, next week, next year—should such a benevolent man as Talaat—forty-seven years away from birth—be taken from us?

"'The prisoner committed political murder on orders from his political superiors. His hatred of our Islamic faith finally exploded in violence—political assassination. These 'alleged massacres' these desperate Armenians refer to, is an effort to escape lawful punishment. Before the laws of Germany—the world—Soghomon Tehlirian must surrender his life at the gallows for the political assassination of Talaat Pasha. May Allah forgive him.'

"This communication was signed by Secretary Shia Bey, of the Turkish Embassy in Berlin and dispatched on June 14, 1921, from Constantinople."

The major clicked his heels, bowed and sat down. A pleased Kolnig thanked him. "No further questions—you are dismissed."

Lemberg banged in protest. "The witness must be cross-examined!"

Von Gorton immediately began this task. "Major Djami, are you at all familiar with the massacre of the Armenian people?"

"Objection!" Kolnig erupted. "Your Honor, I—"

"If the Court please—I would like to answer that question," the witness interrupted. "These are merely rumors, Dr. von Gorton. It was the Turkish people who were massacred. The Armenians alleged the massacre of their people to avoid exposing themselves, don't you see?"

"Can you explain what happened to 1,850,000 Armenian Christians who resided in their 4,000-year-old homeland just six short years ago—yet not *one* is there today?"

"Sir, I am not a statistician—I am a statesman. I do not deal in cold numbers. I did not come here to be interrogated like a common *criminal!* I performed my duty—I read you the message from Secretary Shia Bey. I *demand* to be dismissed!"

"Your Honor," von Gorton addressed Judge Lemberg, "I request that you order the witness—"

Lemberg cut him off, glaring at the witness. "Major, I don't like the word 'demand'—this is a court of law. You'd better start answering questions, Major, you're under oath. Refuse and *you'll* not only be dismissed, but so will your testimony and the telegram."

"But your Honor—" Kolnig protested.

"Don't *but* me!—just instruct your witness to answer."

"He *must* refuse, your Honor—those are his orders," von Gorton interjected. "These reports in my possession are from my investigators. If it please the court, this witness appeared here on orders from Kemal Pasha. The telegram—the substitution of this witness for Secretary Shia Bey—is a planned effort to avoid cross-examination, yet enter Turkish propaganda into the records. These reports—"

"—Is that all you have, reports?" Lemberg interrupted. "I want documented proof that can be introduced into a court of law."

Von Gorton was prepared. "Your Honor, these *are* documented. The telegram read by the witness is fraudulent—a show of cowardice, an act of hypocrisy; words distorted and woven into a chain of lies. I suspected that the Turks, in desperation, would attempt one final move—to camouflage the mass-murder of the Armenians. Therefore I had Secretary Shia kept under surveillance by my investigators for the last four days. Shia Bey is not ill. At this precise moment he is aboard a train, which departed Berlin forty-eight hours ago, en route to Constantinople; and, by direct order of Kemal Pasha, in a deliberate move to prevent the appearance of the Secretary at this trial—where he could be cross-examined. He *did not* dispatch this telegram—he *could not* — simply because he is hundreds of miles from his destination—from where this telegram was sent. This move by Kemal Pasha to becloud the facts introduced to this court, concerning the massacre of the Armenians by the Turks, is a farce. It is common knowledge that less than three months ago, Kemal Pasha officially refused to claim Talaat's body nor allow it to be returned to Turkey. He wanted to avoid involvement in the crime. His decision was quoted in newspapers throughout the world. Although shocking, it is understandable—Kemal had ulterior motives.

"I demand that this man's testimony be declared invalid and stricken from the records, and this obnoxious witness dismissed immediately. He is a fraud, a mockery to this court and German jurisprudence." Turning to face Shia Bey's proxy, von Gorton warned, "Major Djami, if you did not enjoy diplomatic immunity as a member of the Turkish Embassy staff, I would demand your imprisonment for perjured testimony."

"Let me see those reports, Dr. von Gorton!" Lemberg said angrily, reaching across the bench.

The Turks had again exposed themselves as past-masters of the art of deception; fortunately, my attorney had arrested them in the act. God bless him! Hurriedly the three justices studied the reports and came to a decision. Lemberg removed his glasses. "There are laws of a judiciay nature and laws of decency—both have been violated. I hereby order the testimony of this witness and the contents of this—*this* concocted telegram deleted from the records. Major Djami, you are dismissed. Were it not for the legal clause 'diplomatic immunity'—and for that reason alone—I would personally have you placed in confinement. I order you to leave this courtroom immediately—or, I'll have you escorted out."

Lemberg gavelled, "Court is recessed for ten minutes—at which time we'll hear the summations."

* * * * * * * * * *

Only one word would describe the feeling throughout the courtroom when the hearings reconvened: *Tension!*

My attorney explained that Dr. Kolnig would present his summation first. He reassured me that, although the prosecutor had a right to a brief statement later, we had the last word. "That's the one that counts—the one we expect the jury will remember the most," he concluded. Kalousdian gave me an encouraging nod. I felt a little better.

Heinrich Kolnig appeared poised and self-assured as he placed both hands on the polished rail before the jury and leaned forward, an ingratiating smile on his face. His manner was intimate, as though he was about to confide a cherished secret or share a mutual problem with them. Grudgingly, somewhat apprehensively, I was forced to acknowledge that here was an adversary to test any man's mettle; von Gorton's included. Kolnig opened up like a swirling hurricane:

"Fellow citizens, we are charged with a grave responsibility. This is not just another local trial, but one with international implications. You see here in this courtroom the representatives of the world press and telegraphic services. There are, among the spectators, official observers from many distant lands. Your findings will be watched closely by courts of justice in every civilized nation on earth.

"I know that you will bring in a verdict consistent with the honor and integrity for which German justice is noted; that you will render the only verdict possible—guilty of premeditated, political murder."

Now Kolnig, his voice ringing, pointed dramatically in my direction. "There sits a man who invaded our State, accepted our hospitality and then repaid us with a crime as cold-blooded and calculated as any I have encountered in my seventeen years as a prosecutor. He has not retracted a single word of his confessions nor has he ever expressed a syllable of remorse. He is today the same arrogant killer that he was on the morning of March 15, 1921 when he extinguished the God-given light in another man's soul.

"Take a hypothetical case. Let us say that a stranger here in this very courtroom suddenly strikes and kills another man—an innocent man—someone who might even be sitting beside you. Let us say that the victim held a high position in his country, an ally of Germany during the last war, and by his deeds covered himself with fame and glory. To make the crime even more heinous, assume that the victim happened to be an honored guest of this State; but the killer, in contrast, deceitfully enters this country posing as a student. Gentlemen, that is precisely what happened in the case before us.

"My very worthy opponent, in his desperation to find an acceptable motive, would have you believe that the youthful prisoner was overcome with a feeling of piety and righteousness, and because of those feelings he shot a man to death to vindicate the Armenian people, as he so cleverly put it. Is it not a strange reaction for a man who is filled with religious fervor to put a bullet through another man's brain? Does the defense presume to call that a Christian act? No! Let us be done with hypocrisy. Let us consider this case only on the evidence. We have the facts, the *corpus delicti,* the witnesses and the prisoner's own confession. What more do we need to bring in a verdict of guilty?

"Here are the cold facts: on Tuesday, March 15, 1921, at or about 10 o'clock in the morning, on a peaceful Berlin street, the accused culminated a merciless, three-year trackdown. There, Talaat Pasha, a leading Turkish official, was confronted by a vicious twenty-four-year-old killer, Soghomon Tehlirian, and shot dead. Those are the undisputed, bare facts of the case. Now then, the defendant, through his astute lawyer, is anxious that you consider this a compulsive crime." He snorted derisively. "Even the medical experts who testified earlier in the trial could not agree on that score. Yet *Herr* von Gorton seeks to convince you that he is a better, more qualified psychiatrist than his own witnesses."

I was near enough to von Gorton's table to see a flash of resentment on his face. He mouthed a profane word and despite my own jeopardy I almost grinned. I hadn't known he was that human. Now Kolnig discussed each of the medical reports, skillfully interweaving whatever inuendos and opinions he thought might be advantageous to the prosecution. He was so persuasive I could feel goose-flesh dappling my arms. Then I recalled von Gorton's parting shot that we would have the last word. I breathed a little easier.

Kolnig pressed on. "But we need not rely on the reports of the good doctors alone. We also have our common sense which tells us that this was premeditated murder and that the motive was political." Kolnig's voice now changed to one of righteous indignation. "Gentlemen, I certainly do not condone, but I can understand a man who kills in a sudden fit of frenzy. I can understand a man killing another who ravishes his wife. These are terrible crimes to be sure. But, at least, crimes of passion or gain are understandable, abominable though they may be." Here, Kolnig halted and assumed a Shakespearean pose and faced me, even though he was addressing the jury. His voice exuded scorn. "But neither I nor any decent person can ever understand murder for the sheer sake of killing. I say to you that chauvinistic fanaticism is the only force which can be harnessed for political assassination, and Soghomon Tehlirian was consumed by that feeling.

"As if his own degeneracy were not enough, the prisoner now flagrantly attempts to arouse your sympathy with recitals of alleged Turkish killings which he personally knows little about. I grant that there might have been some atrocities committed, but they were committed by both sides. Certainly I would not insult your intelligence by ignoring the oral and documentary evidence presented in this court. But we must remember that war itself is evil and as a consequence we must expect such acts between two warring peoples. The very fact that the Armenians established their own republic after the end of the last war proves that they were in a state of rebellion; this despite the fact that their host, the Turkish Government, had accepted them under its new democratic constitution—a constitution which guaranteed liberty, equality and fraternity to the subject people—to the Armenians.

I do not like to say this about a people who suffered so much, but their conduct can only be termed base ingratitude to the Turkish host to whom they owed so much."

I wanted to shout, "You are wrong! *You are wrong!* We were not at war with Turkey; we were subjects of the Empire. We had no arms, no organized militia. The Turks, as a policy of State, killed our wives, our mothers, our babies. We fought to establish a republic outside Turkey—because the Turks stole our ancient nation." I ignored his references to me personally; I had expected as much. But surely this man, whose reputation I conceded was an honorable one, could not—must not—mislead the world. Every man in the press section was scribbling furiously as the prosecutor spoke and I could have shouted in despair. But I caught the calm, confident eye of my lawyer and I restrained the impulse which could have only injured my defense.

Kolnig was in full sail. "We have seen how the Armenians had been given an inch and now demanded a mile; it seems that the God-given rights of liberty, equality and fraternity weren't enough. There was no satisfying the Armenians who did not even understand the meaning of appreciation for the privileges given to them by the generous Turkish Government. In contrast, is it not peculiar that the Greeks and other minorities had no complaints about their charitable Turkish Samaritans? But the Armenians rebelled against their benefactors and went on to set up their own republic. It is no wonder that the post-war Turkish democracy, under the leadership of Kemal Pasha, found it necessary to again subdue the Armenians."

A fever of indignation seized my brain. I could no longer control my outrage. "That is not true!" I shouted. "They murdered our people and then stole our ancient land. Our little republic was established by survivors of the massacre—beyond Turkish borders. It was conquered just seven months ago by Bolshevik Russia with the help of Kemal's Moslem hordes—they thirsted for Christian blood." The words were scarcely out of my mouth when I recalled von Gorton's warning: "Don't make any speeches, Soghomon, please." But I could not then, nor can I now, help the way I express myself.

The courtroom was abuzz with excited whisperings. Someone (I suspect old *Bahbig*) applauded. Judge Lemberg gavelled the court to order and, after a warning from the bench, for which von Gorton apologized in my behalf, Kolnig continued:

"As you can see, the prisoner possesses a vile, uncontrollable temper—the same kind of temper that sent a lethal bullet into an innocent man—Talaat Pasha. But let us go back a little into the history of the prisoner—this Soghomon Tehlirian who now flings his defiance in the very teeth of this court.

"When the accused realized that his confederates' attempts to establish their own government had failed he was filled with a desire for revenge. In other words, Gentlemen, all he wanted to do was to kill one of the Turkish statesmen who was responsible for suppressing this ill-conceived Armenian revolt against duly constituted authority. Additionally, he was determined, with the help of such criminal organizations as the Armenian Revolutionary Federation, the *Hunchaks* and other brands of rebels, to destroy any other Turkish statesmen who might thwart their revolutionary plans of the future. Politics, Gentlemen, pure *politics!* From 1918 onward, when the world had finally found peace, the prisoner declared a personal vendetta against Talaat and stalked his victim for three long years, existing only for revenge; to assassinate a great political figure who might stand in the way of the Armenian plot to establish an illegal Armenian Republic. We know by the prisoner's confessions how he combed the European and American continents looking for his quarry. In the dark of night, skulking in the shadows, he pursued his prey from Constantinople to Paris, from Paris to America, from there to Geneva and finally to our fair city of Berlin. He was obsessed with the urge to kill."

Kolnig extracted a handkerchief from his breast pocket and wiped beads of perspiration from his brow. "Here in this law-abiding community," he continued, "Soghomon Tehlirian, the sinister figure who had abandoned God's commandment, 'Thou Shalt Not Kill,' with murder aforethought, deliberately blotted out the life of another man. Yes, here in our respectable, decent, Christian society he shot a man to death because that man's political thinking did not agree with his."

Kolnig, who could have earned a comfortable living on a lecture platform, continued with a fine show of outrage. "The defense has gone to great lengths to shift the burden of guilt away from the killer and onto the shoulders of the victim. They would have you believe that *Talaat Pasha* is on trial, but let us not be deceived or carried away with emotional outbursts. It is Soghomon Tehlirian who is on trial here, not Talaat, whose body even now moulders in the grave because of Tehlirian's lust to kill.

"Compulsion? That is the pathetic excuse which you will hear from the defense. But I ask you to view this crime in the light of undeniable evidence. I ask you, for the sake of German honor, in the interest of the Fatherland's position among civilized nations, to bring in the only verdict that intelligent Germans can render; a verdict that will in a small way be a consolation, not only to the desolate widow, *Frau* Talaat, but also to Turkey; one that will be a credit to you and to our nation, the only verdict that you, as responsible citizens of a mature State can possibly bring in—*guilty!* Guilty of premeditated, political murder! Soghomon Tehlirian must pay with his life."

The brilliant prosecutor bowed to the jury, to Justice Lemberg and his two associates, to von Gorton, and then resumed his seat. Lemberg's eyes were naked with admiration for the prosecutor; not necessarily because he agreed with Kolnig's arguments but because of the man's shattering presentation.

As for me, Kolnig's genius left me heartsick. I knew that his closing argument had been compounded of insinuations, half-truths and contrivances, and I prayed—oh how I prayed—that von Gorton would recognize the rhetoric for what it was. It was too late for me to make any further suggestions. My life—the burning truth of the holocaust—was now in the hands of my lawyer. I fastened my eyes on von Gorton. *"Toguh Asvadtz arachnorteh koor medatzoumnehroot ardahgidoutune*—May the Lord control your thoughts and guide your tongue," I silently cried.

In that moment of frustration, for some inexplicable reason which I shall never be able to fathom, I was suddenly transported back to my early youth. Once again I was a little boy. The court disappeared and I could smell the lovely fragrance of wild honeysuckle after a spring shower. Mama was reading to me from the Scriptures and she was reciting from the Song of Solomon:

> "For, lo, the winter is past, the rain is over and gone; the flowers appear on the earth; the time of the singing of the birds is come, and the voice of the turtle is heard in our land."

I settled back, strangely at peace, waiting for von Gorton to address the court, placing my life not in my lawyer's—but in God's hands.

* * * * * * * * *

Von Gorton, sensing the inflamed reaction of the audience to Kolnig's mesmerizing oratory, asked for a recess, hoping, I suppose, that the jury would cool down. Judge Lemberg conferred with his two associates and gave his reply. "This has already been too lengthy a trial. The court believes that it would best serve the interest of justice if the case continued without interruption. Motion for recess is denied."

My lawyer, his face mirroring his resentment of the court's decision, rose to present his summation. Scholarly, erudite and girded for battle, he launched his final counter-offensive:

"Judges of Germany, Gentlemen of the jury, Soghomon Tehlirian stands before you in the prisoner's dock, but he does not belong there. The one who should be standing in judgment today is none other than Talaat Pasha himself, whose black deeds resulted in his own death. It has been said that the defendant committed murder. A correction is in order. The defendant's act was that of executing a criminal; a criminal who committed atrocities not only against the Armenian people, but against all mankind. I say to you that in reality, Talaat, by his own dark and devious evils, actually committed suicide! Tehlirian, in his compulsive act, was more than a human being; he was an instrument—an instrument of justice! I ask you, can you blame an instrument? Can you convict an instrument? Of course not. Gentlemen, it was Talaat—and no other—who not only loaded the Mauser automatic but pulled the trigger, sending a bullet into his own brain.

"Talaat was not an innocent man, obviously. It was he—the arch-assassin—who is in reality on trial here. Picture for yourself the horror of seeing an unutterably evil man as he invades your home. See him as he rapes and then kills your cherished mother, murders your precious children. Imagine, if you can, a vast horde of such heathens slaying your countrymen by the thousands, tens of thousands, hundreds of thousands, as though they were vermin. Think of the soul-shattering grief of the survivors, the tears they shed. I beg you to dwell on the little ones who were slain, youngsters not yet emerged from their brief day of frolic; young men and women who perished at the bloody hands of the Turks before they could propagate their kind, thus multiplying the monstrous crime because their progeny would have peopled the earth in the days to come. These babies were murdered even before they were conceived, but it was murder nevertheless. I say to you that Talaat sinned not only against Humanity—but against

God—because Talaat crushed the seeds that would have flowered into millions of tomorrow's souls. He not only annihilated a million-and-a-half sentient beings but aborted the lives of countless millions who would have continued the culture, religion and traditions of an ancient, civilized, Christian people. Talaat's diseased mind denied the Creator's gift, Ladies and Gentlemen," von Gorton glanced at the spectators, "the gift of life to generations of Armenians yet unborn."

He paused dramatically; now he went on. "In the face of all this I know that you will understand Mr. Tehlirian's overpowering need for retribution, his anguished compulsion for ultimate justice. And I say that there would have been *no* justice had the defendant not acted as he did."

Von Gorton turned and signalled to his assistant, Niemeyer, who produced a massive file of bound papers. "Gentlemen of the jury," he continued, "these are copies of the documents already submitted to the court. Chronicled within these pages are the true accounts of the most bloodthirsty campaign ever directed against an entire people. Let us briefly review the satanic story, the mass-murders of suckling babes, of virile youth, the aged. Let us again read the many death-orders in which Talaat Pasha damned himself by his own signatures. When I have finished you will know that there can be no denying the inquisition, nor will there be any doubt that it was Talaat's clenched fist that snuffed out a million-and-a-half Armenian lives."

For the next hour-and-a-half, von Gorton, Niemeyer and Wertenhauer, each in turn, reviewed the documentary evidence, hammering home point after bloody point. (COMMENT: The letter from Father Speropoulos, of the Greek Orthodox Church, which was entered into the official records earlier, was re-read to the court. It revealed, among others things, the massacre of Greeks, many Jews and others; a refutation of the prosecutor's statements during the summation that the Armenians alone claimed mistreatment and massacre.)

One would think that the repetition would have been boring to the jury, the spectators and the many journalists; but on the contrary, the shocking details held everyone transfixed. There were times when even I wanted to blot out the macabre testimony as it fell so painfully on tortured ears. Yet, like the others, I was held by its very brutality. In the audience the ancient *Bahbig* was weeping. So, too, were Dr. Nazariantz, Eftian and his German bride, Leona. The faces of Ayvazian, Hazor, Vaza, Sumpat and

Norire were deathly white. Bishop Balakian, who had testified for me, made the sign of the Cross. Mrs. Terzibashian, the first witness to appear in my behalf, was unable to endure another word. Sobbing, she was assisted from the courtroom by her husband and a guard. Temporarily, silence; then:

Von Gorton was speaking: "... and, my opponent told you that Tehlirian has not retracted a single word of his confession. In addition, *Herr* Kolnig appears to be concerned because, as he puts it, the defendant did not express remorse for Talaat's death. It would seem that the prosecutor has a very short memory when he speaks of the defendant's confessions. Only a few days ago Justice Lemberg ruled that the so-called confession was inadmissible as evidence. His Honor had good reason to reject that pathetic document—the language barrier rendered it unacceptable because it was inaccurate, improper and made under questionable circumstances. Further, it did not even bear the proper signatures. Written confession? Such a document does not even exist.

"Now let us discuss the question of remorse for a few moments—the matter is worth no more of your time. Would you feel remorseful if you killed a rat infected with bubonic plague? Mr. Tehlirian has repeatedly expressed his remorse, directing it where it belongs—sorrow for the tragedy that befell the Armenian people; not once, but twice in five years. I assure you that the defendant regrets the necessity which compelled him to take a human life, but there is a vast difference between execution and murder. Granted, execution is the responsibility of the State. But there was no Armenia left within Turkish borders as the result of the 1915 Massacre. Talaat could not have been tried by the Republic of Armenia—it had been conquered by the Soviet Union. If the Government of Kemal Pasha had not compounded its treachery by secretly joining Lenin's conquest of the Armenian Republic, it is conceivable that the execution of Talaat would have had the sanction of the defendant's country just as many other countries punish criminals.

"One of the reasons why Talaat did not pay for his crimes under due process of Armenian law was because the Republic and its laws were undermined by Talaat, Kemal and Lenin, as well as his other confederates. Is it not ironic that it was the Turks who, along with the Bolsheviks, demolished the Armenian judicial system—an act which led to the death of one of their own kind, here in Berlin?

"In all probability, if the Kemalist administration had caught up with Talaat first, he would have been executed—not because of his crimes against humanity, but for absconding with Turkey's treasury funds. Let me remind you that it was not until after the Turkish mass-murders were exposed in this courtroom that Kemal Pasha acted by recalling Secretary Shia Bey from Berlin to Turkey; pretending that he was gravely ill. Need I remind you of that disgraceful and cowardly act? Need I remind you of the fraudulent telegram and the untruths revealed in the person of Major Djami, who failed miserably in a last-minute attempt to becloud the fact that bloodstained Turkey was guilty of the murder of the Armenian nation?

"And, consider this final bit of irony: if there was an international agency empowered to bring Talaat to trial for crimes against humanity, he would have been put to death in any event. What happened here on a Berlin street was inevitable—the ultimate triumph of justice."

Von Gorton now moved on to Kolnig's argument in which he intimated, in effect, that no one would be safe if I were free.

"The prosecutor asked you to consider a hypothetical case; that of a stranger, here in this very courtroom, who suddenly murders someone who might be sitting next to you. He goes on to postulate the incredible theory that the murdered man had covered himself with fame and glory. *Herr* Kolnig also asks you to regard the victim as an important official of Germany's wartime ally, Turkey. We are told he was an honored guest of our country."

Von Gorton's voice dripped sarcasm. "Let us analyze and answer these statements one by one. Firstly, it is not only improbable but impossible that anyone in this courtroom or anywhere else on earth could have provoked such an attack. Why? Because Talaat Pasha was unique in the world. There was not another man like him. No one in all the history of mankind has ever achieved the dubious distinction of planning and executing systematic murders on such a vast scale. No man in this courtroom, in all the world, can conceivably compare to the evil Talaat. It would not be amiss to invoke the physicists who tell us that for every action there must be a corresponding reaction. That scientific law is well illustrated in the case of Talaat's death. The 'action' was Talaat's cold-blooded murder of a million-and-a-half people and the deportation of three-hundred-and-fifty thousand others. The 'reaction' was the only one that could be expected—judgment! There could never, under any imaginable circumstances, be a repetition of Tehlirian's act because there was only one Talaat—thank God!

"I cannot believe that a man of *Herr* Kolnig's demonstrated honor and integrity really meant what he said when he referred to Talaat as a man who covered himself with fame and glory. He knows, I know, and you Gentlemen of the jury know beyond any doubt, that the only place where Talaat's record would be considered glorious is in Hell. The ridiculous contention is not even worth answering and I think we can forgive the prosecutor for losing himself in his own oratory."

I was proud of von Gorton. His strategy was clear. By "forgiving" Kolnig for an unthinking remark he had weakened the rest of Kolnig's statement to a degree where it carried much less weight. I expected that Kolnig would be furious, but to my amazement, a slight smile played at the corners of his mouth. Then, astonishingly, he grinned. His lips formed the word *"touche."*

Von Gorton went on, his voice hard: "Prosecutor Kolnig then referred to Talaat, hypothetically of course, as an important official of a wartime ally—Turkey—and a guest of Germany. Absurd! Was he an official of Turkey? We know from indisputable evidence that Talaat and his fellow conspirators were in exile; having emptied the official coffers of its gold. It is plain, therefore, that the Turkish Government regarded him not as an official but as a thief; one of their most wanted criminals—despite their recent pretense in this very courtroom. But they were not wanted for their atrocities against the Armenian people.

"The prosecutor also said that the man was an honored guest of Germany. But was he? Here is a man who alters his features through surgery so that he can remain anonymous. He enters this country illegally under the assumed name of Salieh Bey, posing as a Turkish businessman. He conspires with other expatriate Turks to overthrow his native country and continues to undermine the new Armenian Republic, which is another abuse of German law. Honored guest indeed! I say to you that if Talaat's presence and shadowy maneuverings had been known to our authorities he would have been arrested and probably prosecuted by none other than *Herr* Kolnig himself.

"The last point of the prosecutor's hypothetical case is one which I know that you, as respectable and decent people, will readily refute: that Talaat should be favorably considered because he was an official of a wartime partner of Germany. A correction is in order. Turkey was associated with Germany only as it affected the war against the Allies. There is a vast difference between orthodox warfare—its conduct under the Hague and Geneva Convention rulings—and the outright slaughter of innocent, unarmed civilians, especially when they are citizens of your own country. That is not warfare by any stretch of the imagination; it is murder. I submit to you, on the basis of all the evidence, that the chief murderer was Talaat Pasha." Von Gorton filled his lungs. "And that takes care of *Herr* Kolnig's hypothetical and poorly contrived argument."

Heinrich Kolnig evidently objected to von Gorton's descriptive "poorly contrived." He scowled. But von Gorton was obviously not through with him. "It pains me deeply that I am forced to bring up the subject of religion," Dr. von Gorton went on, "but since *Herr* Kolnig introduced the matter I must, in the defense of my client, answer his charge. Gentlemen of the jury, you will of course be given transcripts of the prosecution's case against Soghomon Tehlirian as well as copies of my own remarks. I need not elaborate on my opponent's jeers concerning the defendant's religious convictions. Briefly, he called Mr. Tehlirian a hypocrite. I honestly believe that the prosecutor owes my client an apology. Let us convict or acquit the defendant on the basis of fact, but not, I implore you, because of a man's preference in the worship of the Lord. I need only remind you that Armenia was a great nation more than two thousand years before Christ; centuries before the Turks appeared on earth as nomadic tribes who were about to become acquainted with fire.

"Greater Armenia, for example, and subsequently Lesser Armenia, were outstanding empires. At its height Armenia numbered 33,000,000 souls. (COMMENT: Verified by New Standard Encyclopedia, Vol. X.) She was the first country in the world to adopt Christianity—301 A.D. But consider them today. No longer are they 33,000,000 strong, but scattered remnants of survivors, surrounded by 18,000,000 Turkish Moslems and millions of Russian Bolsheviks. How did this once great nation of people—an Aryan race—diminish to such a pitiful few captives? (COMMENT: An Aryan is a member of the historic people that spoke Indo-European. The Aryans, or Indo-Europeans, included Armenians, Baltic, Slavic, Persians, Hellenic, Germanic, Nordic, Anatolian, Latins, Indic, peoples. The word *Aryan* is used to establish historical fact and should not be accepted with the distorted meaning given to it by Nazi ideology, prior to and during

World War II, in a vain attempt to demean and destroy the wealth of cultural, spiritual contributions of the Semitic peoples; especially the important role played by the Jewish people throughout history.)

"I'll tell you. They were systematically slaughtered like cattle in an abattoir. And why did these slayings continue? Because, as the testimony proved, the killings were sanctioned by Allah and glorified in the Koran, thus assuring the Moslems an exalted place in Valhalla as a reward for extinguishing the lives of this Christian minority. I need not repeat all those pertinent passages in the Koran; you heard them when they were introduced as evidence." As a reminder, von Gorton read two or three of the eight Islamic injunctions which exhort Moslems to abuse and kill Christians and Jews.

Now von Gorton rose to oratorical heights:

"Burning brightly in Soghomon Tehlirian's breast was the flame of an unswerving belief in the risen Christ, the same convictions passed down to him through the centuries by his ancestors whose martyred blood was spilled in Roman amphitheaters. They were the early Christians who chose the Crimson Confession—death in the arenas at the slavering jaws of wild lions—rather than renounce the Name. Yes, Soghomon Tehlirian, in the throes of spiritual agony, was forced to resort to violence. It was no easy task for the spiritually inclined Tehlirian to mete out justice to the barbarian who slew Armenian Christians in the name of Allah. But let us not call him a hypocrite. No right-thinking man can call him that. In all humility and reverence, I ask you, how else was Talaat Pasha to be prevented from continuing his abominations against mankind?"

The testimony of the medical experts was the next item on the agenda. Von Gorton, clutching the transcripts recorded from the testimony given by the five doctors, at once proceeded to shred the prosecutor's arguments to tatters. He pointed out that the preponderance of opinion indicated that I was impelled by an irresistible and justifiable compulsion to destroy the master of immorality who threatened to repeat his past depredations. He proved, to my eternal gratitude, that I killed Talaat for reasons that had nothing to do with insanity. My fainting and dizzy spells, von Gorton emphasized, were a direct result of the mental anguish I had suffered because of the crimes committed against those whose blood also flowed in my veins. When he had finished, I knew intuitively that the jury understood that I was not now or had I ever been bereft of my reason. I whispered a silent but heartful "*shenorahgaul ehm* —thank you"—to my lawyer.

"*Herr* Kolnig argues that this was a political crime," von Gorton declared, taking a new tack. "He attributes to Tehlirian the motive of chauvinistic fanaticism. Let us examine that statement so that we can see how nonsensical a charge it is. A man commits murder for political reasons because he has certain circumscribed motives for his act. He may desire a change in administration and therefore kills one or more leaders in control. It may be an act of vengeance, pure and simple, because those of his own political party were unsuccessful in a bid for power. He may even be an anarchist who looks on all authority with suspicion and hostility. He may be a Bolshevik who believes that force is the only way to establish a Marxian society. Or, he may be a disgruntled citizen who murders out of resentment. There are other reasons which might induce political murder, of course, but I shall not dwell on them because there is no need to do so. This was not political murder.

"Did Tehlirian expect to achieve a change of administration within the Armenian Government as a consequence of his so-called crime? Certainly not. 1,850,000 Armenians remained in 1915, after centuries of persecution and murder by the Turks. Of that number, 1,500,000 were murdered during the massacres which began in 1915. Because of Talaat, not a single known Armenian was alive in Armenia—within the Turkish empire—by 1918. In the Caucasus buffer zone the courageous survivors defeated the attacking Turkish Army hordes which had advanced beyond their borders to destroy completely *all* Armenians. On May 28, 1918—a little over three years ago—the Armenians established the Free Independent Republic of Armenia.

"Kemal, Talaat and Lenin, last December, conspired to launch a sneak attack on the Republic. Just seven months ago their bloody hands plunged the dagger of death into the back of the Armenian Republic and she fell lifeless at the foot of the Cross—the second time in five short years. Talaat gasped his last breath even as the requiem for the dead two-year-old Republic tolled in his ears. The killing had no political motive, obviously, because there was no political entity that could profit by this act.

"The next argument is that of vengeance. Now then, Gentlemen, when a man seeks to exact vengeance he believes that he will settle accounts. But nowhere in Tehlirian's statements has he uttered the word 'revenge.' He did not because vengeance, in this case, would have been empty. Talaat's death could not possibly have balanced the scales. Certainly one Moslem life could not compensate for the loss of one-and-a-half million Christian lives. The accusation, revenge, cannot and does not stand up in the light of objective analysis.

"We now come to Prosecutor Kolnig's senseless charge of revenge because of the defeat of Tehlirian's political party in an election. I reiterate, neither of the two Armenias existed when Talaat was faced with final judgment. Therefore, there were no political parties. True, Talaat had undermined the new nation, but Tehlirian knew, just as we know, that he could not have profited by Talaat's death. We see once again that the charge of political murder is *absurd!*

"We have eliminated most of the leading arguments that a political motive was behind the execution. Let us completely banish the idea. Was Tehlirian an anarchist or Bolshevik? Of course not! Even the prosecutor did not dare suggest that possibility. As to being a disgruntled citizen whose motives might be rooted in political jealousy; it would be silly to discuss the point. Ancient Armenia was extinct. With the help of the Turks—Kemal and Talaat—the Bolsheviks conquered their first victim: Republic of Armenia. Free elections were abolished before Soviet troops had completed their conquest of the ravaged country.

"It must be clear to all that the motive of politics is ruled out, once and for all. You cannot, Gentlemen, commit political murder unless there is a compensating political advantage. Turkish-dominated Armenia has been dead for three years. The Republic lies silent, a victim of Turko-Soviet treachery. The red, blue and orange tricolors over the city of Yerivan have been torn down and replaced with the Bolshevik Hammer and Sickle on a banner of red. Part of that unhappy land was given to the Turks for their participation in the slaughter of the innocents. No act of Tehlirian's could change its present administrative laws. No act of his could revive the slain Armenia. In reality, the question of political motive has no bearing on this case. I ask you to ignore, as the subterfuge it really is, that which the prosecutor, in his dire urgency, would have you consider. There can be no political murder where there is no political State. Unfortunately, in this case, two States."

Judge Lemberg broke into the lawyer's summation. "Pardon me, Dr. von Gorton, but how much longer do you expect to continue?"

"An hour-and-a-half, or two, your Honor—not much longer than that."

"In that case, Counsel, I think we had better call a luncheon recess at this point—we have gone well past the usual time."

"Yes, your Honor," von Gorton agreed.

The jury filed out to the room especially reserved for them. Judge Lemberg, head bowed over the several documents he was studying, looked up briefly and nodded to his two associate justices as they departed. Von Gorton, Kolnig and my friend and interpreter, Kalousdian, were bustling about, preparing to leave. I, too, made ready to visit the barred ante-chamber where I had been taking lunch each day of the trial.

Suddenly there was a commotion in the aisle. Old *Bahbig* again! This time he was weighted down with a huge wicker basket of the type used as a laundry hamper. He managed to reach the rail which separated the spectators from those involved in the trial, when a couple of alert guards pounced on him.

"Just a moment!" Judge Lemberg growled, snatching off his gold-rimmed glasses. He glared at *Bahbig*. "I thought I told you to stay out of this courtroom."

Bahbig drew himself up to his full sixty inches, an eighty-year-old, dehydrated bag of bones in whose skinny chest still beat the heart of the warrior he had once been so many decades ago. "*Yeteh goozeh eentz hed khoseel, toguh Haiererehn khosee* —If you are addressing me, Sir, speak in Armenian. I don't understand German and I have no intention of learning."

Kalousdian thrust forward hastily. "Your Honor," he interpreted with a straight face. "Mr. *Bahbig* begs your pardon and asks that you forgive him for not understanding German. He claims a deep affection for the German language, and hopes that through study he will shortly be able to master it."

Instead of answering him, Judge Lemberg turned to me. "Mr. Tehlirian," he said severely, "if it isn't asking too much, would you be good enough to tell me what in the name of Heaven you are grinning about?"

Grinning indeed! I was choking with suppressed mirth at Kalousdian's altered, quick-witted translation. How he was able to do it so solemnly was beyond me. I made some feeble excuse and offered an apology which escapes me now. Lemberg, scowling, returned his attention to Kalousdian. He pointed to *Bahbig*. "Ask that man if he knows that he is in contempt of court for returning after I had him ejected for his previous disturbance.

I believe, at that time, he displayed an Armenian flag during the proceedings."

Kalousdian interpreted.

"That was my old regimental battle flag!" *Bahbig* exclaimed hotly in Armenian. "The guards took it and never gave it back."

"The Judge wants to know why you returned after he ordered you out," Kalousdian persisted. "Right now he's not interested in your flag," he concluded.

"But *I am!*" the octogenarian snarled through toothless gums. "Tell him he'd better give it back if he knows what's good for him."

Judge Lemberg, his voice oozing with satire, interrupted. "I don't wish to seem inquisitive in my own court, but would I be breaking the proprieties if I asked what the devil he is saying?"

Red-faced, his embarrassment obvious, Kalousdian translated. For a moment I thought that the feisty little judge—he was no bigger than *Bahbig*—would succumb to a fit of apoplexy. Then, to my amazement, his lips widened in a broad smile. "Tell him that his flag will be returned to him at once," Lemberg instructed Kalousdian.

Kalousdian interpreted and *Bahbig* acknowledged the offer with a spectacular Levantine bow. "But he still hasn't answered my question," Judge Lemberg persisted. "I warned him that he'd be in contempt of court if he returned. What's he doing here?"

"Gartzetsee teh meeahien aiehnt orvahn hamar ehr," Bahbig answered in Armenian.

"What does that mean?" Judge Lemberg asked.

"He said," Kalousdian explained, "that he thought you meant he was to stay away only for that day." The interpreter was having a difficult time maintaining a sober face. I bit down hard on my lower lip to keep from laughing aloud. Von Gorton and Kolnig were also having difficulty repressing what would have been uproarious hilarity. As for Judge Lemberg, he was a waxen image. Then his face wrinkled in a sunburst of creases, his shoulders shook and he added his mirth to everyone else's.

Bahbig was offended. "What the hell's the big joke?" he demanded in Armenian.

Kalousdian somehow managed to mollify him. Lemberg, even though court was not in session, promptly lifted the contempt ruling. "What is that you have in your basket?" he asked curiously, the papers on his desk all but forgotten.

The old man lifted the lid. *"Dolma yev baugauch-hatz,*

ahvore dauk eh, yev bolorees hamar gehraugoor gah—shad gah."

"Mr. *Bahbig* brought Armenian food for all of us," Kalousdian translated. "*Dolma,* and *baugauch* —Armenian circular flat-bread—and a few other things, steaming hot."

"What in the world is *dolma?"* Lemberg asked suspiciously.

Kalousdian scratched his head and turned to me. "How do you explain *dolma* to a German?" he asked me in Armenian.

I remembered watching my mother preparing *dolma* for our family back in Erzinga. Kalousdian translated for Lemberg as I explained. "You take ground lamb and add Armenian spices, onions and rice and roll the meat into cylindrical shapes—like small sausages—and then wrap them individually in grape leaves and cook them for about an hour. Then you cover the steaming *dolma* with tomato paste and mmh—delicious!" I blew a kiss with my fingertips, in the manner of the French. Even before I finished, Judge Lemberg's mouth was watering. So was everyone else's, including my own.

"I must admit it sounds quite exotic," Judge Lemberg commented. Characteristically he peered over his spectacles at Heinrich Kolnig. "If the prosecution has no objections and will not hold me partial to the Armenian Cause I might be tempted to try some of that *dolma."*

"Gastronomically and legally speaking, your Honor, the prosecution has no objections," Kolnig said, laughing.

"In that case, the ruling of this court is that we sample Mr. *Bahbig's* culinary concoctions. I've never tasted Armenian food before. This should be a treat."

Bahbig was whispering in Kalousdian's ear. "Everybody is welcome except that stinker—Kolnig," the wizened old soldier declared. "He's a friend of the Turks."

Kalousdian translated and again Kolnig laughed aloud. "Tell him," said the prosecutor, "that I'm only doing my job. But from the looks of that *dolma,* I think we ought to forget the judicial aspects and eat."

Pacified, the aged veteran distributed the delicacies to Judge Lemberg, von Gorton, Kalousdian and Kolnig. Somewhat embarrassed, I accepted the largest portion he had reserved for me, with an added dish of *pilaff*—rice, tender and succulent.

It was a well-fed judge, defense and prosecution who opened the afternoon session on Tuesday, June 14. I braced myself as Dr. von Gorton opened his final arguments. Whatever lunchtime cordiality had existed between the defense and prosecution lawyers had now vanished. Once again I was confronted with the reality that my attorney was making a Herculean effort to save me from the gallows.

"The prosecution intimated that the defense flagrantly attempted to arouse your sympathy with testimony, both oral and documentary, concerning the 'alleged'—as he put it—Turkish atrocities," von Gorton began, plunging headlong into the core of his summation. "He further insinuated that my client has little personal knowledge of the killings.

"Notice the one little adjective, 'alleged,' which the prosecution used when he referred to the Turkish mass-murders. I shall be merciful and say he used it unthinkingly. Gentlemen, that word should not have been 'alleged' but *factual!* I'll not even attempt to remind you of the scores of documents, to say nothing of the oral testimony, that substantiated the many crimes perpetrated by our wartime ally, Turkey. There is no question but that the atrocities were actually committed. Indeed, they are now part of history; sordid perhaps, but history, nevertheless. Consult any modern encyclopedia; German, Italian, French, Scandinavian or English for verification. The archives of all civilized governments also bear documentary witness to these unspeakable crimes.

"And what, I wonder—as you must wonder—did *Herr* Kolnig mean when he said that Soghomon Tehlirian had little personal knowledge of the massacres? Is it not enough that he saw his home in smoking ruins—a funeral pyre for his mother and others of his flesh and blood? Is it not enough that he witnessed the senseless killings and the results of the Turkish madness across the length and breadth of his homeland? Let me remind you that it is because he *did* witness the ravishment of his people that the compulsion for final justice grew within him.

"Now, let us rip away the pretense that one must expect such cruelties in time of war. As I have said, and it merits repeating, no war existed between the Armenian people and Turkey, because the Armenians were subjects of the Turkish Government. Clearly, we can see that the destruction of an enemy military objective is a legitimate target of war. And, unfortunately, many civilians are maimed and killed in the course of nullifying the effectiveness of enemy military targets. But no civilian nation singled out the non-combatants themselves for extermination. People living far from military objectives; the very old, the very young, the halt, the lame and the sightless cannot conceivably be considered as soldiers or even remotely connected with the military. We know that the most able-bodied males were murdered *en masse.* How then explain the shameful Turkish excuse that atrocities were committed by both sides? Just who among the Armenian remnants could commit atrocities? The ancient crones? The nursing infants? The doddering old men? The sick and enfeebled?"

(COMMENT: The continued arrogance of the Turkish Government exceeds even that of the Nazis. Post-war Germany, at least, publicly disavowed the Hitler atrocities but not so the Turks. Even to this date, April 24, 1989—the 74th memorial of the Turkish genocide of the Armenians in 1915—Turkey had not evidenced feelings of remorse for the genocidal assault—they have, for seven decades, denied any such thing could be possible—even in the United Nations where they shamefully signed the Genocide Prevention Treaty.

On September 25, 1961, Mustafa Aksin, First Secretary of the Turkish Embassy in Washington, D.C., and personal spokesman for Ambassador Suat Hayri Urguplu (later Premier of Turkey), in a letter to this author, brushed off the entire bloodbath with this cold statement: "It was found necessary to remove the Armenians from Eastern Turkey. In the ensuing confusion excesses were committed on both sides." Here we find the official mouthpiece for the Turkish Government in our United States, admitting and then dismissing the murder and deportation of an entire people in a few off-hand words. Thus the destroyer attempted to shift the burden of guilt to the victim because of his feeble and unsuccessful attempt to protect the lives of his loved ones and his property—his ancient homeland.

The cruel audacity that continues to permeate Turkish thought is illustrated in Turkish diplomat Aksin's following statement: "We (Turkey) consider this question (Armenian), which was one of forced resettlement resulting from the conditions of war, as closed." Thus did Aksin casually dismiss the deportations and killings of 1,850,000 Christians—the entire population of Armenia—uprooted from their hearths and homes, their 4,000-year-old homeland.

Typical of most other Turks, Secretary Aksin called it a closed incident, but this crime against humanity is still an open wound in the hearts of the survivors, their offspring and every Christian and Jew—all civilized people walking this earth.

Aksin went on to heights of absurdity to say: "It took an entire army corps led by General Kazim Karabekir to forestall the Armenians." The ways of the Turkish mind are strange indeed. Aksin boldly distorted historical fact. The unarmed Christian minority attempting to escape the unholy bloodletting, to save their children from the bayonets and axes of the Islamic marauders, were now termed an organized army fighting for provinces rather than for their lives.

The impudence of the Turks knows no bounds. Here is how Aksin described his hero, the notorious Talaat Pasha, castigated by historians as "The Pig of Asia Minor." Wrote Aksin, not in 1915 but in the year of our Lord, 1961: "Talaat was a devoted and honest statesman whose constant ideal was to serve his country. He was a man of the people, a humanitarian . . . he loved the Armenian people." The final infamy in Mustafa Aksin's letter is the boast that Talaat Pasha, in 1916, was promoted to Prime Minister (he had been Minister of Interior). Aksin failed to point out that Talaat's promotion was not based on his deeds of goodness but because he had directed the genocide of the Armenians. By 1916, a year after the massacre was launched, almost a million of the million-and-a-half who were to die, had already been slain.

I wanted to ask Secretary Aksin and Ambassador Urguplu—what of the 1943 *Varlik Vegisi* impositions on the Armenians and other Christians? How does Turkey explain the documentary report by Noel Barber, correspondent for the *London Daily Mail,* who smuggled the expose of the 1955 Turkish riots in the streets of Istanbul and Smyrna, telling of the September 6th and 7th mob scenes against Greeks, Armenians and Jews? His dispatch told of nearly a hundred Armenian and Greek churches destroyed and eighteen Jewish synagogues and religious buildings damaged. In that melee, the Turks destroyed 450 Armenian shops, 500 Jewish shops and 5,000 Greek shops, in addition to 700 houses. In the churches, embroidered vestments of the clergy were torn to bits and then burned. Altars were smashed to ruins. Armenian and Greek cemeteries were ghastly scenes of open tombs, the corpses, skulls and bones dragged from their resting places.

Finally, I refer to the July 9, 1961 "Constitution" passed by the Turkish Government which further proved the animosity of the Turks for the simplest prerequisites of liberty. At the urgings of a disgusted world the Turks announced their "New Constitution." But the Turk Government, in 1961 under the rule of the "Committee of National Unity," emasculated that document by adding an amendment which stipulated that any person or group of persons who disagreed with the government were to be deported and all their assets confiscated.

The 700-year-old system of tyranny continues. Where it will end nobody knows. This author suggests that the present leaders of Turkey should study the contents of this book; the information revealed should prove most enlightening to them.)

Von Gorton raised his hands dramatically. Then his arms descended slowly, like the folding wings of a butterfly, his questions shooting like machine-gun bullets: "If atrocities were committed by both sides," he thundered, "then why is it that the mountains of corpses in the deserts of Der el Zor, the countless bloated bodies in the Euphrates River and in the Black Sea, and the charred remains of so many cities and villages are all Armenian!? Where?—where are the Turkish bodies, the charred Turkish cities and villages? And why does every Western nation mention Turkish blood-spilling but never Armenian? The undeniable answer is that atrocities were *not* committed by both sides; they were Turkish, through and through, as they were with their predecessors, the Vandals, before the Crusades. This is an example of Turkey's much-vaunted 'liberty, equality and fraternity,'" he snorted.

Von Gorton's oratory so enthralled me, as it had everyone in the courtroom, that I momentarily forgot my surroundings, even my own plight. Reporters were scribbling madly although complete transcripts of the hearings would be made available to them on the following day. A wave of gratitude threatened to engulf me. My lawyer had promised that he would bring out the true story of what happened to the Armenian people at the hands of the Turkish heathens, and he had more than fulfilled that pledge. Yes, I finally knew, in my heart, that I had vindicated myself and my brothers and sisters, wherever and whomever they might be. "*Shenoreaugaul ehm* —I am thankful, my good friend," I breathed.

Von Gorton had almost, but not quite, concluded his summary:

"It has been repeatedly emphasized that it is Soghomon Tehlirian, not Talaat Pasha, who is on trial here. That statement is nothing more than a simple play on words—a dangerous game of semantics. I tell you that Talaat Pasha *is* on trial in this courtroom and that the judgment must be on him and all the others like him who may seek to unsheathe their talons in the future.

Talaat must be condemned today as a warning to the would-be Talaat's of tomorrow. Yes, every Turkish man, woman and child is on trial here; they and their children shall not be free from guilt until retribution is extended to the Armenians. Not a single word of remorse has been uttered by the Turkish leaders or their people. They have been evasive and obnoxious, to the extent that they even blame the victims, let alone accept responsibility for their crime against the Armenians, against humanity itself.

"It is well and fitting that a German court condemns these inhuman monsters who sought to annihilate an entire people. Whether we like it or not, Germany was allied to Turkey during the war. In many cases it was German officers and German equipment that the Turks used, not only for legitimate warfare against their enemies, the Western Powers, but also to bludgeon an unarmed, helpless Christian minority to near extinction. We, too, must be vindicated, lest we be seen by future generations as cast in the same mold as the Turks.

"If Talaat Pasha is on trial today, then so are we Germans and an apathetic world. Nay, our German children and our grandchildren will not be free from guilt unless we condemn these crimes against humanity. And we must do so by acquitting the defendant who, by a quirk of fate, has been placed in the anomalous position of the *accused* rather than the *accuser*.

"Perhaps by our actions we will establish a foundation upon which the structure of an international court, representing the conscience of all men, may someday be built—a court empowered to bring to trial and to pass judgment on individuals who seek to exterminate a race of people. If and when such a court is established, it will be good to know that Germany was in the vanguard to protest man's inhumanity to man. Yes, let this day of Tuesday, June 14, 1921, set a shining example." (COMMENT: It is ironic that fifteen months later an Austrian house-painter named Adolf Schicklgruber—Hitler—wrote his manifesto: *Mein Kampf*.)

A murmur of approval hummed through the courtroom. Lemberg, always in direct command of his court, brought the incipient buzz to an immediate halt with an impatient tattoo of his gavel. Deliberately von Gorton returned to his table and handed over to his assistant, Wertenhauer, the transcripts from which he had been quoting. Now he slowly walked back to the jury. In the pervading stillness I could hear the ticking of the wall clock. Von Gorton's first words nailed me to the back of my chair.

"The confidential nature of a lawyer-client relationship is well known. Gentlemen, I am about to break that confidence. My client insisted that I dwell on the sufferings of the Armenian people instead of defending him personally. I informed him that his life was at stake and that, as deeply as I regretted the horror which enveloped his people, I was retained to represent *him* in the case before this court; not to unfold the misery that befell the Armenian people.

"But this great man—this great patriot—was adamant in his insistence that I bring out the details of the massacre, and to minimize his own role in the eternal fight for freedom. This, in the very shadow of the gallows, when he should really be concerned about his own fate. Gentlemen, I say that Soghomon Tehlirian should not be a prisoner in this courtroom but should be placed in high esteem as an international hero—the young man who placed the first stone for the building that will someday house an international court of justice. The word 'compulsion' has been used time and again throughout the hearings, and with good reason; for that is the essence of the defense's case.

"Now we have the classic, undeniable proof. Here is a man who is only hours away from the ultimate, mortal judgment, yet he minimizes his own participation in the event which brought him before you, only to plead that justice be done to the memory of the dead and to honor the survivors—Christianity itself.

"Gentlemen of the jury, never in all jurisprudence has compulsion been so clearly demonstrated as in this example. Soldier, patriot, idealist and wielder of retribution—instrument of justice—he did that which he was compelled to do. The act of compulsion, I believe, will stand as a monument to his existence in the years to come; a symbol of righteousness over evil.

"You cannot condemn the defendant unless you condemn every force of decency which propelled man from the primeval jungle to modern civilization. I ask, as the world is asking, that you acquit the defendant, Soghomon Tehlirian, by virtue of compulsion."

The climax of my lawyer's summation came so suddenly it caught everyone unprepared. For a moment it seemed that von Gorton would add yet another statement. Instead he clamped his mouth shut, not another word passing the threshold of his lips. He bowed briefly to the jury, to the three justices, to Dr. Kolnig and then to me. Abruptly he turned and resumed his seat.

The hearings were over.

* * * * * * * * * *

Judge Lemberg gathered his black robe around him, exchanged a few comments with his two associates and then spoke, his voice calm, his manner precise, but with overtones of gentleness and insight I had not heretofore noticed:

"Before I instruct the jury," he said, "and also in behalf of my fellow judges, I would like to commend the attorney for the defense, Dr. Adolf von Gorton, and his assistants, and the attorney for the prosecution, Dr. Heinrich Kolnig, and his assistants for their conduct of their respective cases. You gentlemen have displayed a fine sense of duty and adherence to the law. The standards which you maintained throughout this trial may well be emulated by barristers everywhere. The court thanks you. I need not remind you gentlemen that the eyes of the world are focused on us. But whatever the verdict, you have conducted yourselves honorably and for that you have earned the respect of all Germany. Let us place our faith in a merciful Almighty that the circumstances which led to this trial will never again be repeated."

My eyes were moist as I murmured a heartdeep *"amen."* Among the spectators I could hear a soft chorus of agreement.

Judge Lemberg, now that the hearings had come to an end, had somehow synthesized into a composite of all the wise and kindly judges canonized in literature. "Gentlemen of the jury," he instructed, "you have heard the testimony of the witnesses and the reading of the documentary evidence. There have been charges and counter-charges; some of it based on emotional appeal and others based on fact. True enough, a court of law is not a cold, insensitive body; it is comprised of ordinary men who know the meaning of tears and laughter. Nevertheless I ask you to delve beneath the emotionalism displayed in this trial—and understandably so—by both sides. In short, I ask you to consider only the facts.

"There seems to be no question that the defendant, Soghomon Tehlirian, did in fact slay one Talaat Pasha, the former Prime Minister of Turkey. But, as you have heard, this is no routine case of murder stemming from a sudden burst of passion. We are faced with a breech of civilized conduct that is much more complex. First and foremost; was this a crime of cold, premeditated murder with politics as an extenuating circumstance? Secondly; was this crime prompted by compulsion?

"You are entrusted with a grave responsibility, Gentlemen of the jury. You have heard the testimony and the reading of the documents in their entirety. The final penalty, if any, rests with me and my associate justices. But it is upon your decision that we shall base our judgment. Your foreman will be given complete transcripts of the case. Whatever your decision, may it be just and a credit to Germany; to all decent men throughout the world.

"This session, on the fourteenth day of June, nineteen hundred and twenty-one—Tuesday—is now terminated," Judge Lemberg concluded. "I instruct you to retire to your chambers where you will arrive at your decision."

Solemnly the jury filed out. Whether I would live or die rested solely in their hearts. We had done all we could. My ultimate fate rested in the hands of God.

XXIII. THE VERDICT

Thursday, June 16, 1921.

It was almost an anti-climax when Chief Inspector Mandteufel, accompanied by the ever-present interpreter, Gevork Kalousdian, appeared at my cell door on the fifteenth and last day of my trial, and announced: "The jury will be returning in just a few minutes, Soghomon; they've reached a verdict." He opened the barred door. Shakily I rose to go with him but he genially waved me back, offering me a cigarette. "No rush," he said grandly. "You still have time for a smoke."

My heart thumped. Strangely enough, I had felt no fear until now. It was as though I was the central figure in a stage play and that, true to the tradition of the theater, everything would be favorably resolved in the last act. Take Mandteufel himself, for example. When I was first interrogated by him, shortly after my arrest, I envisioned him as something of an ogre. Certainly he had been obnoxious, but now, in retrospect, I could see that he was doing only what he considered his duty as a police official. Agreed, he was no intellectual giant; yet, as the testimony unfolded and the story of the sorrow that engulfed the House of Armenia was revealed in open court, this bluff, gruff, uncouth man grew progressively more sympathetic and friendlier until the innate warmth within him glowed. We were now good friends.

Kalousdian's translation was rapid and accurate, like the flow of a hillside brook. "I've been thinking about something, Soghomon," Mandteufel said soberly, between puffs. "I never killed a man outside the line of duty, and then only in self-defense. Not once have I ever pulled a trigger unless that man had already shot at me first." His voice faltered.

"Go on," I said gently.

The police inspector cleared his throat. "What I'm trying to say is this: If I ever came face to face with a man who killed my mother, children and everyone else I loved, I'd have done exactly as you did. So would any other man." He coughed embarrassedly.

"That's not for the record of course."

I wanted to thank him; to express my gratitude, but I could think of nothing to say. Instead, we silently clasped hands. He flicked his cigarette into a cuspidor. His manner was abrupt, but I did not miss the underlying affection in his voice. "Let's go, Soghomon," he ordered. "We can't keep the jury waiting."

When I entered the courtroom a few minutes later, it was as though I had never been there before. Physically, the scene was the same, but I could sense a new aura of excitement that communicated itself from person to person, like a nervous bee depositing pollen in one flower after another. The jury had not yet come in. Justice Lemberg and his two deputy judges were conversing in low tones. Von Gorton and Kolnig were talking to Rev. Lepsius. They were smiling and I supposed they were talking about other things than the trial.

Among the spectators I recognized and exchanged nods with were many of my friends. The Armenians, I could see, had turned out in force to hear the judgment. The Federation, as usual, made up the majority of the faithful spectators in the audience. There was Sumpat, carefully groomed as though he was about to attend a wedding; my dear friend Hazor, looking more like a Turk than ever, except for the wide smile of recognition he gave me; Ayvazian, whom I first met at *Maxl's* and who took me under the wing of the local Federation. There was Vaza, Levon Eftian and Bishop Balakian; Mrs. Terzibashian, who had appeared as a witness in my behalf just a few days ago, and many others who waved their encouragement to me. Good old *Bahbig,* I noticed, was resplendent in a new suit, evidently purchased just for this occasion. It did little for his ancient frame, but nevertheless, I was proud of him.

Apart from the others, in the rear of the courtroom, was a group of Turks, including several young students who still believed that Hazor was one of them. Among them was Talaat's widow, a rigid portrait in black, her manner haughty, her mien aristocratic. She was bearing up well under the ordeal and I felt sorry for her.

Suddenly there was a commotion at the entrance to the left of the judge's bench. A door opened and the jury filed in, their faces grim, their paces deliberate. When they were seated, Judge Lemberg addressed them: "Will the foreman please stand."

The foreman arose.

Lemberg cleared his throat. "You are Otto Reiniche, duly appointed as foreman of the jury?"

"I am, your Honor."
"Has the jury arrived at a verdict, *Herr* Reiniche?"
"It has."
"The court will hear your verdict."

There was an air of unreality about the proceedings. Every person in the court was leaning forward, expectancy and repressed excitement etched in their faces. Outside, I could hear a bird singing. Somewhere a church bell tolled. This could not be happening to me, Soghomon Tehlirian, age twenty-five, who loved music, good books, every growing thing of nature, God's greening rains; the man who loved Anahid. Not me! I could not be standing here in a strange court, in a strange land, waiting for strange people to decide whether I should live or die. I bit my lower lip until I could taste the salty tang of blood. Someone was humming—no, they were chanting—no, I could hear more clearly now: they were talking. I forced my attention back to the immediate.

"We, the Jury, find the defendant, Soghomon Tehlirian . . . "
—his voice appeared to fade out, then, suddenly boom:
"Not guilty!"

* * * * * * * * *

From the *New York Post* :

"The courtroom applause that greeted the release of Soghomon Tehlirian shows that Germany will yet make unanimous the world's verdict regarding the slaughter of the Armenians. Even a court in Germany, which had been Turkey's ally during the war, could not find it possible to punish this student who avenged the massacre of his people—innocent Christians—by slaying Talaat Pasha, former prime minister of Turkey."

Among the many congratulatory messages I received was this inspiring communication:

"JUSTICE HAS BEEN DONE. I SALUTE YOU IN THE NAME OF OUR MARTYRED DEAD. MAY THIS BE THE BIRTH OF A NEW AND FREE ARMENIA.

> *Simon Vratzian*
> Premier (In Exile)
> Republic of Armenia."

My spirits soared. The elected leader of the former Republic of Armenia had honored me. He spoke in behalf of my martyred countrymen. I felt proud, but very humble. That message was one I would long remember. Overwhelmed, I sat silently for a moment, my surging emotions held back as I dug my fingers into the arm rest of my chair.

XXIV. CONCLUSION

The mission that had begun among the smoldering ruins of my family home in Erzinga had taken three long years to accomplish. Following the trial, and at the insistence of my many friends in America, I visited the glorious United States where, for the better part of a year, a host of old friendships were renewed.

I was feted in many major cities, honored at banquets and glorified as an international hero; a warm experience I shall never forget. Poems, folk songs and stories were written about me, although I must confess, I was always embarrassed when they were read or sung in my presence. From coast to coast the Armenian communities took me to their bosoms. I was never one to seek such honors and I was deeply moved. I knew then, somewhere deep within me, that the execution of the notorious Talaat had rekindled inside my people the flame of liberty and pride of nationality that I had hoped would be the results of my mission.

The dispersed Armenians who settled in America, I quickly learned, had contributed largely to its culture and Christian climate; helped make it the great world power it is today. In literature, medicine, engineering, theology—the gamut of the arts, sciences, industry and agriculture—all were represented by my fellow Armenians.

During my visit to the United States, however—and to my deep regret—I did not see Yeranouhi Danielian. Yeranouhi, now a free-lance writer, was on an assignment in South America.

My sojourn to America, thrilling though it was, delayed my wedding plans, and it was not until 1922 that I returned to Europe where Anahid and I were finally united in marriage. For nearly thirty years we lived happily in Yugoslavia where we were blessed with two fine sons, Shahen and Zaven.

Only twice during that period was my life endangered when Turkish secret agents came close to discovering my whereabouts. Thank the Lord, life was pleasant thereafter.

I began anew. In time I prospered in the food brokerage

business and acquired substantial property. But with the end of World War II, and after the advent of communism in Yugoslavia, our assets were confiscated by the State. What had happened to our Independent Republic of Armenia in 1920, the first democratic nation, the first country to be crushed by the Reds, had now happened in the Balkan lands. Half of Europe, crawling from under the rubble of war, was now pinned under the Soviet heel.

We fled Yugoslavia, as did many others who yearned for freedom, and settled in Casablanca, only to find we were unable to adapt to the customs of that strange city.

We awoke one morning faced by danger arising out of the past: Turkish agents were closing in, the Federation informed me. Our friends in America urged us to proceed immediately to the United States. Strangely, as I considered the message, I remembered, with something of a pang, that Yeranouhi had once written, "In America there is a friend on every street."

In 1956 we arrived in the U.S.A. We were met with a warm reception by our friends who were with the Federation. Eventually, my lovely wife, Anahid, and I went to live in San Francisco—accepting the invitation of my very dear friend, George Mardikian, of that city. Mardikian, respected civic leader and one who had been close to the sufferings of the Armenians, had lost many relatives—and was himself a survivor—in the 1915 massacre. Along with others, he had formed A.N.C.H.A. (Armenian National Committee for Homeless Armenians), following World War II. He was the nephew of Lt. Krikor Amirian, who had been my superior officer in the Armenian Volunteer Regiment.

We had barely settled in our new residence in the "Paris of the West" when the Armenian-American community of Fresno, located in central California, invited us to a picnic which was given in my honor.

It was a typically warm and serene California Sunday afternoon when we arrived at the picnic grounds. Fluttering in the gentle breeze beside the American flag was the red, blue and orange tricolors of Armenia. A corps of journalists and city dignitaries mingled in the large, happy throng. An old fashioned Armenian orchestra, replete with violins, the *oud* and tambourines, struck up "*Maier Haierenik* —Our Fatherland."

The tributes were many, the speeches stirring. My own, as guest of honor, was necessarily brief—I was too overcome to speak at length. One of those who addressed the crowd was the brilliant and kindly Gregorian priest, Reverend Father Yeghishe

Mekhitarian, whose documented experiences as a victim of the massacres served as evidence in my behalf during the trial. *Der Haier* Mekhitarian ended his speech with a moving prayer that brought back many memories. He then stepped from the platform to greet me.

Our conversation was heartwarming but I was saddened to learn of the deaths of so many of my friends; particularly Avak Zakar Avakian, whose written testimony revealing the experiences of his family and that of his lovely wife, Surpoohi, and her family in the 1894 massacre, helped me during my trial. He had passed away just a year-and-a-half previous. Avak's death had been premature for a man as active as he. He was a great patriot, Armenologist, an excellent writer of Armenian history, a devoted fighter and leader for Armenia, the organizer of the Federation on the West Coast and a highly respected American. "Avak was not only a great patriot but a fine family man. He left his charming widow, Surpoohi, eight stalwart sons and two lovely daughters," Rev. Father Mekhitarian told me. But my sadness was somewhat brightened when *Der Haier* introduced me to a young man. "Soghomon," he announced, "I want you to meet one of Avak's sons, Lindy, and his lovely wife, Glynna."

It was fortunate that we met. Vahag (I preferred to call Lindy by his Christian name.) escorted me to a nearby table and introduced me to a delightfully-pleasant lady who appeared to be in her middle fifties. There was something vaguely familiar about those dark eyes and friendly smile.

"I came especially to see you, Soghomon," she said softly— ever so softly.

That sweet voice! Suddenly I knew. My memory reached back over a span of thirty-five years, and saw her again— Yeranouhi's sister, in her nurse's cap and gown. *"Araxie!"* I gasped. We fell into each other's arms.

It was a joyous reunion. We talked as though we would never stop, each interrupting the other and laughing like children. Vahag brought us two glasses of punch and *shish-kebab* sandwiches. "Araxie," I said, as we sipped our drinks and enjoyed the mouth-watering *shish-kebab*—the king of Armenian delectables, "I've wanted to ask you this since we met. How is Yeranouhi?"

Araxie hesitated. When she finally spoke, it was with deep sadness. "She—she isn't well, Soghomon. Yeranouhi is—is in a sanitarium."

"Is she all right?" I asked anxiously.

"Let's say she's tired—terribly tired. Yeranouhi always was a romanticist, I suppose. She waited a long time—just kept hoping, hoping against hope. And then, one day—even that hope ran out."

"I must see her," I said quickly. "Is she here in Fresno?"

"No—near San Francisco. Vahag knows the place. He can bring you right to the door."

In the excitement of meeting Araxie I had almost forgotten his presence. I placed a hand on the young man's shoulder. "I loved the father," I told him, "and now I must be indebted to the son. I want you to take me to Yeranouhi."

Vahag called for me a week later. We drove across the Golden Gate Bridge, traveling past the verdant hills and valleys of Northern California, through the famed redwood forests, and onward toward the Oregon border. At an intersection marked by a log cabin restaurant, we turned off on a side road that was edged on either side with flowering, carefully groomed shrubs. We climbed a winding road for a few hundred feet and stopped before a stately building that looked more like a colonial mansion than a rest home.

We entered the building and were greeted by the superintendent of nurses who escorted us to a glassed-in patio; three of its walls serving as huge picture windows through which the green hills beyond could be plainly seen.

A tiny figure was seated in a wheel chair. I had planned an informal little introduction, but now I could only falter; "*Yeranouhi*—my dear—do you remember me? I'm Soghomon—Soghomon Tehlirian," I said in Armenian.

She lifted her eyes and I saw that they were still as liquid, infinitely tender and warm as they had been so long ago in Constantinople. But the vibrancy was missing. Her hair, white as the coat of a baby lamb, fell softly to her shoulders. Her eyes penetrated me as she studied my every move.

A little smile played at the corner of her mouth. "You must be my new doctor," she said softly.

My throat constricted. "Is there—there anything I can do for you?" I asked inanely, my voice husky.

"*Busheeshg, zeese doun guh danesk? Yhes ahveli lavuh guskahm* —Oh, Doctor, will you take me home? I feel so much better today."

Unable to utter a single word, I took her little hand in mine and pressed her tiny fingers to my cheek; two silhouettes in the gathering dusk. I kissed the valiant lady's tremoring hand. She was warm, ever so warm. I knew that she was struggling with every breath, yet somehow I knew that she would live on forever. A nurse entered the room and politely motioned that it was time for me to leave.

There was so much I had hoped to say—so many things I wanted to thank her for. I wanted to shout to the sky, beg for time to reel backwards so that I could have Yeranouhi understand every word—but her rapid breathing, her weary and aging, uncomprehending face halted me. I could not thank her; I did not, for my voice was near to breaking.

Yeranouhi pointed a shaking finger to the picture window, through which could be seen the rolling hills of Northern California. Her expression was ecstatic: "Doesn't—doesn't Mount Ararat look beautiful this evening?" she murmured. Now she leaned forward. "Oh, how I love Armenia!—only the Lord knows." Her frail figure straightened and a look of unutterable pride diffused her features.

She sat upright in her wheel chair; proud, courageous, ever faithful—glowing with spiritual love—the eternal symbol of our people.

Crying, I walked out into the night.

EPILOGUE

> "God's finger touched him,
> and he slept."
> Tennyson

Soghomon Tehlirian went to his glory in the arms of his loving wife, Anahid, in San Francisco, California, on May 23, 1960, at the age of sixty-four.

The international hero of the Armenians, of all free people, was laid to rest in Fresno, California, near the vineyards and orchards he had learned to love so much. In addition to the flag of the United States, the red, blue and orange tricolors of his beloved Armenia draped his casket.

Services were held at the Holy Trinity Armenian Apostolic Church. Officiating were the Very Reverend Father Vahram Yeghiayan, Rev. Father Papken Kasparian, Rev. Father Vartan Dulgarian, Rev. Father Kourken Koudoulian and Rev. Father Vahritch Shirinian. In attendance were his still lovely widow, Anahid; their two sons; Soghomon's brother and other close family members. Also attending were honor guards of the Federation; Tehlirian's old unit, the Armenian Volunteer Regiment; members of the Armenian Red Cross; countless dignitaries from all over the world and hundreds of others who came to pay their final respects, including this author, his wife and other members of his family.

Soil and sacramental oil from the Armenian Holy See at Cilicia were sprinkled on his resting place, the Armenian cemetery—appropriately named *Ararat*—in the same shrine that once held the remains of his former Field Commander and intimate friend, General Antranik.

On May 28, after lying in state for five days, Soghomon Tehlirian's body was laid to rest, forty-two years to the very day that the Republic of Armenia enjoyed its brief rebirth.

The Soviet Union and Turkey now hold the former Independent Republic of Free Armenia captive. When Armenia's struggle for independence is again successful, it will be, in no small measure, due to the inspiration and unflagging dedication of a truly great man—the Patrick Henry of Armenia:

Soghomon Tehlirian.

INDEX

Abel, 170
Acts, Book of, 171
Adana, 19, 177
Aharonian, Avedis, 78
Aknouni, 56
Aksin, Mustafa, 235, 236
Albac, 171
Alchemy, 10
Aleppo, 26, 29, 201
Alexander the Great, 170
Alexandropol, 43
Allah, 21, 37, 55, 90, 91, 193, 214, 228
Allied Powers, 18, 181
Amirian, Lt. Krikor, 34, 35, 247
Ankara, 206
Antoyan, Corporal Girar, 41-2
Antranik, General, 33-4, 36
Apelian, Yervant, 101, 124
Ararat, Mt., 10, 16
Ark, Noah's, 10, 12, 16-7, 170
Armageddon, 10
Armenia, Independent Republic of, 45, 85, 89, 91, 101, 220, 224, 245
Armenia, Kingdom of, 170
Armenian Revolutionary Federation (A.R.F.), 12, 33, 49, 52, 63, 67-8, 81, 86, 99, 102, 109, 112, 119, 124, 134-5, 158, 185, 190, 243, 247-8
Armenian Volunteer Regiment (Army), 28, 33-4, 50, 189, 247
Armenians (throughout)
Arsacid Dynasty, 170
Artaxiad Dynasty, 170
Artaza, 171
Ashubashian, 56
Asia Minor, 212
Associated Press, 64, 211
Assyrians, 170
Ataturk (see Kemal Pasha)

Avakian, Avak Zakar, 12, 86, 99, 185-6, 248
Avakian, Surpoohi, 186
Ayvazian, 86-124, 243

Bahgradian Dynasty, 170
Bailunzon, Leona, 102-3, 124, 141-4, 223
Baku, 40
Balakian, Bishop Krikorees, 49, 55, 186-7, 192-4, 243
Barabbas, 10
Barber, Noel, 236
Bartholomew, Saint, 10, 171
Bash Abaran, 44
Bashkaleh, 171
Bedri, 55, 93
Beirut, 16
Beria, Lavrentia, 94
Berlin, 14-5, 88, 95, 97, 100, 102, 118, 121, 124, 126, 134-6, 163, 199, 204, 206, 212, 214, 217, 224-5
Berliner Tageblatt, 131
Bitlis, 31, 36, 170, 186
Black Sea, 26, 28, 46, 170, 173
Bolsheviks, 39, 99, 209, 224, 230
Boston, 14, 79, 81-2, 109, 190
Bradenburg Gate, 118
British Blue Book, 23
British Embassy, 105
Bronsart Pasha, 65
Bryce, Lord James, 17, 64, 170
Bulgaria, 20
Burton, Rev. James, 65

Cain, 170
Caligula, 64
Cappadocians, 170
Casablanca, 247
Caspian Sea, 170, 173
Caucasus, 27, 34, 40, 46, 70, 92, 170, 209
Charlottenburg, 116, 143

Chavoushian, 56
Chinkil, 43
Christ (see Jesus), 22, 25, 91, 113, 161, 193, 227
Christian Science Monitor, 64
Christianity, 10, 16, 54, 114, 172, 192, 194, 204, 207, 210, 227, 239
Cilicia, 177
Communists, 39, 51, 92
Constantinople (Istanbul), 34, 47, 52, 55-6, 58, 60, 77-8, 80, 83-5, 93, 97, 104, 187, 191-3, 201-3, 212, 214-5, 220, 249
Crusades, 11, 114

Daghavarian, 56
Danielian, Araxie, 71-4, 79-81, 191, 248-9
Danielian, Yeranouhi, 48-92, 119, 189-91, 246-50
Darbinian, Reuben, 85
Dardanelles, 24
Demad, Grand Vizier, 90-1
DeMirjian, Arto, 188
Der-el-Zor, 26
Deukmejian, George, 1
Deutchland Barrister, 144
Deyirmen, 28
Diliman, 34
Diliman, Battle of, 35-6
Djami, Major, 212-6
Djemal, 24, 63, 65, 93-7, 106, 108, 111, 167, 176
Dro, General, 34, 44
Dutton, Samuel, 65

Edirne, 212-3
Eftian, Levon, 101-4, 124, 223, 243
Egypt, 186
Eichmann, 53
Elliott, Charles, 65
Enver, 24, 39, 63, 65, 94, 100-1, 167, 176, 197

Erzeroum, 25, 160, 170, 180-1, 187
Erzinga, 16, 39-42, 48, 89, 125, 160, 170, 184, 233, 246

Fedeii (Armenian Fighting Elite), 33-4, 40
Ferdinand, Archduke Franz, 178
Fevi Pasha, 90
Foerster, Dr. Edmund, 148-51, 155
France, 77-8, 179, 186
Fresno, California, 12, 185-6, 247

Gaidzag, General, 34, 40
Garden of Eden, 12, 170
Garin, 40
Garo, Armen, 83-6, 108, 190
Garrini, Signor, 27
Genesis, Book of, 170
Geneva Convention, 227
Geneva, Switzerland, 85-6
Genocide Prevention Treaty, 235
Genocide, 1, 10-3, 67, 91, 159, 194, 235
George, Lloyd, 20
Georgia, 27
Ghengis Khan, 180
Gibbons, Cardinal, 65
Gibbons, Herbert Adams, 177
Gibralter, 172
Gihon (Araxes), 170, 187
Gladstone, Sir, 113, 172
Gnass, Heinz, 117, 136
Gorton, Dr. Adolf von, 121-243
Greece, 20
Greeks, 90, 167, 188-9, 219, 223, 236
Greene, Rev. Frederick, 22
Gulf of Persia, 170

Hagen, Dr. Bruno, 147-8, 155
Hago, 106-8
Hague Conference, 198, 227

Haiguzum Dynasty (Yervantian), 170
Haik, King, 170
Hairenik, 85
Hakka, 93
Halim Pasha (Prince Said), 19, 24, 93
Haloian, Miss Aroos, 180-3
Hamazsasb, General, 34
Handles-Zeitung, 122
Hazor, 94-112, 121, 223, 243
Herod, 64
Hiddekel (Tigris), 170
Hitler, Adolf (Schicklgruber), 18, 53, 235, 238
Holocaust, 11
Holy Ghost, 171
Hrap, 106
Hunchak Party, 49, 220
Hurie, 50, 71, 74-5

Igdir, 34
Inonu, Ismet, 11, 90
Isaiah, the Prophet, 172
Islam, 20
Istanbul, 236
Ittihad Terraki Party (Young Turks), 11, 19, 30-1, 50, 94, 98, 100, 104, 107, 175-7, 213

Jagadamard, 47-8, 59, 61, 70, 75, 77
Jehad, 16, 24, 196
Jerusalem, 186, 188, 202
Jesus (see Christ), 10, 24, 171-2, 191
Jewish Holocaust, 13
Jews, 1, 17, 21, 90-1, 167, 188-9, 223, 228, 236
John the Baptist, 171-2
Jongiulian, 56
Journale Il Messagooro, 28

Kagizman, 34
Kajag, 56

Kalousdian, Gevork, 118-242
Karabekir, General Kazim, 213, 236
Karakilisseh, 44
Kassirer, Dr. Richard, 106, 153-5
Kemal Pasha (Ataturk), 45, 49, 51, 90-1, 96, 110, 190, 206, 212, 215, 219, 224-5
Kemalists, 51, 225
Kennedy, Robert, 10
Keri, General, 34
Khalil, 24
Khamroian, Parantzie, 30
Kharpert, 25, 187
Kiazim Pasha, 90
Kolnig, Heinrich, 124-243
Koran, 21, 55, 177, 228

Larentz, 56
Lemberg, Judge Erich, 125-244
Lenin, Nikolai, 39, 91, 224
Lepsius, Rev. Johannes, 164-80, 243
Liebmann, Dr. Hugo, 152, 155
Locke, Karl, 125, 139
London Daily Express, 30
London Daily Mail, 236
London Times, 26

Madatian, Khosgrove, 50, 57, 59-60
Madatian, Levon, 48
Madera, California, 12
Magou, 171
Mamigonian, Vahan, 171
Mamigonian, Vartan, 171
Mamikonians, 170
Mandteufel, Chief Inspector, 120, 138-9, 184, 205, 208, 242
Manhattan, 82
Manif, Djelel, 65
Marash, 91
Mardikian, George, 247
Marseilles, 78

INDEX / 255

Mayflower, 170
Mecca, 21, 172
Mekhitarian, Rev. Father Yeghishe, 186-8, 247-8
Mesopotamia, 173
Mezre, 25
Middle East, 34, 209, 212
Mithridates, King, 170
Mohammed, 21, 113, 172
Morgenthau, Henry, 17
Moscow, 94
Mourad, General, 34, 40
Moush, 36, 170, 172, 185-6
Mugurditchian, Harootoun, 49-76, 87, 125, 193-4

Nazariantz, Dr. Libarid, 99-101, 211, 223
Nazi (Nazis), 1, 18, 227, 235
Nazim, Dr., 105, 108
Neanderthal, 173
Nestoria, 20
New York American, 64
New York Post, 244
New York Tribune, 27
New York, 82, 188
Niemeyer, Dr. Kurt, 122, 124-5, 141, 223
Nobel Peace Prize, 11, 90
Norire, 106, 224
Norman the Conqueror, 170
Novorossiysk, 46

Ohanessian, Parantzie, 31
Ottoman Empire, 1, 16-7, 27, 33
Ourfu, 36

Palestine, 93, 183
Papazian, Mrs. Bertha, 112-4
Papert, 40, 160
Paris, 73, 77, 79, 220
Parthians, 170
Pashayan, 56
Pathe, Ernest. 125, 146, 152-5
Pentecost, Feast of, 171

Persia (Iran), 28, 170-1
Pesan Valley, 36
Phrath (Euphrates), 170, 182, 201, 237
Pison (Cyrus), 170
Pompey, 170
Poork, 37

Queen Translation, 10, 172

Reiniche, Otto, 243-4
Reuters, 64, 211
Rhupen, Prince, 113
Rhupenian Dynasty, 113, 170
Romans, 36-7, 171
Rome, 107
Roosevelt, Franklin Delano, 17
Rumania, 34

Salamaust, 34
Salonika, 213
Samsek, 162
San Francisco, 247, 249
Sanders, General Limon von, 179, 194-201
Sardarapat, 44
Sarikamis, 34
Sassoun, 36, 113, 170
Saudi Arabia, 187
Schultzen, Inspector Max, 119-20, 136-8
Sebouh, General, 34, 40
Serbia (see Yugoslavia), 16
Serkoyan, Berge, 63-7, 97, 124
Sevan, 170
Shabin Karahissar, defense of, 36-9
Shadakh, 36
Sharigian, 56
Shekir, Dr. Behaeddin, 93, 105, 108
Shellendorf, Erich von, 65
Shia Bey, 110, 204, 206, 211-5, 225
Shroud of Jesus, 171

Siamanto, 56
Silikian, General, 44
Smyrna, 91, 188-9, 236
Soviet Union, 85, 91, 94, 100
Speropoulos, Father Alex, 188-9, 223
St. Charles Monestary, 185
St. Gregory the Illuminator, 171-2, 184
St. Mesrop, 172
St. Paul, 172
St. Sahag, 172
Stalin, 53
Stelbaum, Frau Mildred, 141
Stoemer, Dr. William, 146-9, 153, 155
Sultan Abdul Hamid II, 19, 83, 176, 178, 185
Sultan Ariz, 176
Sultan Mahmoud, 176
Sultan Mejit, 176
Sumpat, 104-8, 124, 223, 243
Sumpat, General, 34
Swing, Raymond Gram, 24
Syria, 20, 26, 93, 170, 177, 202

Talaat Pasha (throughout)
Tarsus, 172
Tatigian, Anahid, 45-6, 62, 67, 70, 80, 89, 92, 184, 190-1, 205, 244, 246-7
Tehlirian, Soghomon (throughout)
Tekir Pasha, 57-61, 69, 72, 75-7
Terzian, 78-9, 82
Terzibashian, Mrs. Christine, 160-4, 224, 243
Thaddeus, Saint, 10
The Armenian Review, 85
Tiedman, Frau Mae Lena, 141
Tiflis, 34, 45, 76
Tigranes the Great, 170
Tomajanian, 56
Trebizond, 26

U.S. Congressional Record, 177
United Press International, 27, 64, 211
United States, 20, 44, 92, 184, 246-7
University of Leipzig, 173
Urguplu, Suat, 11, 235-6
Urumiah, 170

Van, 35-6, 170
Varoujan, 56
Vaza, 106, 109-10, 112, 223, 243
Vratzian, Simon, 25, 245

Wagner, Armin T., 30
Washington, D.C., 85, 235
Wehib Pasha, 44
Wertenhauer, Dr. Johannes, 121, 124-5, 141, 144, 223
Wilhelm, Kaiser, 16, 167, 194, 197
Wilson, Woodrow, 29, 180, 183
Wise, Rabbi Stephen S., 65
Wolf-Metternich, 197
Wood, Henry, 27
World War I, 18, 90
World War II, 247

Yeprod, 188
Yerevan, 43-4
Young Turks (see *Ittihad Terraki* Party)
Yugoslavia (see Serbia), 246-7

Zakarian, 56
Zakarian, Vahan, 141
Zaven, Archbishop, 68-70, 77-8, 191
Zeitoun, 113
Zoroastrianism, 171